Metaphors *of* Genre

THE PENNSYLVANIA STATE UNIVERSITY PRESS
UNIVERSITY PARK, PENNSYLVANIA

Metaphors *of* Genre

The Role *of* Analogies in Genre Theory

David Fishelov

Library of Congress Cataloging-in-Publication Data

Fishelov, David.
    Metaphors of genre : the role of analogies in genre theory / David
Fishelov.
        p.   cm.
    Includes bibliographical references (p.   ) and index.
    ISBN 0-271-00886-5 (acid-free paper) ISBN 0-271-02325-2 (pbk)
    1. Metaphor. 2. Literary form. 3. Symbolism in literature.
    4. Literature—History and criticism—Theory, etc. 1. Title.
    PN228.M4F57   1993
    808'.001—dc20   92-12151
                                                                    CIP

Published by The Pennsylvania State University Press,
Suite C, Barbara Building, University Park, PA 16802-1003

It is the policy of The Pennsylvania State University Press to use acid-free paper
for the first printing of all clothbound books. Publications on uncoated stock
satisfy the minimum requirements of American National Standard for Information Sciences—Permanence of Paper for Printed Library Materials, ANSI
Z39.48–1984.

To my Mother and Father

with Love

Contents

Acknowledgments   ix

Chapter 1   Analogies, Theories, and the Concept
               of Genre   1

               The Four Analogies
               Analogies, Theories, and the Scientific
                  Paradigm
               Genre: A Working Definition
               Examples: Scope and Language

Chapter 2   Literary Genres as Biological Species   19

               Life, Death, and Evolutionary Concepts
               One Exception, Two Problems, Three Stages
               Darwinism: Alive and Kicking
               Dominance and the Periphery: The Indirect
                  Path of Evolution

Chapter 3   Literary Genres as Families   53

               The Family Analogy: The Logical Aspect
               The Family Analogy: Parent-Child
                  Relationships and Beyond
               Growing Up In and Through the Novel
               A Final Familial Thought

Chapter 4   Literary Genres as Social Institutions   85

               Conventions in the Theater: The Semiotic
                  Connection
               Life Is But a Stage, the Stage Is But Life
               The Role of the Blocking Figure: The *Alazon*
               Some Variations on the Role of the Blocking
                  Figure

Chapter 5   Literary Genres as Speech Acts   119

Literary Genres as Speech Acts
Literary Genres as Imitations of Speech Acts
Carpe Diem or *Vivamus atque Amemus*
The *Amemus,* Speech Acts, and Literary Genres

Chapter 6   Concluding Remarks   155

Bibliography   161

Index   171

Acknowledgments

It is my pleasure to thank various teachers, scholars, and colleagues who contributed to the shaping of my ideas throughout this book. Robert Alter, with his broad knowledge of different kinds of literature, his keen awareness of the theoretical problems involved in literary studies, and his sensitivity to the subtleties of the text, offered indispensable comments. In Thomas Rosenmeyer I found the erudition of a classicist expressed with the vigor of a modern theorist. His deep interest in genre theory made his comments the more helpful and informative. Reading Chana Kronfeld's detailed critique, I had the feeling that she understands not only everything I actually write but also what I intend in what I write. Her special combination of theoretical knowledge and interpretative insight made her contribution vital.

I have also much profited from the careful and perceptive comments of Charles Altieri and Wendell Harris, the two readers of Penn State Press, and Philip Winsor, the senior editor, offered all the help and encouragement I needed during the final stages of writing and production.

I want also to thank Paul Alpers, Benjamin Harshav (Hrushovski), and Yeshayahu Shen with whom I have shared some of my ideas and who offered useful suggestions. In writing the final draft, Mira Reich's stylistic suggestions gave the manuscript of a non-native English speaker a more elegant shape. Thanks are also due to the Hebrew University of Jerusalem for a special grant to cover the technical costs involved in the preparation of the manuscript.

Part of Chapter 3 was published as "Genre Theory and Family Resemblance—Revisited" in Poetics *20 (1991), and I would like to thank Cees Van Rees, the editor, for permission to reprint.*

Finally, I wish to thank my wife, Nitsa Kann, a gifted poet, for her understanding support of my academic interests. To elaborate on my thanks to her, however, would bring me far beyond the boundaries of the subgenre of Acknowledgments into territories more poetical.

Satire exists as literary fact . . . as the existence of mammals is a "fact" of the physical world. Though whales suckle their young and grow hair, they have at least as many traits in common with sailfish as they do with men; our selection of the particular similarities to define a class called mammals is justified only because, when we lump whales together with elephants, hyenas, and men, we facilitate the knowledge of the biological universe, contained, for example, in Darwin's theories.

    —Sheldon Sacks, *Fiction and the Shape of Belief*

Representatives of a genre may then be regarded as making up a family whose septs and individual members are related in various ways, without necessarily having any single feature shared in common by all.

    —Alastair Fowler, *Kinds of Literature*

The literary kind is an "institution"—as Church, University, or State is an institution. It exists, not as an animal exists or even as a building, chapel, library, or capitol, but as an institution exists. One can work through, express oneself through, existing institutions, create new ones, or get on, so far as possible, without sharing in polities or rituals; one can also join, but then reshape, institutions.

    —René Wellek and Austin Warren,
    Theory of Literature

The notion of illocutionary action was developed by philosophers of language, particularly Austin, Strawson, and Searle, in order to discuss the phenomena of asserting and commanding, promising and questioning, which are as important in constituting language as grammar or propositions. Just as speaking is made up of different types of action carried out by means of language, the system of actions carried out through literature consists of its various genres.

    —Elizabeth Bruss, *Autobiographical Acts*

Chapter 1

Analogies, Theories,
and the Concept of Genre

THE FOUR ANALOGIES

Anyone who has done even some casual reading on the theory of literary genres will be amazed by how often writers use analogies—such as the four quoted above—in trying to understand and illuminate the nature of literary genres.[1] This tendency to resort to analogy suggests, among other things, that the literary genre is an elusive and multifaceted phenomenon that resists explanation by any one simple, straightforward approach. In this book I examine the role that such analogies play in different theories of genre; I look at how these analogies broaden, yet at the same time limit, one's understanding of the complex phenomenon that is the literary genre.

Each of the above four statements represents an entire theoretical framework constituted and encapsulated as an analogy (or, as one might also call it, a "deep metaphor").

1. *The Biological Analogy.* The major issue under this heading is

---

1. Heather Dubrow (1982), for instance, refers to analogies with biological species, human personalities, social codes, and shadings of color. Alastair Fowler (1982) mentions analogies with biological species and families, among others. Globinsky (1969) refers to the biological analogy and to the analogy between the system of literary genres and the grammar of language, and he elaborates on the analogy between literary genres and social institutions. Paul Hernadi (1972) proposes the analogy between a genre and a visual Gestalt. And this is by no means an exhaustive list.

evolution. Although some of the "evolutionary" theories applied to literature in the late nineteenth century are inadequate, I contend that evolutionary concepts (notably those of Darwin!) can bring some fresh insights into genre theory.

2. *The Family Analogy.* In order to avoid rigid models for defining a genre, Wittgenstein's notion of *family resemblance,* according to which not all the members of a genre share even a single trait, has been introduced to genre theory. In addition to this logical aspect of the analogy, one may point to some sociopsychological implications it has for genre theory: the dialectics of imitation and innovation within a generic tradition may be taken as analogous to the parent-child relationship, or to growing up within a family.

3. *The Institutional Analogy.* Here my main purpose is to explore some structural and functional similarities between the two phenomena. Social institutions, like literary genres, provide a network of norms through which our experience is made culturally meaningful. Concepts such as conventions (and deviations from conventions) and institutional roles stand at the core of the institutional analogy.

4. *The Speech-Act Analogy.* One may relate literary genres to speech acts by describing genres as complex, written counterparts of or as imitations or representations of speech acts. I will attempt to show how the concept of a representation of speech acts can be operative in describing literary genres, but also to warn against its pretension to explain *all* literary genres.

I have three overall goals. The first is to demonstrate the importance of these four conceptual analogies in genre theory. They are present, whether explicitly or implicitly, in many of this century's theoretical discussions of literary genres. Although they are not the only ones to occur in theoretical discussions, they seem to me to offer a rich network of implications and hypotheses.

My second goal is to propose, within the framework of each of these four conceptual analogies, my own perspective—first by distinguishing between different theoretical interests and implications expressed through the same analogy, and second by pointing to some aspects of the analogy that seem to bring new understanding and insight into the field of literary genres.

My first two undertakings—demonstrating the importance of conceptual analogies in genre theory and suggesting some distinctions and hypotheses during the discussion of four such analogies—should support the third. By showing how different conceptual analogies can illuminate the heterogeneous field of the literary genre, I shall advocate a *pluralistic approach* to genre theory. According to such an approach, a given conceptual framework may be fruitfully applied to some aspects of the generic field, such as some particular literary genres or some aspects of their interrelations and development. The key word here is *some:* a given theoretical model may be highly relevant to some kinds of genres, or to some aspects of their evolution, but only partially relevant or even totally irrelevant to other genres or other problems in the field. Note that this pluralistic view is *not* a relativistic one, because not every conceptual analogy is relevant to the same degree (or even necessarily relevant at all) to genre theory.

Finally, in the course of my discussion I shall also analyze and interpret some specific generic traditions and literary texts in order to illustrate the theoretical approaches. The specific generic traditions were chosen because they lend themselves most readily to the conceptual framework suggested by a particular analogy: the epic for the biological analogy, the novel for the family "metaphor," comedy for the institutional perspective, and the lyrical *carpe diem* for the speech-act analogy. By illustrating the different conceptual frameworks with different genres, I am also indirectly arguing that the plural nature of the range of genres is a major reason for embracing a pluralistic approach.

My study is thus primarily a metatheoretical one insofar as it presents, compares, and criticizes certain existing theories. It also has theoretical aspects in that it raises new hypotheses that may be related to these existing theories. Then, too, when it discusses texts of a specific generic tradition, it is at least intermittently descriptive and interpretive, although this latter aspect of the work is clearly subordinate to the theoretical issues.

However, before I start presenting the theories and their implications, I should raise two preliminary issues. First, I should justify the very method that underlies my study—that is, the presentation of theories of literary genres as elaborate and complex formulations built around conceptual analogies. Second, we need a working definition of the term "genre" as a point of departure for further discussions. This working definition will also help me to show how, and why, my study differs from other approaches (especially certain current ones) to the concept of literary genre.

ANALOGIES, THEORIES, AND THE SCIENTIFIC PARADIGM

To justify my basic assumption that analogies are very important in theories of genre, it will be useful to make a brief foray outside the literary field to look into the role of analogy in theoretical and scientific discourse in general.

Voltaire's *Micromegas* provides an amusing view of this role. Micromegas, a giant inhabitant of Sirius, is trying to have a scientific discussion with the Secretary of the Academy of Saturn concerning variety in nature. Micromegas opens the conversation:

> "It must be admitted," he said, "that there is plenty of variety in nature."
> "Yes," agreed the Saturnian, "nature is like a flower bed of which the flowers . . ."
> "Enough of your flower bed," said the other.
> "Nature," resumed the secretary, "is like a company of fair women and dark women whose apparel . . ."
> "What have I to do with your dark women?" said the other.
> "Well, then, nature is like a gallery of pictures whose features . . ."
> "Oh, no!" said the traveler. "I tell you once more—nature is like nature. Why speak to compare it with anything?"
> "To please you," answered the secretary.
> "I do not want people to please me," replied the traveler, "I want them to teach me."[2]

According to these two characters—both the Secretary, who is using analogies, and Micromegas, who rejects them with contempt—analogies have only an ornamental (or "poetical") function whenever they occur in serious scientific discourse. This attitude would have made our two travelers welcome in the Vienna Circle of the twenties (Schlick, Carnap, and others). These advocates of logical positivism considered propositions meaningful "only if they were *either* confessedly logical, and thereby tautologous or inconsistent, or *else* genuinely empirical, in which case their semantic value would be determined by cashing them in for actual or possible observation reports or *Protokollsätze*."[3] Analogical language (metaphors, similes, etc.) should be expelled from the realm of scientific and true philosophical discourse. As a sign of good will, these analogical expressions would not be totally ignored, but rather lumped in with other suspect discourse (such as ethical statements) and would be labeled "emotive" language, as distinct from serious, scientific, "cognitive" language.

Accepting this attitude toward analogy in any theoretical discourse

2. Voltaire, *The Portable Voltaire*, 416–17.
3. Allan Janik and Stephen Toulmin, *Wittgenstein's Vienna*, 213.

would require rejecting the four quotations that open this discussion as mere poetic, "emotive" play on language with no cognitive value. This would compel me to discard my fundamental assumption that conceptual analogies should be seriously considered.

To argue on behalf of my perspective here, and to counter some of these positivistic attitudes of Micromegas and his heirs from the Vienna Circle, let us turn to M. H. Abrams's famous presentation of neoclassical and romantic theories of literature.[4] One of the things that makes *The Mirror and the Lamp* so interesting and illuminating is the very fact that Abrams bases his discussion on two analogies (as the title indicates). His book is a fine example of the fruitfulness of the method I am trying to follow in my own.[5] Abrams also shows a keen awareness of the methodological assumptions that underlie his work, and he formulates them in a lucid and persuasive manner. I would like to quote his remarks on the role of metaphor in cognitive discourse at some length, since they can be applied almost verbatim to my own study:

> The task of analyzing the nature and function of metaphor has traditionally been assigned to the rhetorician and to the critic of literature. Metaphor, however, whether alive or moribund, is an inseparable element of all discourse, including discourse whose purpose is neither persuasive nor aesthetic, but descriptive and informative. . . . Even the traditional language of the natural sciences cannot claim to be totally literal, although its key terms are often not recognized to be metaphors until, in the course of time, the general adoption of a new analogy yields perspective into the nature of the old. And in the criticism of poetry, metaphor and analogy, though less conspicuous, are hardly less functional than in poetry itself. A particular aim of this book is to emphasize the role in the history of criticism of certain more or less submerged conceptual models—what we may call "archetypal analogies"—in helping to select, interpret, systematize, and evaluate the facts of art. While many expository analogies, as conventional opinion proposes, are casual and illustrative, some few

4. M. H. Abrams, *The Mirror and the Lamp: Romantic Theory and the Critical Tradition.*
5. Another example of the fruitfulness of this method can be found in Peter Steiner's critical presentation of the Russian formalists, in his *Russian Formalism: A Metapoetics.* To present their theoretical presuppositions, Steiner uses three "deep metaphors" (or, to use Abrams's term, "archetypal analogies"): the machine, the organism, and the system. By doing so, he succeeds not only in illuminating some basic assumptions of Russian formalism, but also in depicting an interesting line of development within the formalist theoretical framework.

seem recurrent and, not illustrative, but *constitutive:* they yield the ground plan and essential structural elements of a literary theory, or of any theory. By the same token, they select and mold those "facts" which a theory comprehends. For facts are *facta,* things made as much as things found, and made in part by the analogies through which we look at the world as through a lens.[6]

These statements gain credibility from certain contemporary developments in the philosophy of science associated with Thomas Kuhn's concept of the scientific paradigm, in his controversial *Structure of Scientific Revolutions.* To clear up certain arguments and unnecessary misunderstandings, Margaret Masterman has meticulously analyzed the meaning of the term "paradigm" in Kuhn's theoretical framework. She first sorts through what appear to be many different meanings of the term in order to focus on three basic ones. The first, the "metaphysical paradigm," does not seem to her to be essential to Kuhn's conceptual framework. The second, the "sociological paradigm," is a model for action governing and regulating the scientific community in its "puzzle solving" (to mention another central concept in Kuhn). The third, however, is what seems philosophically to be the central meaning of the term: the "artifact" or "construct" paradigm. Setting aside some of Masterman's sophisticated formulations, we may say that a scientific paradigm, that innermost characteristic of scientific activity, is none other than an extended analogy. Or, as Masterman puts it, "[Kuhn's] paradigm is a concrete 'picture' of something, A, which is used analogically to describe a concrete something else, B."[7]

To illustrate this "double view" provided by a scientific paradigm, Masterman cites the example of the genetic code, which can be described by drawing an analogy between language (or rather one concrete "picture" of language) and biochemical processes. Later on, she summarizes her conclusions concerning the nature of the scientific paradigm: "If a paradigm has got to have the property of concreteness, or "crudeness," this means that it must either be, literally, a model; or, literally, a picture; or literally, an analogy-drawing sequence of word uses in natural language; or, some combination of these. In any of these cases, I wish to say that a paradigm draws a 'crude analogy.' "[8]

Thus the logical positivists' ideal of a pure scientific discourse, uncon-

6. Abrams, *The Mirror and the Lamp,* 31.
7. Margaret Masterman, "The Nature of a Paradigm," 77.
8. Ibid., 79.

taminated by confusing metaphors and analogies, is a chimera. Analogies are not merely a tolerated element at the periphery of scientific discourse; rather, they constitute the innermost productive core of the whole scientific endeavor.

If I apply the label "ornamental approach" to the view of analogies held by Micromegas and the logical positivists, the opposing point of view may be called the "cognitive approach." This view, which I follow, perceives the four quotations that open my discussion as serious theoretical pronouncements rather than mere ornamental flourishes. In treating scientific analogies seriously, Richard Boyd suggests:

> One should seek to discover more about the relevant similarities or analogies, always considering the possibility that there are no important similarities or analogies, or alternatively, that there are quite distinct similarities for which distinct terminology should be introduced. One should try to discover what the "essential" features of the similarities or analogies are, and one should try to assimilate one's account of them to other theoretical work in the same subject area (that is one should *attempt* to explicate the metaphor).[9]

However seriously one treats these analogies, one should not confuse them with scientific theories: the fact that a given theoretical discourse is saturated with analogies does not in and of itself guarantee that the discourse constitutes a valuable research paradigm. "Deep metaphors" may be a necessary element of a scientific paradigm, but they alone do not constitute such a paradigm. Moreover, even though literary theory has become quite sophisticated, it is not yet scientific, at least not to the standards of a natural science (in which Kuhn is basically interested). This is demonstrated by the fact that literary theory offers a number of paradigms simultaneously, whereas Kuhn holds that in the natural sciences only one paradigm at a time may prevail. Thus my reference to Kuhn's philosophy of science is not intended to "elevate" the use of analogy in literary theory to the status of a true ("exact") scientific paradigm, but rather to support the basic methodological "cognitive approach" that I will adopt.

9. Richard Boyd, "Metaphor and Theory Change," 406. For similar treatment of analogies in scientific discourse, despite some philosophical disagreements with Boyd, see also Thomas Kuhn's "Metaphor in Science."

GENRE: A WORKING DEFINITION

Having elaborated on the method to be used in this research, I must now clarify the concept of literary genre that will play a key role in the coming chapters.

At this point I shall supply only a general working definition of genre. I will expand and explain the key terms used in this definition, but I do not intend it to solve all theoretical problems concerning the nature and function of literary genres. Rather, it should provide a ground for my discussion and serve as a point of departure for my exploration of different genre theories. Of course, this definition is influenced by my views and presuppositions, which are, as I will explain, opposed to certain current trends in literary theory; nevertheless, my definition of genre should still be acceptable to the different schools or "paradigms" of genre theory. The fact that I can propose the four analogies already referred to, each of which has its own perspective and preoccupation, and still adhere to one general working definition of genre is a reliable sign of its flexibility.

I define genre as *a combination of prototypical, representative members, and a flexible set of constitutive rules that apply to some levels of literary texts, to some individual writers, usually to more than one literary period, and to more than one language and culture.*

This definition is intended first of all to distinguish genre from certain other types of groupings of literature (e.g., by period, school, style, or author). Thus, for example, a literary period is defined, however elusively, with reference to specific historical periods, whereas genre is presented here as crossing the boundaries of literary periods. To take another example of a neighboring concept: in describing texts in terms of a specific literary style we are confined to discussing their linguistic and stylistic features, whereas the concept of a genre as stipulated by our working definition refers to a dynamic cluster of formal, stylistic, and thematic features.

The working definition is also supposed to apply to all existing (and future) "historical genres." Here I use the term "historical genre" (though later I will use only "genre") to distinguish our domain from certain other major, usually triadic, divisions of literature, sometimes called "modes" (such as poetry, fiction, and drama, or drama, epic, and lyric). These latter divisions can be misleading, because they tend to assign to particular modes of presentation (such as monologue, dialogue, first person, third person) metaphysical or psychological attributes (such as subjectivity, objectivity, or introversion),[10] and also because they represent a futile effort to determine the existence of three (or four, or two) elementary, fundamental "genres"—an approach that turns out to be only one of many possible ways of dividing up literature.[11]

Tzvetan Todorov's criticism (1975) of Northrop Frye's generic schema (1957) distinguishes "historical" from "theoretical" genres. The former are abstracted from concrete historical texts, the latter are deduced from a theory of literature. Todorov accuses Frye of being inconsistent in his theoretical framework because of his inclination toward historical criticism. Todorov himself proposes a consistent theoretical framework and a dialectical approach to concrete historical genres that both achieves theoretical consistency and describes adequately historical genres. He tries to apply his method to what he calls "the fantastic."[12] But Todorov was himself criticized by Christine Brooke-Rose for certain flaws in his approach to the relationship between his theoretical framework and his concrete historical analyses.[13] Brooke-Rose defends in strong terms the need for a consistent, comprehensive framework for "theoretical genres." It is no accident, however, that she herself does not provide such a "grammar" of genres.

In all these cases, the construction of "theoretical genres" seems to be either problematic or, as a means of describing and explaining actual literary genres, simply useless. Obviously any description of an actual literary genre must make some theoretical distinctions among various levels of the literary text (such as its formal level, its thematic level, or its representational status), but it seems pointless to try to construct innumerable abstract tables of theoretical genres when they are of no help in dealing with actual historical genres—which are, after all, the raison d'être of my inquiry.[14]

10. An interesting reinterpretation of these triads, associating them with various psychological and linguistic categories, can be found in Emil Staiger's *Les Concepts fondamentaux de la poétique*.

11. For a discussion of the "historical kinds" and the three "ultimates," see René Wellek and Austin Warren, *Theory of Literature*, 227–29. In leaving these "ultimates" aside and focusing on the "historical kinds," I follow their method. For an excellent survey of the history of the concept of "elementary" genres, and of the confusion accompanying this history, see Gérard Genette, *Introduction à l'architexte*.

12. Robert Scholes, in his *Structuralism in Literature*, 117–41, claims to be following Todorov's dialectical method as presented in *The Fantastic*, but is actually relying heavily on only one textual dimension: the relationship between the fictive and the real world. Because of this restriction, which does not do justice to the multilayered nature of the literary text (and hence, of the literary genre), Scholes's schema falls short when he tries to apply it to the rich and complex field of actual historical genres.

13. See her "Historical Genres/Theoretical Genres: A Discussion of Todorov on the Fantastic," 145–58.

14. For persuasive theoretical as well as practical arguments against such an abstract

My concept of "historical genre" can be best elucidated by contrasting it with three alternative views. First, I consider genres "historical" in the sense that they are *transmitted through history* and oppose the view that confines a literary genre to only one literary period. During the process of transmission some significant changes may of course occur, but still, literary genres serve as a network of linkages between different literary periods, sometimes successively, sometimes through chronologically discontinuous "leaps" (e.g., the Renaissance reintroduction of classical genres). Alastair Fowler, for example, rightly points out that "rewriting of genre history can only be achieved through acknowledging continuities."[15] Second, I consider genres "historical" in the sense that they are *concrete configurations of texts in specific periods and literatures,* and oppose abstract, atemporal classificatory schemata, which produce numberless and unfruitful "empty" rubrics. Third, I consider genres "historical" in the sense that they *actually shape how writers produce, and readers respond to, literary works.* This last point opposes the view that statements about literary genre are merely pragmatic conveniences. According to this approach, labeling something a "genre" is nothing but a convenient way to group literary works. Whenever the critic's goals change, his generic labeling may change as well. There is nothing "out there" that the critic is expected to describe and to explain; only the critic's goals and presuppositions are real, and, as they change, so do the literary groupings known as "genres."

Because this "neopragmatic" view of literary genres, with its strong relativistic implications, has been advocated in some important and sophisticated contemporary contributions to genre theory,[16] I would like to explain why, and how, I disagree with it.

One might willingly admit that any statement about literary genres is made by a critic (or writer, or reader) who has certain goals and presuppositions. But then every statement about anything is made by somebody who has certain purposes. This does not automatically prove

---

"grammar" of genres, see Uri Margolin, "On Three Types of Deductive Models in Genre Theory," 5–19. The tension between proposing abstract classificatory "grammars" of genres and describing actual literary genres can be traced back to Aristotle's *Poetics:* see, for instance, Genette, *Introduction à l'architexte;* Thomas Rosenmeyer, "Ancient Literary Genres: A Mirage?"; Jean-Marie Schaeffer, *Qu'est-ce qu'un genre littéraire?* 10–25; and my "Aristotle's Approach to Literary Genres: Classification, Description, Evaluation."

15. Alastair Fowler, "The Future of Genre Theory: Functions and Constructional Types," 303.

16. The emphasis on the "purpose" of the critic and theorist as a major factor in "constituting" genres can be found in Gary Saul Morson, *The Boundaries of Genre;* Adena Rosmarin, *The Power of Genre;* Ralph Cohen, "History and Genre"; and Jean-Marie Schaeffer, "Literary Genres and Textual Genericity" and *Qu'est-ce qu'un genre littéraire?*

the relativism of the neopragmatic view. Thus, at its most basic level, the neopragmatic approach sounds trivial. But, in stressing the decisive role of the critic's preoccupations in genre theory, advocates of this view usually mean something more radical—namely, that the critic's purposes ultimately *determine* the validity of his theory. The more "conservative" factors for corroborating a certain genre theory, such as conspicuous patterns of similarity between literary works, the work's title (or subtitle) that signals a certain generic tradition, testimonies of writers and readers about how they compose and read the texts, critical pronouncements of the discussed period that make explicit or implicit generic divisions, and how other participants of the literary community label a work as "belonging" to a certain genre (e.g., publishers, teachers, librarians)—all these considerations are diminished and totally subordinated to the critic's present purposes.[17] It follows that there are no stable paradigms of genres, because if the critic's purposes shift, so do his "generic" groupings of works. Ralph Cohen expresses one version of this pragmatic-relativistic view: "Since the purposes of critics *who establish genres* vary, it is self-evident that the same texts can belong to different groupings of genres and serve different generic purposes."[18] These formulations clearly overstate the critic's role, and ignore many other important factors that participate in "establishing genres."

Gary Morson likens generic groupings to the process of shelving books in one's office according to the courses one is teaching,[19] and Adena Rosmarin goes even further in stressing the "neo-Kantian" assumption that all groupings of objects are made only "as if" they were similar, and there are no objective criteria for checking our generalizations: "A genre is a kind of schema, a way of discussing a literary text in terms that link it with other texts and, finally, phrase it in terms of those texts. . . . We can always choose, correct, invent, or define a class wide enough to make the desired mistake possible."[20]

Now I think these "pragmatic-relativistic" views are inadequate as a basis for genre theory not only because critics should be generally more modest about their role in the constitution of literary genres, but mainly because their overemphasis of the "pragmatic" aspects of genres comes usually at the expense of a serious attempt to describe the intersubjective

17. An interesting attempt to depart from the pragmatic-relativistic approach and to establish generic studies on empirical grounds can be found in some works published during the last decade in *Poetics*. The "empirical" emphasis may sometimes sound too restrictive, but I think it is basically a promising approach.

18. Cohen, "History and Genre," 204 (italics added).

19. Morson, *The Boundaries of Genre*, viii.

20. Rosmarin, *The Power of Genre*, 21.

factors of literary genres (what I described earlier as the "conservative" factors) and how literary genres actually function in the literary communicative situation. Let me challenge the "pragmatic-relativistic" view in a somewhat indirect way. Consider, for example, a statement made about the metrical pattern of a poem (e.g., "This poem is written in dactylic hexameter"). Surely a critic making such a statement has a certain theoretical purpose; it is also obvious that he has some presuppositions about what constitutes a metrical pattern and how this abstract pattern relates to the concrete phonetic level of the poem. There might also be some deep disagreements among critics about these prosodic questions (how to define the prosodic units, how to *group* literary texts that demonstrate the *same* metrical pattern), but no one will deny that there is something "out there" in the poem's phonetic organization that serves as a referent for corroborating (or undermining) a given statement about the poem. Literary genres are, needless to say, far more complex and elusive than prosodic patterns. Still, the critic's obligation to respect the varied historical evidence that is part of the communicative situation of literature should be the foundation of genre theory, not an auxiliary, marginal part of it, subordinated to new, original critical purposes.

Otherwise, we get a picture of the critic, settled in his ivory tower, preoccupied in grouping and regrouping literary texts to achieve interesting (what Rosmarin would call "edifying") interpretations, but paying little attention to what is going on "down there" beneath the haze of his critical preoccupations. Confronted with such an approach, my counterargument may be reduced to the adamant restatement of certain generic paradigms. Ultimately my argument against such views may be encapsulated in statements such as "*The Odyssey,* the *Aeneid, Paradise Lost* are epics are epics are epics." Perhaps such statements do not have much logical force, but any genre theory that does not accept them as its foundation loses its credibility as a descriptive and explanatory tool. Hence the stipulation of prototypical, representative members of generic categories in the first part of my working definition of genre. In every generic category we witness an intimate, hermeneutical relation between paradigmatic instances and the associated rules: generic rules are drawn from, and exemplified by, those representative cases. To cut this Gordian knot connecting prototypical members and the associated generic rules would result either in disregarding the stable, paradigmatic instances, or else in denying that authors and readers (consciously or unconsciously) draw from those instances a flexible set of generic rules.

Whereas the neopragmatic approach to genre theory may lead to overestimating the critic's role in "constituting" genres, and to underestimating historical evidence (in the broad sense discussed above), one should also note its merits in cautioning against the uncritical acceptance of generic groupings and labels, and of course against any essentialistic bias of genre theories, i.e., describing genres as ideal entities existing outside of historical developments. Thus the current neopragmatic approach may serve as a useful corrective against essentialistic approaches to literary genres.

These fruitful corrections of genre theory, however, are difficult to find in another trend in contemporary literary studies—deconstruction. If the special issue of *Glyph* devoted to the topic of genre (1980) is representative of this school's contribution to the subject, then I am afraid it is a highly problematic contribution. Deconstructionist pronouncements about literary genres as decategorized categories, unbounded bounds, and decodified codes seem either to reiterate (rather tiresomely) paradoxes borrowed from set theories according to which literary genres demonstrate the law "of participation without belonging—a taking part in without being part of . . . the boundary of the set comes to form, by invagination, an internal pocket larger than the whole,"[21] or to adopt romantic metaphysical terminology according to which "Genre is 'more than a genre.' . . . It is an Individual and an organic Whole capable of self-engenderment. . . . The literary genre is Literature itself, the *Literary Absolute*."[22] Needless to say, such statements deserve careful exegesis from sympathizers of the deconstructivist school, but their usefulness as a basis for a serious, theoretical as well as descriptive, study of how literary genres function within literary communities and how they are actually organized, interrelated, and develop, seems to me a bit questionable.

After this brief interlude concerning the concept of historical genres and the need to counter certain neopragmatic and deconstructionist trends, I shall go back and clarify some of the terms in my working definition that I left deliberately vague and undetermined. I described the set of rules as flexible, but without specifying the degree of flexibility. It will suffice here to point out that the degree of flexibility is itself flexible—from genre to genre and from literary period to literary period. Classical and neoclassical literatures are less flexible than modern literature; and literary genres whose organizing principles are basically thematic or rhetorical (e.g., satire) enjoy greater flexibility than those with conspicuous formal organizing principles (e.g., the sonnet).[23] By stipu-

---

21. Jacques Derrida, "The Law of Genre," 206.

22. Philippe Lacoue-Labarthe and Jean-Luc Nancy, "Genre," 10.

23. In their interesting suggestion that generic rules might be described in terms of a flexible "preference model," Ellen Schauber and Ellen Spolsky, in *The Bounds of Interpretation*, 39–77, point out the different degrees of flexibility of generic rules when applied to structural as opposed to rhetorical ("functional") genres. Jean-Marie Schaeffer's distinction,

lating a flexible set of rules I emphasize the dynamic aspect of literary genre that allows some rules to be reshaped or loosened, but insists that writers who wish to participate in the dialogical framework of a generic tradition adhere to some norms associated with that tradition.

By speaking of rules (or norms) rather than of traits or characteristics, I seek to depict genre as a kind of "mediator" between author and reader. Robert Scholes, for example, says that, "the reading process and the writing process—are fundamentally generic in nature."[24] And Marie-Laure Ryan makes a similar point, using linguistic terminology, when she says that "the 'communicative competence' of the members of a culture includes a generic component through which they are able to handle a variety of linguistic artifacts such as tragedies, poems, jokes, and advertisements."[25] Whereas generic rules stand before the writer as an exemplum, challenge, or red flag, they appear to the reader as heuristic "reading directions," which may be obeyed or rejected. In all these cases, reference to *rules* (rather than to traits) stresses the institutional, conventional nature of the process of literary production, transmission, and reception.

By saying that the set of rules is constitutive, rather than regulative, I wish to emphasize the intimate connection between the abstract "rules of the genre" and the literary texts that are its manifestations. John Searle explains the distinction between constitutive and regulative rules in a way pertinent to my intention: "Regulative rules regulate a pre-existing activity, an activity whose existence is logically independent of the rules. Constitutive rules constitute (and also regulate) an activity the existence of which is logically dependent on the rules."[26]

For example, it is pointless to think of specific, concrete sonnets preexisting the rules of sonnets. These rules need not necessarily be explicit, or in some cases even consciously known to the writer. Sometimes, generic rules are grasped intuitively rather than known consciously. Going to the theater to see a comedy involves having certain expectations, but does not depend on having an articulated, theoretical understanding of a construction known as "Comedy." These expectations need not necessarily be fulfilled, but they do form an integral part of the communicative situation of watching that play.

---

in "Literary Genres and Textual Genericity," 183, between "synthetic genericity" and "analytical genericity" also points out the different degrees of flexibility in different generic traditions.

24. Scholes, *Structuralism in Literature,* 130.

25. Marie-Laure Ryan, "Introduction: On the Why, What and How of Generic Taxonomy," 112.

26. John R. Searle, *Speech Acts: An Essay in the Philosophy of Language,* 34.

The rules apply to some levels of the literary text, and in any case to more than one. This point must be introduced into the definition in order to distinguish generic rules (or norms) from types of rules that operate on the text, but on only *one* level of it. Prosodic rules, for example, are also constitutive rules, but they differ from generic rules in that they operate on only one level of the text (the phonetic). Prosodic rules have, of course, played decisive roles in constituting genres (especially in classical literature), but the concept of genre involves a combination of rules operating on more than one level. For example, a sonnet is a *junction* of certain prosodic patterns, of meter and rhyme, of graphic pattern, and of other more flexible thematic and structural rules (e.g., some conventional topics; the couplet as a conclusion or an antithesis to the quatrains).

The rest of my definition is intended to relate the concept of literary genre to certain other common groupings in literature, and to distinguish it from them.

Although I do not propose to determine how many authors should write within a generic framework, there is no doubt that a genre cannot remain an individual endeavor. No matter how important a specific writer is in a given generic tradition, he is always only a part of that tradition. An individual writer may found a genre (e.g., Homer and epic poetry), but this implies "offspring" who carry on the generic tradition thus established. A writer's idiomatic style or thematic preoccupations may modify a genre or mark a key stage in its development (e.g., the Petrarchan sonnet and the Shakespearean tragedy), but the poetic principles that characterize an author are not identical with the princples that characterize a genre. In other words, the poetics of an individual writer include characteristics that are "variables" from the point of view of the genre. Elements essential to any description of an individual writer are options in the genre's tradition. This becomes evident when the same poetic traits of the same writer are expressed in *different* genres (Pope's elegant heroic couplets, for example, which may appear in a satirical poem, a didactic treatise, or a pastoral), without being considered a constitutive element of any of these genres.

The fact that a genre extends beyond any individual writer seems quite obvious, but it is more problematic and controversial to postulate that it should also transcend the boundaries of any single literary period. Here one may raise counterexamples such as Attic Old Comedy. If, however, we consider the links between Aristophanes' works and the great chain of satirical writings, his plays seem less isolated and their generic principles less confined to one literary period. We may, of course, stress the uniqueness of Aristophanes' satirical comedies, and to do so—

since I qualify this clause in my definition with "usually"—would not undermine my basic claim, which applies to the bulk of literary genres. In any case, this element of the definition seems necessary if we are to distinguish the rules of a genre from the norms that characterize a literary school or movement or, more generally, the concept of a literary period. These poetic norms do of course play an enormous role in shaping and in modifying literary genres (e.g., Greek tragedy, Elizabethan comedy, futuristic poetry, or the modernistic novel), but they do not encompass the entire range of possibilities and tradition of these genres.[27]

This point is reinforced by the simple linguistic fact that the same term is used to refer to different periods; for example, we use the word *tragedy* when we speak of classical tragedy, Renaissance tragedy, and neoclassical tragedy. This presumably reflects some continuity. An opposing point of view would have to make a nominalistic argument that no real affinities exist between such manifestations of the genre in different periods. I admit that this is logically possible and that many disputes could only be resolved by analyzing the concrete evidence supported by the texts in question. However, I would still argue that it is simpler (and therefore better, all other things being equal) and more fruitful to assume the existence of connections between the different historical phases of a given genre, just as the linguistic usage suggests. In other words, the burden of proof lies with those who claim that despite the same term, there are no affinities between the various historical phases of a given genre.

In order to resolve this sort of argument by the nominalistic approach, it might be useful at this point to introduce the concept of the *subgenre*. The concrete configuration of the generic rules *and* poetic norms that characterize a literary period or movement would constitute a subgenre. A subgenre could also emerge as a result of the introduction of a new, dominant element (or elements) into the generic system. This conspicuous new element could be thematic (the historical novel) or formal (the English sonnet) or a mixture of the two (as with the detective novel).

My last point in the working definition—namely that a genre transcends the boundaries of languages and cultures—is also qualified, because national literatures sometimes become isolated from one another for geographical or political reasons. In such cases, where the very

---

27. For an alternative view of literary genre that confines it to only one literary period, see Uri Margolin, "The Concept of Genre as Historical Category" and "Historical Literary Genre: The Concept and Its Uses." But even Margolin concedes from time to time that literary genres can be described as transcending the boundaries of one literary period (see, for instance, "The Concept of Genre," 45 and 55). Perhaps my disagreement with Margolin is merely semantic: what he calls a "genre," I call a "subgenre."

channels of intercultural and interlingual communication are blocked, the generic system will remain confined within its linguistic boundaries. However, this situation in its pure form seems to be the exception in literary history; interlingual and intercultural contacts are the norm. Where such contacts occur, literary genres commonly migrate across the borders and establish "colonies" in neighboring countries or languages.[28]

The fact that a genre can retain its identity in the face of sometimes radical changes in its linguistic and cultural environment illustrates the flexibility of the genre's rule and its ability to absorb "culture shock." At the same time, the generic rules often change as a result of these migrations, creating a variant, or a subgenre—e.g., the sonnet, while migrating from Italy to England, changed its rhyme scheme. These variants to which a genre's "expansionism" gives rise can be used as a means of further subclassification within a given phase of the genre; for example, we can speak of neoclassical French tragedy or of the English romantic sonnet.

A genre may be permitted to join the "club" of genres only after it has gained a number of followers, has some claim to longevity, and has (preferably) traveled from its homeland to visit foreign countries and leave behind some offspring.

EXAMPLES: SCOPE AND LANGUAGE

I would like to make a final note in this introductory chapter about how I selected the texts to be analyzed or cited in the following chapters. Of course, the most important criterion is relevance to the issue or specific theory involved. In addition to this, I tried to confine myself to central texts of Western literature. The reason for this is simple: an elaborated theoretical framework that can accommodate only marginal or esoteric examples to support itself will lack credibility as a sound theory. On the other hand, if a theory can account for both central and marginal cases, that would be a mark of its validity.

In confining myself to the paradigmatic cases, to texts that have become widely recognized as representative of certain genres, I also avoid futile arguments about the generic "identity" of different marginal cases. These problematic cases, interesting and important as they may be, should not make us abandon all generic divisions, as the existence of

---

28. Normally the move will be from a complete, developed literary system to an incomplete one. On these issues see Even-Zohar, *Polysystem Studies,* 53–72.

amphibious vehicles does not make us abandon the distinction between cars and ships.

Still, even with these methodological restrictions, I am left with a wide variety of examples, ranging from epic poetry to modern novels, and from classical comedies to Renaissance lyric poetry. The texts I cite are drawn from widely differing times, languages, and cultural backgrounds. It would be foolish or idle of me to claim that my expertise covers this range of genres, languages, and periods (and, of course, it would also be untrue). Nevertheless, I have decided to venture into these multifarious literary territories because of my basic conviction that the crossing of linguistic and national borders, as well as crossing literary periods, is a hallmark of my subject matter. And wherever it goes, I should follow.

Since the texts to be used are taken from a variety of linguistic backgrounds, I have decided to use modern English translations in all cases. I will refer to the original only where the translation does not succeed (in my judgment) in conveying a specific point relevant to my discussion.

Chapter 2

Literary Genres
as Biological Species

Today, so long after it has become a subject for sober obituaries,[1] my reintroduction of the biological analogy into genre theory may seem a necrophiliac impulse. One might, of course, welcome a postmortem analysis of this conceptual analogy, which flourished around the turn of the century, but regard with skepticism any attempt to consider the biological analogy a promising conceptual framework for the field of contemporary genre studies. Nonetheless, my objective in this chapter is precisely that, to advocate the fruitfulness of the biological analogy today.

I should state at the outset that I do not expect the biological analogy to provide a comprehensive model for genre theory. Its usefulness appears to be restricted to questions of generic evolution and interrelationship, the complex process of the emergence of new genres on the literary scene, and the decline of old ones. Other issues central to genre theory, such as the internal structure of a genre, the relationship between a specific text and the generic conventions, or the place of these conventions in interpretation, have very little to do with the biological analogy.

1. See, for instance, Wellek's article "The Concept of Evolution in Literary History," 37–53; the critical presentation by Ehrenpreis in his *"Type" Approach to Literature*, 38–42; Margolin's dissertation, "The Concept of Genre," 135–38; and Schaeffer's astute discussion in *Qu'est-ce qu'un genre littéraire?* 47–63.

LIFE, DEATH, AND EVOLUTIONARY CONCEPTS

When Benjamin Harshav (Hrushovski) titled one of his lectures "Why Can We Have Romantic Realism and not Doggy Cats?" he was hinting at one of the major differences between biological species and literary groupings (movements and schools as well as genres). Whereas the former very rarely produce hybrids, literary genres (and movements) intermingle constantly. Further, any biological hybrid is likely to be sterile, especially when there is a great genetic distance between its parents. Literary hybrids, however, are often very prolific, no matter how different the "parents" are: tragicomedy is perhaps the most conspicuous example, but by no means the only one. Thus hybridization in . literature is not only more common than hybridization in nature; it is also more productive.

To this point, one may add another important sense in which the analogy does not hold. Todorov clearly formulates the contrast between biological species and literary genres:

> Being familiar with the species tiger, we can deduce from it the properties of each individual tiger; the birth of a new tiger does not modify the species in its definition. The impact of individual organisms on the evolution of the species is so slow that we can discount it in practice. . . . The same is not the case in the realm of art or of science. Here evolution operates with an altogether different rhythm: *every* work modifies the sum of possible works, each new example alters the species.[2]

A similar statement can be found in Uri Margolin's criticism of the biological analogy: "In contrast to biology, many specimens always deviate from the genre concepts of their time, every such deviation is significant, and a number of them could very well signal the emergence of a new 'species.' "[3]

And Wellek, in his well-known attack on the biological analogy, opens his list of arguments by rejecting the fixed generic concept implied by the biological analogy: "Darwinian or Spencerian evolutionism is false when applied to literature because there are no fixed genres comparable to biological species which can serve as substrata of evolution."[4]

So far, the critics I have quoted have objected forcefully to the careless

2. Tzvetan Todorov, *The Fantastic: A Structural Approach to a Literary Genre*, 6.
3. Margolin, "The Concept of Genre," 118.
4. Wellek, "The Concept of Evolution," 45.

application of the analogy. They do so by stressing the points where the two domains differ.

Two aspects seem to be central in these criticisms. First, compared to a biological species, a literary genre looks like a far more flexible, open-ended, and undetermined kind of "population." Second, concerning the relationship between the individual unit (organism in the case of species, text in the case of genre) and its related group (species and genre, respectively), in biology the individual can only manifest or exemplify the group, whereas in literature each of the individual units to some extent modifies and changes the group.

This degree of modification of relationships between the group and the individual is striking on the diachronic level: thousands of years may pass with no perceptible impact on most biological species, but the same span of time will alter most radically an entire literary system, including most of its genres.

These two basic points seem to me valid and illuminating. But do they thwart any attempt to use the biological analogy? According to the perspective I present later, not necessarily. They should, however, ensure that any future attempts to apply the biological analogy will be more cautious. Note by the way that even these two critical points may be challenged. This is not to say that the points are not valid; they are. But the question is whether the differences between the two domains are differences of kind, or just of degree.

Assuming, for instance, that we can reach an algorithm that will translate "biological time" into "cultural time": the former, needless to say, seems very slow compared to the latter. Comparing these two systems we may find that what seems fixed and stable in a biological species seems so only because it is viewed from within the perspective of cultural time. If a year in cultural history is "translated" into a thousand years (for example) of biological history, perhaps the two realms will start to look more alike than we had anticipated. Projecting natural history on the screen in this way, with an accelerated projector, would probably enhance the similarities between natural and cultural evolution. And such a perception may lead us to qualify some of the objections quoted above.

But even if we grant the validity of these objections, they need not undermine the whole analogical approach. Analogy, after all, is not identity, and stressing some dissimilar aspects does not discredit the entire project. A look at some further objections to the biological analogy reveals that the fault is sometimes not with the analogy as such, but with some of its formulations and hasty applications.

Wellek's second argument against the analogy is that with literary genres, unlike biological species, "there is no inevitable growth and decay."[5] This point, with some related issues, is elaborated by Margolin:

> I do not believe that there is any one predetermined generic essence inherent in all historical genres and embodied to various degrees of perfection in different works and phases of each genre. I reject the conception of an inevitable, unidirectional, and irreversible movement of striving towards one single predetermined peak and of ensuing decline. This also entails a rejection of the teleological view of genre dynamics. Accordingly, I cannot subscribe either to the idea that each genre has any one immanent "telos" and perfect instance, or to the assumption that it is a closed system.[6]

Now, I can heartily agree with all these statements, and still advocate the biological, evolutionary analogy as a pertinent perspective for genre theory. How is such an apparent contradiction possible? The answer is simple: the points that both Wellek and Margolin are making here have nothing to do with true evolutionary concepts. In order to understand the virulence of these attacks and to expose the fundamental misunderstanding that clouds the issue of the evolutionary analogy, a brief look at some loci classici might be helpful.

The two most famous and important figures in the application of the biological-evolutionary analogy to the literary field are Ferdinand Brunetière in France and J. A. Symonds in England, both working around the turn of this century.[7] Brunetière is perhaps the more fascinating of the two, because one can find in his theoretical pronouncements (as well as in his descriptive historiography) a mixture of new insights and old fallacies. The most problematical point is that Brunetière, even as he declares his advocacy of evolutionary theories, is actually referring to something else. Under the heading "De la fixation des genres" he speaks of the existence of a genre as analogous to "une existence individuelle, une existence comparable à la vôtre ou à la mienne, avec un commencement, un milieu et une fin."[8]

5. Ibid., 51.

6. Margolin, "The Concept of Genre," 136–37.

7. Ferdinand Brunetière, in his *L'Evolution des genres dans l'histoire de la littérature*, especially the first chapter, and in his *L'Evolution de la poésie lyrique en France au dix-neuvième siècle*; J. A. Symonds, "On the Application of Evolutionary Principles to Art and Literature," 42–83. For a good retrospective account of the growth and decline of the biological analogy around the turn of the century, see Wellek, "The Concept of Evolution," and Ehrenpreis, *The "Type" Approach to Literature*.

8. Brunetière, *L'Evolution des genres*, 12.

This confusion between the life cycle of an individual and the concept of a species is ubiquitous in Brunetière's "evolutionary" theory of genres. Note, for example, the following passage from L'Evolution de la poésie lyrique:

> Comment naissent les genres, à la faveur de quelles circonstances de temps ou de milieu; comment ils se distinguent et comment ils se developpent—à la façon d'un être vivant—et comment ils s'organisent, eliminant, ecartant tout ce qui peut leur nuire, et, au contraire, s'adaptant ou s'assimilant tout ce qui peut leur servir, les nourrir, les aider à grandir; . . . telles sont, Messieurs, les questions que se propose de traiter la methode evolutive.[9]

First, I should note that to depict biological species as actively, almost volitionally, adapting to their environment is more appropriate to Lamarck than to Darwin. But aside from this, Brunetière's fundamental fallacy reappears here. The evolutionary, sometimes characteristically Darwinian terminology only camouflages Brunetière's true model: the life cycle of an individual organism. Parenthetical phrases may sometimes betray one's deepest convictions, as in this case, where amid all the talk about adaptation, nourishment, and transformation, Brunetière says "à la façon d'un être vivant." This, not evolutionary species, constitutes Brunetière's archetypal analogy, despite his evolutionary rhetoric.

Adherence to the analogy of the life cycle of an individual organism rather than of a species, clearly traceable in Brunetière's formulations, becomes even more explicit in Symonds's "evolutionary" theory. Discussing Elizabethan drama, Symonds claims that: "This type of art exhibits qualities analogous to those of an organic complex undergoing successive phases of germination, expansion, efflorescence, and decay."[10] The difference between an evolutionary model based on the species and a model based on the individual organism cannot be overemphasized. Most important, there is no line of development from birth through maturity to death with biological species. Some species reach "mature" form very quickly and maintain it, with no conspicuous signs of development or "decay," for millions of years. Further, species that have become extinct did not die of some intrinsic "aging" but because of some combination of geological and environmental changes with which it was not able to cope (despite its "maturity"). Thus, carelessly mixing the two metaphors may result in serious confusion.[11]

9. Brunetière, L'Evolution de la poésie, 5.
10. Symonds, "On the Application," 58.
11. Stephen J. Gould, in his Ever Since Darwin: Reflections in Natural History, 42–43,

Going back now to modern criticism of the biological analogy, it is easier to see what triggered the strenuous attacks—not a consistent application of truly evolutionary concepts, but rather a bewildering confusion of Darwinian and "organistic" analogies. Modern criticism, instead of pinpointing the fallacies of the biological analogy, tried to discredit any attempt to use this analogy. Wellek, for instance, rightly rejects Brunetière's concepts of "fixed genres" and of an "inevitable growth and decay" of genres. He is less persuasive, though, when he goes on to claim that there is "no transformation of one genre into another, no actual struggle for life among genres."[12] He offers some arguments against Brunetière's "transformation assumption" in discussing the latter's claim that "French pulpit oratory of the seventeenth and eighteenth centuries was thus changed into the lyrical poetry of the Romantic movement."[13] To this, Wellek critically responds: "But the analogy will not withstand close inspection: at most, one could say that pulpit oratory expresses similar feelings (e.g., about the transience of things human) or fulfills similar social functions (the articulation of the sense of the metaphysical behind our lives). But surely no genre has literally changed into another."[14]

Since no analogical model claims that the features compared in an analogy have to be identical, Wellek's final sentence in the quotation seems truly strange. Moreover, Wellek's formulations, with only minor modifications, might quite easily fit into an "evolutionary" framework. If pulpit oratory in France was declining as a viable genre, and, in the subsequent literary period, a new genre was emerging, in romantic poetry, which "expresses similar feelings," why not interpret the transfer of some poetic feature (in this particular example an expressive one) from a disappearing genre to a new, emerging, one as the "transformation of the genre"?[15] Consider another issue: Assume that writers who create within a specific generic framework direct their works to a certain kind of reader. Assume further that similar generic frameworks must compete for overlapping target readerships, which can consume only so

---

presents the theory that "evolutionary lineages, like individuals, had cycles of growth, maturity, old age, and death (extinction)" as *incompatible* with Darwinism because it assumes that, at some point, "old," crippled forms of a species prevail. For Brunetière's confusion between the evolutionary model and the life-cycle model, see Jean-Marie Schaeffer, *Qu'est-ce qu'un genre littéraire?* 59–62.

12. Wellek, "The Concept of Evolution," 51.

13. Ibid., 44–45.

14. Ibid., 45.

15. For Elton Hocking, for instance, the fact that some of a genre's "qualities pass into surviving or newer forms" is an excellent example of "transformation of the genre." See Elton Hocking, *Ferdinand Brunetière: The Evolution of a Critic*, 171.

many works associated with only a limited number of literary kinds (e.g., adventure stories and science fiction compete for nearly the same target readership). Does not then the concept of a "struggle for survival" seem more pertinent to the dynamics of literary kinds than first suspected?

Thus one can either be ready to perceive the analogical implications of evolutionary concepts such as "transformation of genre" and "struggle for survival," or else adamantly stick to the letter, which is exactly what Wellek does.

ONE EXCEPTION, TWO PROBLEMS, THREE STAGES

Amid widespread contemporary dismissal of the biological analogy, there is one serious dissenting voice. Alastair Fowler merits our sympathy and praise when, despite the critical consensus, he dares to revive the biological analogy and apply it to genre theory.[16]

Fowler poses the right questions concerning the evolutionary issue. His answers to these questions, however, do not seem satisfactory. He starts his discussion of "the life and death of literary forms" with a very useful distinction between the "life and death" of individual works and the "life and death" of literary genres: "The historical duration of works need not coincide with the duration of the forms they use."[17] He then defines the "death" of a genre: "Pronounce a genre dead if works related to it directly are no longer widely read, so that its forms have become unintelligible without scholarly effort."[18]

One can raise some objections to the vagueness of some key terms in this definition. How many works should be read? In what sense are these works directly related to the genre? How widely read? Finally, how is a scholarly effort defined (a preface, notes, a closely annotated edition)? These questions pose difficulties in any attempt to make Fowler's definition workable. But my main objection to this definition of a genre's "death" is that it is based on a misleading concept of what a genre is or what generic rules are. According to Fowler, generic conventions are similar to the rules of signaling systems; thanks to them we are able to interpret and understand literary texts:

16. Alastair Fowler, "The Life and Death of Literary Forms," 199–216. The principles advocated in this article were later incorporated in his *Kinds of Literature*, 149–90.
17. Fowler, "The Life and Death," 199.
18. Ibid., 209.

Traditional genres and modes . . . enable the reader to share types of meaning economically. Moreover, his subsequent understanding is also genre-bound: he can only think sensibly of *Oedipus Tyrannus* as a tragedy, related to other tragedies. If he ignores or despises genre, or gets it wrong, misreading results. Johnson's blunder over *Lycidas* and the more recent and even more spectacular critical error of taking *Paradise Lost* as classical epic with Satan the hero are dreadful examples. Clearly, generic forms must rank among the most important of the signal systems that communicate a literary work.[19]

To me, a statement that one can think sensibly of *Oedipus Tyrannus* only as a tragedy seems a little tyrannical itself. Why not think of it, at least in some context, as the first detective story? Perhaps Fowler has overemphasized the role of generic rules in literary interpretation. Although I believe that genres play an important role as orienting devices in literary history and communication, I think that Fowler loads a far greater burden onto genre than it can sustain. Genre as a "signal system," producing and ensuring correct interpretations, is an unrealistic picture of how generic conventions function. We may approach a text with some assumptions about the generic tradition on which it relies, but there is always a *dialectical relationship* between these assumptions and expectations and what the text itself tells us. It is true that our interpretation is (at least partly) a product of our assumption about the generic tradition on which the text relies, but it is equally true that this very assumption is a product of our interpretation. Thus, generic assumptions are not protected from the "hermeneutical circle"—where the significance of the whole is a function of its constituting elements and the meaning of these elements is determined in its turn by the significance of the whole—evident in any act of interpretation.

Whereas according to Fowler's picture the interpreter has to be equipped with the generic "code" in order to "decipher" a specific text, I propose a more complicated, and to my view a more truthful, picture of how generic assumptions function in the act of interpreting a literary text: the specific text activates our relevant knowledge and assumptions concerning various genres of whose tradition the text reminds us, and those generic frameworks contribute, on their part, to our understanding and integrating various elements of the specific text. Interpreting the text involves generic knowledge, as well as other types of knowledge, but it is by no means *determined* by this knowledge.

19. Ibid., 201.

Taking Satan to be the hero of *Paradise Lost*, for example, is perhaps a romantic fallacy. However, it can be said that Milton's poem enables, and to some extent even encourages such a "fallacy." To some extent, we may even argue that the fact that *Paradise Lost* allows different interpretations of the identity of its "true" hero is a mark of its complexity. But the crucial point is that rejecting Satan as hero, and deciding that the true hero is the Son, ensues from a careful examination of the part played by Satan in the poem and a close inspection of the other possible "candidates" for the role of "hero." It is by no means a conclusion that we reach because we were told that the true "signal system" of *Paradise Lost* is that of Christian epic. This last proposition might serve at best as a working hypothesis, or a heuristic assumption, but not as a mechanism that produces an interpretation. Furthermore, even if we accept *Paradise Lost* to be a "Christian epic," we can still prefer Adam, for example, as the "true hero" of the text (an interpretation I personally favor). As a matter of fact, one source for the power of Milton's epic is precisely this conflict concerning the "true and only" hero of the poem.

But it is the general methodological warning against assigning too great an interpretative weight to generic concepts that I want to stress here, not any specific interpretation of Milton's *Paradise Lost*.[20] If we assume that generic rules function like the rules of a signaling system, then losing these rules, so necessary for "correct reading," can be seen as the "death" of the genre. Hence Fowler's emphasis on the need for scholarly reconstruction of the lost code as sign of the genre's "death." I argue that this perception of generic conventions assumes too much about their role in the actual process of interpretation.[21] There are only a few genres whose conventions bear any real similarity to the "deciphering code" envisioned by Fowler. I can think of some allegorical traditions in poetry that cannot be understood without a "key" and some highly formalistic devices that are not apparent to a casual reader.[22] Most generic conventions, however, can be understood from the text by sensible and sensitive reading.

20. Such a methodological warning was persuasively formulated by John Reichert in "More Than Kin and Less Than Kind: The Limits of Genre Theory," 64.

21. It is ironic that Fowler refers to Hirsch's *Validity in Interpretation* throughout his discussion, despite the fact that the latter assigns a very minor and heuristic role to the traditional concept of genre. Hirsch introduces the concept of "intrinsic genre" as an alternative to the traditional concept of genre, which he considers too shaky and ephemeral. However, on precisely such a concept Fowler greatly relies. The problem with Hirsch's concept of "intrinsic genre" is that it is almost inseparable from the meaning of a specific text.

22. For instance, poems that can also be read backwards, a form in which some of the Jewish poets of Spain, especially in the late eleventh century, excelled.

Thus Fowler's definition of the "death" of a genre is problematic because it relies on a doubtful assumption about the role of generic conventions in the interpreting and understanding of literary texts. But there is a second major problem in this theory. According to Fowler, if we can define a genre's "death," we are also able to describe the *three* main phases of its "life," and these phases are "organic and invariable in sequence."[23] It is easy to recognize the return of the organistic fallacy in Fowler's "organic and invariable," but it is interesting to see how he specifies the stages of this "invariable sequence": "During the first phase, the genre-complex assembles, until a formal type emerges. . . . In phase two, a 'secondary' version of genre develops: a form that the author consciously bases on the earlier primary version."[24]

The flexible opposition of primary and secondary phases in a genre's tradition seems satisfying. It is a relative-contrastive definition according to which a text is not intrinsically and constantly "primary" or "secondary," but rather acquires these labels with respect to a specific historical situation.[25] Thus we may talk about Theocritus as "primary" when compared to the "secondary" Virgil in the pastoral tradition; but from Spenser's viewpoint, it is possible to describe both Theocritus and Virgil as "primary" and Spenser himself as "secondary."

But then, why and how do we need the tertiary phase that Fowler introduces later? I am afraid that this question has no clear answer in Fowler's conceptual framework. Having made the primary-secondary opposition that, at least in principle, can cover any generic development, he falls back on a "triadic" way of thinking that is incompatible with the concepts he himself is developing. One starts to suspect that the answer to the question "Why a tertiary phase?" does not lie in any coherent conceptual framework, but in an almost unconscious lapse into the "organistic fallacy" usually associated with three steps: birth or childhood, maturity, and decay or death.

In addition to the methodological and conceptual flaws that stem from this mixture of binary and triadic divisions, Fowler's triadic scheme raises some problems of validity even when taken on its own terms. Whereas his descriptions of the first two phases sometimes disclose a vacillation between a relative-contrastive ("empty," i.e., without specific characteristics for either of the two phases) and a substantive definition, the tertiary phase is given specific thematic and structural characteristics: "The tertiary form may be burlesque, or antithetic, or symbolic modu-

23. Fowler, "The Life and Death," 212.
24. Ibid.
25. Fowler, *Kinds of Literature*, 161–62.

lation of the secondary. . . . Tertiary development seems often to constitute an interiorizing. Thus *Paradise Lost*, like *The Faerie Queene*, has little wholly exterior action."[26]

One may wonder why the secondary phase could not take the form of, say, a symbolic modulation of the primary one, but instead of posing more perplexing questions, let us discuss some literary examples. More than once, Fowler illustrates his three "organic" phases with the epic tradition. Homeric epic represents, according to this scheme, the primary phase, Virgil's *Aeneid* the secondary, and Milton's *Paradise Lost* the tertiary. To corroborate Fowler's schema even further we may mention the mock-epic that flourished in the eighteenth century in England (*The Rape of the Lock* is perhaps the most famous, but by no means an isolated case) as another example of the tertiary phase, this time a burlesque. Thus at face value, an organic, three-phased description of the history of the epic seems valid. A closer look, however, will reveal many difficulties with this rigid, unidirectional schema.

Let me start by recalling that we can find mock-epic—a burlesque, supposedly "tertiary" phase—almost as early as we find the Homeric—"primary" phase—epic. Although the date of *The Battle of the Mice and Frogs*, an anonymous burlesque epic, continues to be uncertain, it was surely composed long before the *Aeneid*.

Even on its own grounds, then, the triadic schema is rendered vulnerable by the example of the ancient burlesque. In order to loosen this "organic and invariable" schema even further, I would like to discuss another example, this time a modern epic poem whose very existence challenges the rigidity of the scheme. This is *Pan Tadeusz*, written in the nineteenth century by the "national" Polish poet Adam Mickiewicz.[27] If, to use Fowler's phrase, "we know epic by, among other things, its high style, formulae, episodes and similes"[28] then *Pan Tadeusz* is an epic *par excellence*. We may add some more distinctive marks to this list, like stating the epic theme at the beginning of the poem:

> O Lithuania, my fatherland,
> Thou art like health; what praise thou shouldst command
> Only that man finds who has lost thee quite.[29]

And the invocation, addressed to some holy source of inspiration:

26. Fowler, "The Life and Death," 212–13.
27. Adam Mickiewicz, *Pan Tadeusz, or The Last Foray in Lithuania*, trans. Watson Kirkconnell (1962).
28. Fowler, "The Life and Death," 202.
29. Mickiewicz, *Pan Tadeusz* (1962), 7.

> O holy Virgin, who dost oversee
> Bright Czenstochowa and in Wilno shinest
> Above the Ostra Gate! . . .
> Meanwhile bear
> To those treed hills my spirit of despair,
> To those green meadows, stretching far and wide
> By the blue Niemen; . . . [30]

To these, we may add the structural division into twelve books, in imitation of Virgil, and that each book is preceded by an "argument" after the classical tradition (which was also adopted by Milton in *Paradise Lost*). On the level of the plot, we have a father (Jacek Soplica) returning, disguised, to his native land and being revealed to his son (Tadeusz).

And if this accumulation of evidence has not already convinced us, we might refer to the situation often represented in an epic—the so-called epic situation of a bard, telling and singing his epic poem to the native audience. Compare, for example, the epic situation of the Phaeacian poet Demodocus described by Homer in the *Odyssey*:

> The crier soon came, leading that man of song
> whom the Muse cherished; by her gift he knew
> the good of life, and evil—
> for she who lent him sweetness made him blind.
> Pontonoos fixed a studded chair for him
> hard by a pillar amid the banquetters,
> hanging the taut harp from the peg above him,
> and guided up his hands upon the strings;
> placed a bread basket at his side, and poured
> wine in a cap, that he might drink his fill. [31]

And here Mickiewicz's description of Jankiel, the Polish Jew who plays the dulcimer and sings of Poland's history:

> Jankiel loved Zosia greatly, beyond measure,
> And bowed his beard in token of assent.
> So to the centre of the throng he went
> And on his knees the dulcimer they slide; . . .
> Jankiel with half-closed eyes in silence lingers
> And holds the hammers sleeping in his fingers. . . .

---

30. Ibid.
31. Homer, *The Odyssey*, trans. Robert Fitzgerald, 8.27–36.

He played anew; the strings now trembled soft
With motions light as though a fly's faint wing
Sounded a gentle buzz upon the string.
The master gazed intently at the sky
For inspiration; with a haughty eye
He looked down at his silent instrument;
Then raised both hands, dropped them with firm intent
And with both hammers all the strings coerced.[32]

In addition to all these formal, structural, and thematic points that
make *Pan Tadeusz* a welcome member of the epic club, it is crucial to
note that the work played a central role in Polish literature and culture,
paralleled perhaps only by Homer's epics in Greece and the *Aeneid* in
Rome.[33]

If we adhere to Fowler's triadic scheme, we would expect that after
Milton's *Paradise Lost*, every epic would either be another demonstration
of "symbolic" tendencies or some debased "burlesque" form, or some
"antithesis," whatever that may mean. But *Pan Tadeusz* cannot easily be
fitted into one of these rubrics. According to Fowler's scheme, after
Milton's "symbolic" epic and after the burlesque mock-epics of the
eighteenth century, we stand at the genre's deathbed, and no new,
vigorous instance of it can be expected.

To be sure, *Pan Tadeusz* has some mock-heroic playfulness. But this
humorous aspect is not dominant in the poem, and is often a factor in
shaping important themes. To illustrate this intermingling of the mock-
heroic with serious thematic patterns, I will quote at some length an
episode in which Tadeusz, the young protagonist of the poem, sees
Telimena, an aging coquette who is having an affair with him:

But Telimena suddenly outspread
Her arms to left and right, leaped from her seat,
Jumped clear across the brook in wild retreat;
Pale, with dishevelled hair, she sought the wood,
Leaped in the air, and knelt, lay down for good,
And helpless to arise, writhed on the turf.
'Twas plain to see how sore in passion's surf
She suffered there; he saw the lady seize
Her breast, her neck, her foot-soles and her knees.

---

32. Mickiewicz, *Pan Tadeusz* (1962), 363–64.
33. See Wiktor Weintraub, *The Poetry of Adam Mickiewicz*, 264. See also the description
of *Pan Tadeusz* as the "only successful epic our century has produced," in George Brandes's
introduction to *Pan Tadeusz, or The Last Foray in Lithuania*, trans. George Rapall (1917), ix.

> He sprang to help her, thinking she'd gone mad
> Or had a fit.[34]

It is not difficult to see that this scene is a pointed allusion to the fourth book of the *Aeneid,* when Dido becomes frantic after hearing that Aeneas is to depart:

> But Dido, desperate, beside herself
> with awful undertakings, eyes bloodshot
> and rolling, and her quivering cheeks flecked
> with stains and pale with coming death, now bursts
> across the inner courtyards of her palace.
> She mounts in madness that high pyre, unsheathes
> the Dardan sword, a gift not sought for such
> an end.[35]

This literary allusion is reinforced by some decisive indications. First, in *Pan Tadeusz* Telimena fills Dido's function in the *Aeneid,* that of a loving woman abandoned for the sake of a better, purer, and more promising young bride who symbolizes a fresh start on the national as well as the personal level. And as if these local and structural marks were not enough, Mickiewicz goes out of his way to make the allusion conspicuous by explicitly introducing Dido's name into his text—in the "Argument" that precedes book eight of *Pan Tadeusz* and in an anecdote about Dido that one of his characters tells.[36]

But now, after establishing the seemingly dramatic episode in which Telimena is associated with the tragic figure of Dido, he gives a realistic explanation of her seemingly distraught behavior:

> Beside a neighbouring birch grove stood a hill
> Of ants, mighty mound piled up with skill;
> These frugal insects through the grass would crawl,
> Mobile and black; and, whether at the call
> Of pleasure or of need one cannot tell,
> Fair Meditation's temple they loved well;
> Had trodden from their hillock to the spring
> A path by which they led their mustering.

34. Mickiewicz, *Pan Tadeusz* (1962), 149.
35. Virgil, *The Aeneid of Virgil,* trans. Allen Mandelbaum, 4.888–95.
36. Mickiewicz, *Pan Tadeusz* (1962), 138, and his own note 90, on page 379, about the source of this anecdote—another way to emphasize the importance of the intertextual relationships.

Unfortunately, Telimena sat
Right in the middle of their highway flat;
The ants, allured by snowy stocking's sheen,
Crawled up through all her clothes, with tickling keen,
And bit her everywhere. She ran, she shook,
Then sitting down, their capture undertook.[37]

The mock-heroic comic clash is obvious. On the one hand we have the tragic figure of Dido rushing to her death, caught by terrible *furor*, and on the other—the coquettish Telimena, attacked by ants. The ants, by the way, are not totally original: Virgil introduces them in book four of the *Aeneid* (lines 553–60), the book of Dido, but there they appear only on the figurative level, as part of a simile. Here, Mickiewicz brings them into the (fictional) world of the poem, as part of his realistic approach.

But this incident is incorporated into a larger thematic pattern of the poem: the process of disillusionment that the young Tadeusz is undergoing. His disenchantment with Telimena's charms is a true process of personal maturation (almost in the manner of a bildungsroman). This psychological process has some nationalistic overtones, because Telimena also represents foreign, Russian, influences from which the Poles need to be liberated in order to achieve a mature and independent status as a nation.

This amusing, down-to-earth explanation of Telimena's behavior is part of Mickiewicz's attempt to write a *realistic epic*. This attempt can be found on various levels of the poem, but perhaps it will be revealing to concentrate on one of the most famous marks of a true epic poem—its similes.

In one long and elaborated simile, Mickiewicz likens a tavern to a praying Jew:

Thus, from afar, the likeness clear one sees—
The tottering crooked inn was like a Jew,
Nodding himself in prayer; the roof, in view,
Was like his cap, the touzled thatch his beard,
The smoky, dirty walls his frock appeared;
While at the front the carvings, I avow,
Jut outward like the buttons on his brow.[38]

37. Ibid., 149.
38. Ibid., 113.

But the interesting point is that the simile here, unlike those in a classical epic, is *realistically motivated:* the tavern is likened to a Jew because it is Jankiel the Jew who runs and dominates the place:

> Jankiel, the host, stood in their midst and wore
> A long black gown that fluttered to the floor,
> Fastened with silver clasps. . . .
> The Jew was old, and famed for probity;
> For many years he'd been the licensee;
> Peasants and gentry loved him in accord;
> None ever went complaining to his lord.[39]

Now, if the hallmark of realistic literature is the metonymy that stands behind (or "motivates") the metaphor, as Roman Jakobson's dictum goes, then the example just discussed is a nice illustration of Mickiewicz's realistic intentions, and achievements.

To conclude my brief argument: Mickiewicz's epic poem can be described as a successful attempt to embody a new nationalistic ethos in old epic patterns, and to try to create a synthesis between the lofty epic world and the realistic, down-to-earth world.[40] At any rate, it is living proof that Fowler's triadic schema is too narrow and restrictive compared with the rich, everchanging, and basically unpredictable possibilities of the evolution of literary genres.

To shake Fowler's "organic and invariable" schema even further, we can take a brief look at the list of modern epic poems discussed by Paul Merchant in his short introductory book on epic: Wordsworth's *Prelude* and *The Recluse;* Byron's *Don Juan;* William Carlos Williams's *Paterson;* Pound's *Cantos;* Whitman's *Leaves of Grass;* David Jones's *Anathemata.* And among non-English modern epic poems he mentions Ivo Andric's *Bosnian Story* (Yugoslavia); Saint-John Perse's *Anabasis* (France); Koetis Palamas's *Twelve Lays of the Gipsy;* Odysseus Elytis's *Worthy It Is;* Kazantzakis's *Odyssey;* and Takis Sinopoulus's *Deathfeast* (Greece).[41] Per-

---

39. Ibid., 113–14.

40. Here Fowler might argue that Mickiewicz's poem is not truly an epic but rather a fusion of two different genres: the epic and the historical novel. Thus, I cannot claim it as a counterexample for Fowler's description of the tertiary stage of a genre, because it simply is not a tertiary stage of epic. This seems to be a strong argument, but actually it relies on circular reasoning: every tertiary development in a generic tradition that does not fit into Fowler's specific characteristics can be automatically dismissed as "something else" (a fusion of two genres, a mode, a subgenre). I hope that the evidence I have provided concerning the central epic patterns in *Pan Tadeusz* would make the retreat to such circular argument difficult.

41. Paul Merchant, *The Epic,* 83–94.

haps it is possible to "squeeze" all these works into Fowler's "tertiary" phase, but at what cost? I believe that such a "squeezing" is possible only if one first squeezes dry many important and vivacious aspects of these works.

But if Fowler's attempt to revive the biological analogy results in various conceptual and descriptive inadequacies, what do we have left? My basic, and to some extent provocative answer would be—a true evolutionary framework, inspired by certain Darwinian concepts.

DARWINISM: ALIVE AND KICKING

The major recurring objection to Darwinian concepts made by literary scholars is that Darwinism is a deterministic way of thinking that suppresses the free individual spirit. When Darwinian principles are cautiously applied, these accusations prove groundless.

Stephen Jay Gould, one of the best advocates of Darwin today, summarizes Darwin's arguments concerning natural selection as follows:

1. Organisms vary, and these variations are inherited (at least in part) by their offspring.
2. Organisms produce more offspring than can possibly survive.
3. On average, offspring that vary most strongly in directions favored by the environment will survive and propagate.
   Favorable variation will therefore accumulate in populations by natural selection. . . .
   The essence of Darwin's theory lies in his contention that natural selection is the creative force of evolution—not just the executioner of the unfit. . . .
   [V]ariation must be random, or at least not preferentially inclined toward adaptation. For, if variation comes prepackaged in the right direction, then selection plays no creative role, but merely eliminates the unlucky individuals who do not vary in the appropriate way. . . .
   Evolution is a mixture of chance and necessity—chance at the level of variation, necessity in the working of selection.[42]

According to these formulations, the parameters of a comparison between the biological and the literary fields can be established as follows:

42. Gould, *Ever Since Darwin*, 11–12. The dialectics of chance and necessity as characterizing evolutionary processes have been elaborated by Jacques Monod in *Chance and Necessity*.

The individual organism is analogous to the individual text, the biological species to the literary genre, and the natural environment to the "cultural environment." Natural selection will turn out to be, from this perspective, literary and cultural selection. It is essential to demonstrate at this preliminary stage that Darwinism does *not* entail determinism. Any mechanistic and deterministic approach that considers literary texts in the context of culture and society (like some simplistic Marxist approaches) will stress that literary texts are but a *product* of this cultural environment. True Darwinism, on the contrary, as an analogy to literary production, leaves great leeway: new works, new variations, new directions (or, for that matter, old and epigonic ones) are *not determined* by the environment, but rather are *assumed* by the theory. It is on this level of basically free production that the mechanisms of cultural selection operate, and here processes are bound by certain restrictions.

In other words, this evolutionary approach allows full poetic license; every eccentric innovation, every avant-garde (or epigonic or archaizing) movement has equal standing as a legitimate manifestation of literary production. This evolutionary framework does not require accepting a mechanistic, deterministic approach on the level of production.

If we assume that only a portion of the literary productions that enter the cultural scene can "survive," then the variations face the restrictions and mechanisms of selection. Some variations are fostered, encouraged, and elevated, and some are suppressed. Following this interpretation of the Darwinian approach, there is no deterministic assumption on the level of literary production. In other words, such an approach does not predict "what literature will be written," although it may venture some answers (at least in principle) to questions such as "what literature will be accepted and promoted, or coerced and restricted, in a given cultural environment." In other words, the question that a true evolutionist will ask concerning literary genres is not "how is a genre produced by its cultural environment?" but rather "how does a generic tradition, having been produced, succeed in establishing itself on the literary and cultural scene?"

In culture, we should remember, the forces that select are guided (unlike in nature) by value systems. The literary environment is a cluster of institutionalized values (aesthetic, ideological, political) that promote some parts of the literary production and suppress others. It is also important to note that the literary environment is much more dynamic and changeable than the natural environment (although the latter is by no means static); there is a dialectical relationship between the literary production and the literary environment in which the former may not only adapt itself to the latter but also contribute to reshaping it.

In any case, to know what prevails culturally would require us to look into a complicated mechanism of hierarchical systems and institutions, including publishers, readership, critical discussions, educational systems, and translations.[43] All these complicated and interrelated factors participate in shaping what Daniel Milo calls our *"bagage culturel,"*[44] including, I may add, the literary-generic system of that *"bagage."* A truly evolutionary perspective is, of course, not satisfied with enumerating the prevailing genres in a given "cultural environment." Certain key evolutionary concepts, when cautiously used, may throw light on the intricate relations between literary genres and the cultural scene in which they operate.[45]

The first pertinent evolutionary concepts that I would like to introduce are those of generic survival and generic productivity. In fact, in the perspective I propose, the real hallmark for the survival of a genre is not whether its works are read or interpreted "correctly" (as Fowler argues), but whether new works associated with a specific generic tradition are *produced*. The stress on *productivity* goes hand in hand with the biological analogy that regards the *procreation* (not merely the existence of individuals) of a species to be the hallmark of its survival. A necessary condition, of course, if new works are to be produced, is that important manifestations of the genre are available and become part of the "cultural middle ground." A work must first be published and read to be a model, or an inspiration, or a challenge for further writers who wish to participate in a generic dialogue, as in the biological analogue an organism must procreate to contribute to the survival of the species. Thus survival of literary genres should be perceived in terms of production and not of reception.[46] The latter is a necessary, but not a sufficient condition for generic survival. Literary genres, like biological species, are recognized as such only "retrospectively." It is not enough that we recognize a new work as fitting no existing generic system; only after that work has

43. For an interesting attempt to examine these cultural systems from a Darwinian perspective, see Daniel Milo, "Aspects de la survie culturelle."

44. Ibid., 13–14.

45. I should mention in this context Richard Dawkins's thought-provoking study, *The Selfish Gene* (chapter 11), in which he suggests that biological replicators (genes), characterized by "longevity, fecundity, and copying-fidelity" (208) have their analogue in cultural *memes* (his coinage). He illustrates those "memes" mainly with specific ideas and social codes transmitted throughout history, but some of his insights may also apply, with some modifications, to genres.

46. As a matter of fact, I believe that the ultimate test for the survival of an individual text is also a function of its "productivity": i.e., its ability to serve as a source of influence (in the form of motifs, images, phrases). The more we find literary allusions to a specific text, for example, the more its ability to survive is increased.

inspired emulation can we say that we are witnessing the emergence of a new genre, as the detection of a novel biological variant is not sufficient to proclaim it a new species, but rather the fact that this new biological variant has engendered progeny.

Some further distinctions concerning generic survival and productivity are called for here.

Generic survival should be measured, first and foremost, by *generic productivity*. Generic productivity can have two basic forms: primary and secondary. *Primary generic productivity* occurs when the works of a genre serve as a "stimulus" for the production of further texts that are perceived as "belonging" to this genre, i.e., the new texts bear some distinct resemblance to an existing generic tradition and this resemblance is recognized in the communicative situation of writer and reader. *Secondary generic productivity* occurs when the new texts related to the genre are produced according to some "fixed" formula, and have some definite relationship to this genre: translation (the relation of equivalence), parody (the relation of comic imitation and distortion), "imitation" (in the eighteenth-century sense of preserving the "form," changing the "content"), or adaptation (preserving the "content," but changing the "form" or the medium). These secondary texts are, relatively speaking, highly predictable, but the primary texts move in unpredictable directions.[47]

Now it is possible to try and formulate the opposite of generic survival, namely, generic extinction. But the term "extinction" poses two preliminary problems. First, it is impossible to speak of the material extinction of a genre or a text in our post-Gutenberg world. Although we can use the term literally to apply to antiquity, the huge libraries and sophisticated information retrieval systems of the post-Renaissance world make the use of the term highly metaphorical, indeed too metaphorical for my taste.

Furthermore, the term seems unhappy because in those cases where we can trace an *unproductive genre,* in the sense defined above, there is always the possibility that this genre, unproductive in one literary period, will become productive in the next (through primary or, more likely, secondary productivity). The Renaissance, of course, provides some examples of "revival" of literary forms. In this respect the Renaissance is not exceptional in literary history, but rather typical.

---

47. In making the distinction between primary and secondary forms of productivity, I am indebted to Ziva Ben-Porat's "Intertextuality, Rhetorical Intertextuality, Allusion, and Parody," as well as to Even-Zohar's distinction, in *Polysystem Studies,* 20–22, of primary and secondary literary types.

In the face of these preliminary terminological problems, I propose an alternative, *generic sterility*. In accordance with my previous definition of generic productivity, generic sterility can be defined, mirror-like, as the condition in which a genre has no generic productivity. Sterility does not imply a material absence of the works of this particular genre, nor does it exclude the possibility of becoming productive again after some period. At any rate, this term seems to escape some of the obvious shortcomings of "extinction," without discarding the biological analogy. It is also important to stress that "productive" and "sterile" are the ends of a continuum, not mutually exclusive and exhaustive categories. A genre is more or less productive, on primary or secondary levels (or both). It would be difficult, if not impossible, to find a totally sterile genre. Thus what we have in fact is a continuum of different degrees of generic productivity, where the "zero point" is labeled as "sterility," but is not necessarily realized. It is also important to emphasize that the "survival" of a genre is not an inherent property of the genre as an isolated system. Rather, it refers to the *relationships* between the production of texts "belonging" to the genre and the literary and cultural environment and how this environment coerces (or thwarts) the genre's production—as in biology, where "survival" designates the intricate relationships between species and their natural environment.

Now it is easier to see how my approach differs from Fowler's. Fowler proclaims a genre alive if its works are widely read and understood without the help of scholarly crutches. I take the alternative view, stressing the productive nature of generic rules. A genre may exist as part of our cultural "archive," but only its productivity, the fact that it plays an active role on the literary scene, ultimately ensures its survival. This perspective emphasizes the active role assigned to generic rules. According to Fowler, generic rules are a "piece of knowledge" (like a Morse code) to be acquired in order to correctly interpret literary texts. By accentuating the productive orientation of generic rules, we no longer need perceive them as fixed and passive, something to be pulled out of a drawer, but can appreciate them as a constant challenge that activates writers and propels them, in turn, to redefine and reshape these very rules.

To illustrate the concepts of generic productivity just defined, and some of their implications, I will now focus on the epic in English literature in the seventeenth and eighteenth centuries, because, it seems to me, it may provide us with an example of different forms of generic productivity and show how an active and prestigious genre—heroic epic poetry—can lapse into relative sterility. A brief glance at some standard modern anthologies of English literature reveals no typical epic after

Milton's *Paradise Lost*.[48] However, a closer look at some specialized historical studies reveals a more complicated picture. Epic poems were still produced and read, but the complex relationships between literary productivity and literary and cultural environment resulted in the relative sterility of at least one species of heroic verse. And to exemplify some aspects of this mechanism, it is worth taking a closer look at one writer of epic poetry in the seventeenth century: Richard Blackmore.

Not only are Blackmore's epic poems not mentioned in many respectable anthologies of English literature, but even some books devoted to presenting the rich scope of the epic tradition overlook his work[49]—a sign of the strength of the sometimes cruel mechanism of literary selection.

Even if we believe that the harsh critical judgment that sentenced Blackmore's epic poetry to near oblivion over the last three centuries is basically justified, we still have the responsibility, as literary historians, of describing the interaction between generic forms of productivity and the "literary environment" with its aesthetic and ideological norms.[50] The situation is complicated even more by the favorable reviews and the popularity Blackmore's epic poems enjoyed when they were first published.[51]

Further, at least at face value, one of these works could have been *the* epic that Britain had long been seeking, the peak of a series of attempts to create the truly *British* epic by combining the classical heritage with the English subject *par excellence*—the legends of King Arthur.[52]

Alexander Pope (who became the sharpest of Blackmore's critics), for instance, wrote a humorous prescription for composing the long-desired English epic, in his *Receipt to Make an Epic Poem* (1713):

> For the Fable.
> Take out of any old Poem, History-books, Romance, or Legend

48. See, for instance, Frank Kermode, John Hollander et al., eds., *Oxford Anthology of English Literature*, or M. H. Adams et al., eds., *Norton Anthology of English Literature*.

49. See, for example, Merchant's study, *The Epic*, and C. M. Bowra's *From Virgil to Milton*.

50. In his *English Epic and Heroic Poetry*, William M. Dixon makes some excellent critical observations about Blackmore's epics, but his only explanation for Blackmore's failure in the long run—his lack of "genius"—has too strong a romantic flavor, and one cannot accept it as the only ground for a satisfactory historiography.

51. For a balanced and objective discussion of Blackmore's faults and significance, and his place in the literary society of eighteenth-century England, see Harry M. Solomon, *Sir Richard Blackmore*.

52. In this context it is worth mentioning a later, and far more successful, attempt to use the Arthurian legend in a long poem, Tennyson's *Morte d'Arthur*. But Tennyson's poem, which was later incorporated into his *Idylls of the King*, is probably more idyllic poetry than epic.

(for instance *Geoffrey of Monmouth* or *Don Belianis of Greece*) those parts of story which afford most Scope for long Descriptions. . . . Then take a Hero, whom you may chuse for the Sound of his Name, and put him into the midst of these Adventures: There let him *work*, for twelve books.[53]

Pope's first source for proper subject matter in his *Receipt* is Geoffrey of Monmouth, the twelfth-century author of *Historia Britonum,* a work that established the lore of Arthur and his knights. Humorous and parodistic in intent as this passage may be, the legend of King Arthur represents a very serious option for writers of English epic poetry: it would be the equivalent of the Greek and Roman myths and legends that served as models for Homer and Virgil. And it would be authentically British.

Paul Merchant, after quoting a passage from *Paradise Lost* in which Milton refers to Uther's son (Arthur) and Lancelot (book I, 579–81), makes the following comment: "The reference to Arthur (Uther's son) and Lancelot, the Armoric knight, acts as a reminder that Milton had originally intended his epic to have King Arthur as its hero. Arthur is of course the natural choice for the hero of a British epic; and had Milton been seriously determined to write the English *Aeneid,* Arthur would no doubt have remained the hero."[54]

The opening lines of *Prince Arthur,* Blackmore's most successful heroic poem, nicely fit, at least formally, into what would be expected of a British epic in the seventeenth century:

> I sing the *Briton,* and his righteous arms,
> Who bred to suff'ring, and the rude alarms
> Of bloody war, forsook his native soil,
> And long sustained a vast heroick toil,
> Till kinder fate invited his return,
> To bless the isle that did his absence mourn.
> To re-enthrone fair liberty, and break
> The Saxon yoke, that gall'd Britannia's neck.[55]

Thus, Blackmore's choice of hero and story may be regarded as the *entelechia* of British epic (to use the Aristotelian organistic term). What,

53. Quoted in Merchant, *The Epic,* 64.
54. Ibid., 57.
55. Richard Blackmore, *Prince Arthur,* 1. The fact that I could obtain only a scholarly reprint rather than a new edition is another indication of the process of literary selection.

then, reduced this work from promise to fiasco? In order to provide an adequate historical, evolutionary answer we should turn to the relationships between the form of generic productivity expressed in Blackmore's epic poem and the literary environment of his time.

To make my point about Blackmore's *Prince Arthur* more cogent, compare it to Milton's *Paradise Lost* and consider both as front-runners in the race for the British epic championship. Today we take Milton's honorable place in the literary canon for granted, but this was not always so. Milton published his epic almost thirty years before Blackmore's appeared in 1695, but the first reactions to *Paradise Lost* did not make it the great poetic success story of the seventeenth century. Harry Solomon, in his enlightening book on Blackmore's literary career, refers to Milton's limited success: "Perhaps nothing indicates the limited familiarity Milton enjoyed at this time so clearly as the fact that no reviewer of *Prince Arthur* suggested its indebtedness to Milton despite resemblances which would strike a modern reader as unmistakable."[56]

In order to better understand why Blackmore failed where Milton prevailed, one must recognize Milton's indisputable poetic talent and superior handling of language and structure. Establishing historiography on laudatory terms (e.g., "genius") and confining it to literary summits is unsatisfactory, but it is equally mistaken to deny the existence of these summits. My argument is that in explaining why and how Milton's epic is one such "summit" of the epic tradition, evolutionary concepts of generic productivity play a decisive role.

According to the distinctions of generic productivity that I introduced earlier, Blackmore's work is an excellent example of *secondary* generic productivity. One can easily detect the basic "formula" that generated *Prince Arthur:* a close imitation of Virgil's epic model applied to British history. In a way, it is a Virgilian epic, updated and tailored to a British audience, rather than an original work that relies on, but also develops, the epic tradition. Needless to say, there is nothing wrong in secondary generic productivity as such. But, compared to primary forms of generic productivity, the secondary forms are much more transient. Pope's translations of Homeric epics seem "old," and Johnson's imitation of Juvenal's tenth Satire is less appealing to a contemporary reader than is the original text.

Milton's epic, however, is an exemplum of *primary* generic productivity. Milton molds the generic rules of the epic in unpredictable ways to create an original text that is still part of the generic tradition. There is no single formula that can easily sum up the move from classical epic to

56. Solomon, *Sir Richard Blackmore,* 56.

Paradise Lost. Furthermore, there is a constant tension between the classical model with its concept of heroism and Milton's concept of heroism, as well as the more global tension between the pagan and the Christian texts and world views embedded in Milton's epic. Again we must conclude that the productivity of a genre expresses itself in the dialectical relationships between the generic rules and the new texts carrying on that generic tradition.

We should also note that, in general, the subsequent literary period is almost as important as the period in which this genre is written to the literary survival of a given genre. From the eighteenth century onward, complexity, subtlety, originality, and the concept of an autonomous artistic text became the dominant values of literature. Heroic poetry such as Blackmore's epic (and many others), declarative in tone and reducible to simple allegory, was at odds with all these. We might say that heroic poems in general were not welcomed in the eighteenth century with its new sensibilities. The dominance of the mock-heroic throughout the eighteenth century underscores how unfavorable was the atmosphere for a serious epic. Tillyard states this point very clearly in his erudite book on the tradition of the English epic: "The vogue of the burlesque heroic mode revealed a lack of confidence in the possibility of exploiting the mode itself in a straightforward way."[57]

And Harry Solomon refers to the paradoxical clash between the explicit poetics of the period, which set epic at the pinnacle of literary endeavor, and the true, inner aesthetic convictions that guided its literary practice: "Perhaps the temper of the times was simply uncongenial to epic, despite the profusion of contemporary opinions to the contrary. Perhaps, as one critic suggests, the Augustans moved away from epic to excellence in mock-heroic and other varieties of satire 'without fully realizing what they were doing—almost against their will.' "[58]

Blackmore's epic was a typical victim of this new literary environment. The dominant literary figures of the time were not just "uncongenial" to Blackmore. First came Dryden with his hostile response to *Prince Arthur.* But it was Alexander Pope, first in his *Peri Bathous* and later in the *Dunciad,* who mounted the really devastating attack. As a matter of fact, coming as it did after Blackmore's literary reputation had already suffered innumerable critical and satiric blows, the *Dunciad* was almost a coup de grace. Blackmore moved from enjoying modest but substantial success in the initial stages after the publication of *Prince Arthur* (three editions, supportive reviews) to suffering constant attacks

57. E.M.W. Tillyard, *The English Epic and Its Background,* 495.
58. Solomon, *Sir Richard Blackmore,* 32.

from the dominant wits, declining popularity, and in the end caricature as a priggish and valueless writer: "By mid-century he was remembered, when at all, as an illustration that it is genius and not rules that distinguished a poet from a poetaster, a Milton from a Blackmore. . . . Before the end of the century, Blackmore ceased to be a distinguishable poetic entity; he merged into that troop of poetasters whose only excuse for immortality is to bear abuse."[59]

One major factor that contributed to the mechanism of suppression in the case of Blackmore's epic is its very choice of hero. It seems that there is one crucial factor that has not received due attention in historical and critical discussions of epic poetry: the literary and cultural environment has consistently suppressed, from the seventeenth century onward, any epic that has a king as its hero.[60]

This is true not only when we observe Blackmore's case with its conspicuous contemporary allusions (King William is its almost undisguised "Arthur"); this applies also to Abraham Cowley's *Davideis* and to many other epics written in the seventeenth century. Milton's *Paradise Lost* does not have a king as its hero, and direct allegorical readings of it, if made at all, are subordinated to deeper and more complex thematic structures in the work.

Thus Milton's epic succeeded in winning the appreciation of the reading public partly because of the new, "non-royal" concept of heroism presented in *Paradise Lost*. Even more important than appreciation are literary influence and productivity: Milton's poetic images left their mark on the dominant Augustan wits. Dryden's depiction of Achitophel in *Absalom and Achitophel* is largely modeled after Milton's Satan, and Pope's *Dunciad* is saturated with allusions to *Paradise Lost*.

Concerning the complex mechanism of literary survival, I claim that both the contemporary literary period and the subsequent one are crucial. Consider the extent to which the nineteenth century and romanticism gave new vitality to *Paradise Lost*—over and above its already established reputation—by reinterpreting Satan's role. Problematic and questionable as this interpretation may have been from the historical perspective, it can be regarded (to use Escarpit's term) as a "creative treason," a legitimate and complex way a work can reach beyond its immediate readers to new and diverse audiences.[61]

---

59. Ibid., 180.

60. One might cite Voltaire's *Henriade* as a counterexample to this generalization concerning the decline of "royal" epics, but a closer look at the fate of this poem only corroborates my hypothesis. Today Voltaire is perceived as the author of *Roman et Contes* and of philosophical essays rather than of epic poetry.

61. Robert Escarpit, *Sociology of Literature*, 85. Escarpit illustrates this notion of "creative

Whereas Milton's epic was revitalized through this "creative treason," Blackmore's sank deeper into oblivion. When Alexander Chalmers, for example, argued in the early nineteenth century, in *The General Biographical Dictionary,* that it was time to judge Blackmore more evenhandedly, there was no echo to his call.[62] And in the twentieth century Milton's complex rhetoric still appealed to reader (and critic), but Blackmore's "royal" heroic tomes were already covered in dust.

Yet another Darwinian concept seems highly pertinent to literary genres, namely that the "struggle for survival" is strongest between the closest forms: "It is the most closely-allied forms—varieties of the same species, and species of the same genus or of related genera—which, from having nearly the same structure, constitution, and habits, generally come into the severest competition with each other."[63]

The basic assumption can be applied to the relationships between the epic, the mock-epic, and the novel in eighteenth-century literature. It is clear that the emergence of the two latter genres is closely associated with the decline of the former. And whereas one branch of the epic—the "royal" epic—has become virtually sterile, the novel has gradually emerged as the new dominant genre of English and world literature.

My argument here is that the mock-epic forms suppressed the epic and forced it to yield to its heir in the evolutionary chain of literature— the novel. This statement is not entirely new. Hegel made popular the idea that the novel is "a manifestation of the spirit of epic under the impact of a modern and prosaic concept of reality."[64] But this idea has attracted some pertinent criticism.

Ian Watt, for instance, after referring to Hegel, devotes a whole chapter in his book on the rise of the novel to refuting what seems to him to be too close an association between these two genres. His main effort is to show that Defoe's and Fielding's references to the epic were marginal to the major conventions of the new genre of the novel.

Mikhail Bakhtin, again after citing Hegel, goes a step further and radically opposes these two genres.[65] On the one hand we have the monological, conservative, hierarchical, fixed genre of the epic with its "frozen" past tense, and on the other the dialogic, progressive, challenging, and dynamic genre of the novel with its "open" present tense.

---

treason" with the transformations undergone by *Gulliver's Travels* and *Robinson Crusoe*— from serious, satirical, and philosophical works to children's adventure books.

62. See in Solomon, *Sir Richard Blackmore,* 180.

63. Charles Darwin, *The Origin of Species,* 154.

64. This summary of Hegel's argument is quoted from Ian Watt, *The Rise of the Novel,* 272.

65. Mikhail M. Bakhtin, "Epic and Novel."

Although one can argue against certain details in Watt's or Bakhtin's more radical theories, or perhaps accept some of their ideas (however overstated), one can still contend that the novel is the "evolutionary heir" to the epic. The main point is that the line of evolution does not present a smooth, linear progression in which one subspecies simply resembles its ancestors in all or most of its features. Certain interesting, unpredicted mutations usually occur during the evolutionary process.

Similarly, one need not prove that the epic resembles the novel in all or most of its features. It is enough to note that the novel shares some basic characteristics with the epic, and that there is a detectable line of transformation. The large-scale plot, the versatile and diverse modes of representation, the variety of characters, and the mixture of comic and tragic effects are examples of such important characteristics.

Furthermore, the end of the seventeenth and the bulk of the eighteenth century can be seen as the transitional phase between the decline of the one genre and the rise of the other. In this period we see works such as Fenelon's *Télémaque,* a didactic prose tale modeled closely on the classic epic, and—more important—an abundance of mock-epics whose basic function, from the evolutionary perspective, was to blaze the path for the mundane and realistic new genre. By creating the comic clash between classical epic conventions and "low" day-to-day reality, these mock-epics helped to cultivate new sensibilities, the expression of which would culminate in the novel. Viewed from this perspective, Fielding's remarks in *Joseph Andrews* and *Tom Jones* that make explicit reference to affinities with the epic are neither playful slips of the pen nor, as Watt argues, ultimately insignificant.[66]

To these considerations, I might add the functional argument according to which the novel is the "evolutionary heir" of the epic because it strove, successfully, to take the most powerful position in the literary system, held until then by the epic. The novel became powerful both in its popularity and, ultimately, in the serious status that it gained after long being considered an unserious, even uncanonical (sometimes corrupting) literary endeavor.

The biological analogy may seem relevant also in the important role it assigns to the variability of a species as a criterion for its survival. Darwin makes this point clear when he discusses the number of individuals in a population: "A large number of individuals, by a better chance for the appearance within any given period of profitable variations, will compensate for a lesser amount of variability in each individual, and is, I believe, an extremely important element of success."[67]

---

66. Watt, *The Rise of the Novel,* 282–95.
67. Darwin, *The Origin of Species,* 147.

Darwin here emphasizes the importance of the size of a population, but only as compensation for the absence of variability. It is the capacity of a given population to produce *variety* that guarantees its survival in the long run.

Applying this principle of variability to the generic field may help explain why certain genres seem to survive during relatively long periods and others are relegated to our literary "baggage" (e.g., some classical genres) without playing a productive role. When we think of genres such as the epic, or satire, or the novel, or the sonnet—all four highly productive for many centuries—we soon discover that when they first established themselves on the literary scene they were markedly diverse and variable. Homer and Virgil, for example, are quite different in poetic sensibilities and thematic focus. Even if we restrict ourselves to Homer, we can still see different generic paths taken by the *Iliad* and the *Odyssey*. Satire offered, from its first stages as a distinct genre, at least two different models associated with Horace and Juvenal. And if we take into account also Attic comedy, and Menippean satire, the principle of variety seems indispensable. When it comes to the novel, the principle of variety is most conspicuous: the "founding fathers" of this newcomer to the generic field include writers such as Cervantes and Defoe, Richardson and Fielding, each representing different novelistic techniques and thematic sensibilities. Even the sonnet's high degree of formal constraint may still illustrate the principle of variability when we take into account the fact that during the first stages of its establishment on the literary scene, it allowed formal and thematic variability: Petrarch and Shakespeare, the two major "founding fathers" of the genre, not only organized their poems differently, but also differed significantly in poetic sensibilities, with Petrarch emphasizing idealistic and Shakespeare worldly concepts of love.

Finally, to conclude this chapter, I would like to suggest one more interesting similarity between biological and literary evolutionary theories.

DOMINANCE AND THE PERIPHERY: THE INDIRECT PATH OF EVOLUTION

Biological thinking, like literary theory, does not shun metaphor. One such metaphor that proves fruitful in contemporary biological thinking is that picturing evolution as a "bushy" pattern, as opposed to the traditional metaphor of the "ladder" that dominated biological thought for decades: "The metaphor of the ladder has controlled most thinking about human evolution. We have searched for a single, progressive sequence linking some apish ancestor with modern man by gradual and continuous transformation."[68]

If we substitute "literary evolution" for "human evolution" in this passage, we can easily see that the metaphor of the ladder, in some form or another, has also dominated our perception of literary history, and most of our literary historiographies. This "ladder" approach, says Gould, is inadequate and should be replaced by the metaphor of the bush:

> Evolution usually proceeds by "speciation"—the splitting of one lineage from a parental stock—not by the slow and steady transformation of these large parental stocks. Repeated episodes of speciation produce a bush. Evolutionary "sequences" are not rungs on a ladder, but our retrospective reconstruction of a circuitous path running like a labyrinth, branch to branch, from the base of the bush to a lineage now surviving at its top.[69]

An important consequence of this perspective is how speciation is explained and described. The "bush" approach enables biological theorists to offer the "allopatric theory": "*Allopatric* means 'in another place.' In the allopatric theory, popularized by Ernst Mayr, new species arise in *very small* populations that become isolated from their parental group at the *periphery* of the ancestral range. Speciation in these small isolates is *very rapid* by evolutionary standards."[70]

The crucial point in this description of evolution is that it assigns to the periphery an indispensable role in the mechanism of evolution, unlike traditional views, which either neglect or, at best, give the periphery a very marginal role in their theories.

The allopatric theory also gives a new twist to the debate between the view of evolution as a gradual process and the view that it proceeds by abrupt leaps.[71] According to this theory, we should not look at evolution as a sudden leap occurring in the dominant area, but rather as a combination of gradual changes in the dominant population and very

68. Gould, *Ever Since Darwin*, 58.

69. Ibid., 61.

70. Ibid.

71. John Manly, for instance, influenced by the concept of "mutation" in modern biology, tried to undermine the traditional perception of unilinear and gradual development by suggesting that generic evolution may be more like a sudden, mutation-like leap. See his "Literary Forms and the Origin of Species," 1–19.

rapid change in the peripheral, which intermittently invades (and supplants) the dominant to create the impression of a sudden leap. Again, one can see the immediate implications that such a view may have for genre theory. It is clear that the gradual and sudden approaches are not mutually exclusive. The allopatric theory combines the merits of both.

But how are we supposed to apply the allopatric theory? Periphery in biology is literal, i.e., geographical. What would be the literary equivalent to this concept? Sometimes, of course, geography may play a role in defining literary dominance and periphery (e.g., Paris, as the dominant location of French literature), but even in these cases geography is not the primary consideration. A literary area is usually geographically dominant as a function of other social and cultural factors, and the geographical location is just an auxiliary or a derivative factor. The concept of a "dominant literature" is in fact closely related to cultural and literary values: it is this part of literature that becomes the cultural "middle ground"; the part "approved" by the dominant milieu.

This notion of the well-established, "high" literary culture is sometimes opposed to various types of trivial literature thought of as "low" or "marginal." I would like, however, to introduce one major qualification to such a definition, namely, that the periphery should contain not only those works, trends, and genres that are "below" high literature but also those "above" it: avant-garde literature in its various forms. Thus the dominant area consists of all "well-established" literature, whereas the periphery is everything else, either because it is considered too "low" or too "advanced." The major point is that it is "outside" as far as the mechanism of status-gaining in the literary system is concerned.[72]

Talking of literary evolution in terms of dominance and periphery was one of the contributions of Russian Formalism for establishing literary historiography on more solid and adequate grounds. Thus by using this pair of concepts I am not only revivifying the biological analogy but also paying tribute to their highly illuminating and vanguard position in the theory of literary evolution. It was Roman Jakobson who introduced the term "dominance" into literary theory in his article "The Dominant," where he first defines it in terms of a single text as "the focusing component of a work of art: it rules, determines, and transforms the remaining components."[73] Later he applies it also, rather elusively, to the works of an author, of a genre, of a period, or of an entire culture.

---

72. The role of the educational system in this process of status gaining (what, and how much, to teach of a writer) is explored in Milo, "Aspects de la survie culturelle," especially 160–67.

73. Roman Jakobson, "The Dominant," 82.

It is important to stress that the formalists do not use the term "dominant" in any evaluative sense. Calling a certain work or genre "dominant" is not praising it for meeting undisputable aesthetic criteria. The statement means only that the "literary environment" of a certain age has accepted it as "good" or respectable.

The formalists were first to insist on the importance of "peripheral" literature within the major (seemingly ladder-like) trend of literary evolution. Victor Erlich faithfully summarizes one of their ideas concerning the role of peripheral forms: "In order to renew itself literature draws upon motifs and devices of sub-literary genres. Products of popular culture, leading a precarious existence on the periphery of literature, are thus admitted into the parlor, raised to the status of *bona fide* literary art, or, as Sklovskij put it, 'canonized.' "[74]

Some subspecies of the novel emerged in accordance with this pattern. Daniel Defoe's *Moll Flanders,* for example, which succeeded in obtaining a respectable place in English literature, is but the tip of the iceberg of a peripheral genre that flourished toward the end of the seventeenth century. Ian Watt, discussing possible models for Defoe's novel, concludes that

> The closest analogy in point of subject matter to *Moll Flanders* is provided by the rogue biographies, a native tradition which was much more exclusively devoted to realistic social documentation than were the picaresque novels. The genre had begun in completely factual compilations, such as Thomas Harmon's *Caveat for Common Cursitors* (1566), and had developed into a partly fictional form influenced by picaresque tales and jest-books.[75]

The point to be observed here is that from the viewpoint of well-established literature the rogue biography was a typical peripheral form, and what is even more important, from around the middle of the seventeenth century on it grew in size and popularity.[76]

Thus the allopatric theory seems to work: before being introduced into dominance, the new subgenre has to establish itself in the periphery. And if the new subgenre first appears in avant-garde circles, as often is the case, then again according to the allopatric theory we should expect a relatively rapid production of this new subgenre before it gains dominant status.

74. Victor Erlich, *Russian Formalism: History—Doctrine,* 260.
75. Watt, *The Rise of the Novel,* 119.
76. See, for instance, James Sutherland, *English Literature of the Late Seventeenth Century,* 210–13.

Milton's "Christian epic" of *Paradise Lost* may also be called upon in this context. Its way to the dominant position it enjoys in English literature was opened by other biblical and Christian epics. Any respectable historiography will mention Cowley's *Davideis*, which appeared shortly before *Paradise Lost*. But a closer look at English literature of the seventeenth century (encouraged by the assumptions of the allopatric theory) reveals other such works. These biblical and Christian epics can be found not only in English literature itself, but also in some neighboring literatures. These instances can also be considered peripheral—from the point of view of English literature. Thus, in addition to attempts by English writers to produce Christian epics in the seventeenth century, one can find also French attempts, which were known, sometimes through direct translation, to English readers and writers.[77]

This example reinforces my conviction that the "periphery" to which we should look for some interesting and new production of literary forms (preceding the emergence of such forms in the dominant area) is not to be confined to subcanonic literature as Victor Shklovsky defines it. A similar broad view of the "periphery," which does not restrict itself to the noncanonic literature, is suggested, for example, in Hans Robert Jauss's discussion of the emergence of new literary genres in medieval literature: "The new genres of the courtly verse-romance, the first prose romances, and the allegorical epic are not canonization of lower genres, but rather proceed from a shift of functions (the paired, or respectively, narrative eight-syllabic line was found in rhymed chronicles; the prose in historiography; and the allegorical form in spiritual poetry)."[78]

I was first attracted to the allopatric theory by its similarities to the formalist perspective on the issue of literary evolution. But in addition to these shared premises about the indirect path of evolution, allopatric theory contributes one interesting feature not stressed by Russian Formalism and its disciples: the concept that the new form must develop in the periphery before it "infiltrates" the dominant area.[79] It seems that in at least the two cases I have briefly examined—some forms of the novel, and the Christian epic—this hypothesis is corroborated.

The allopatric theory and the Russian Formalist evolutionary theory

77. For a listing of these peripheral biblical and Christian epics, both English and foreign, see Douglas Bush, *English Literature in the Earlier Seventeenth Century, 1600–1660*, 371–76.

78. Hans Robert Jauss, *Toward an Aesthetic of Reception*, 106.

79. Note that I do not claim that every aspect of the allopatric theory is relevant to the literary field. The new subgenre, for instance, does not necessarily acquire its followers in a totally isolated, peripheral environment (as in the biological case). As a matter of fact, dominant and peripheral forms of literature interact continuously.

both reject the smooth, linear path of evolution. Instead, the formalists presented a picture made up of constant "struggles" and "breaks" as summarized by Erlich: "[A] twisted path, full of detours, of zigs and zags. Every literary trend represents a crisscrossing, a complex interplay between elements of tradition and innovation."[80]

Now these "zigs and zags," these constant reshufflings of the line of evolution, are not random. Rather, their contour can be captured in a "law" of literary evolution formulated by Shklovsky: "According to the law . . . in the history of art the legacy is transmitted not from father to son, but from uncle to nephew."[81]

Thus, after surveying various aspects of the biological analogy, especially some of its evolutionary implications, it seems that I have unexpectedly reached new metaphorical territory, that of my next chapter, the familial analogy. This should not surprise us, because a family is partly a biological and partly a cultural concept (though probably more of the latter). Consequently, some aspects of genre evolution—notably those concerned with generic productivity and generic "struggle for survival"—can be addressed through the biological analogy, whereas other aspects, on which I will focus in the coming chapter, can be illuminated through the family analogy.

---

80. Erlich, *Russian Formalism*, 259.
81. Quoted in ibid., 260.

Chapter 3

Literary Genres as Families

Most evocations of conceptual analogies focus on only one aspect of the two domains to be compared. When Ortega y Gasset, for instance, presents the biological analogy, he is not interested in its wide range of implications (some of which were discussed in the previous chapter). The aspect that interests him is the limited, confined, and exhaustible nature of a literary genre: "Just as every animal belongs to a species, every literary work belongs to a genre. . . . A literary genre, the same as a zoological species, means a certain stock of possibilities; and since in art only those possibilities count which are different enough not to be considered replicas of one another, the resources of a literary genre are definitely limited."[1]

To illustrate these questionable statements, Ortega y Gasset chooses as a representative of literary genres the novel, which is perhaps the most varied, dynamic, and protean of them all. And since it is not the theoretical implications of the biological analogy that interest him, but the purported closed nature of literary genres, later on in his discussion he evokes another analogy (this time a more original one), which likens a generic tradition to a mine: "As a routine production, as an exploitable mine, the novel may be finished. The large veins, accessible to any diligent hand, are worked out."[2]

1. José Ortega y Gasset, "Notes on the Novel," 58.
2. Ibid., 99.

In both cases, the analogies interest him only to the extent that they support the point he wants to make about the genre as a closed, exhaustible system. Perhaps it was this description of the novel that moved Robert Alter to declare, in a chapter of his *Partial Magic* titled "The Inexhaustible Genre": "I suspect that death in the novel might be a more useful focus for serious discussion of the genre than the death of the genre."[3]

In opposing the rigid perspective proposed by Ortega y Gasset, Alter joins the dominant trend in modern critical theory, with its stress on the flexible and dynamic nature of literary genres. This dominant trend, in attempting to establish a philosophical foundation for its undogmatic approach, introduces Wittgenstein's concept of family resemblance into genre theory. According to this view: "Representations of a genre may then be regarded as making up a family whose septs and individual members are related in various ways, without necessarily having any single feature shared in common by all."[4]

This notion seems, at least *prima facie*, to be a happy medium between the Scylla of closed, uncompromising concepts of literary genres, and the Charybdis of denying all generalizations concerning them (as Croce does, for instance). Wittgenstein's appealingly loose concept began to permeate genre theory during the sixties, and its popularity made Eliseo Vivas refer ironically to the new "handy" solution to the problem of literary classes as "the evangel of Saint Ludwig."[5]

I would like to suggest that Wittgenstein's concept, at least in one of its interpretations, has perhaps become too fashionable, too little scrutinized. Instead of being a methodology of last resort, it has become the first and immediate refuge in the wake of disappointment with one or other rigid definition made up of a confined list of characteristics.

In the following discussion, I first show that the very transfer of the concept from Wittgenstein's philosophical framework to genre theory involves a shift that may call into question the outcome of the application. I also argue that there is sometimes a discrepancy between the loose concept of family resemblance and the practical assumptions made about genres, even by the advocates of the concept. And finally, I propose certain ways in which Wittgenstein's concept, as well as other aspects of the "kinship analogy" can be, after all, fruitfully applied to genre theory.

3. Robert Alter, *Partial Magic: The Novel as a Self-Conscious Genre*, 244.

4. Fowler, *Kinds of Literature*, 41. The "family resemblance" approach, with different stresses and degrees of sophistication, is advocated by Paul Alpers, Robert C. Elliot, Claudio Guillén, Graham Hough, Uri Margolin, Jean-Marie Schaeffer, John Reichert (1978), Marie-Laure Ryan (1981), and Morris Weitz (1956, 1964, 1977), among others.

5. Eliseo Vivas, "Literary Classes: Some Problems," 101.

THE FAMILY ANALOGY: THE LOGICAL ASPECT

Instead of presenting a homogeneous description of language centered around its cognitive function, Wittgenstein proposes a highly pluralistic picture. By so doing he opposed some of the logical positivists of his time (Schlick, Carnap, and others), as well as the author of the *Tractatus Logico-Philosophicus*, namely himself in an earlier phase of his philosophical development.

In order to illuminate the radically heterogeneous character of language, Wittgenstein introduces the games analogy. This analogy is meant to illustrate the crucial statement that linguistic activities not only differ from each other in various respects, but have, as a set, nothing in common:

> Consider for example the proceedings that we call "games." I mean board-games, card-games, ball-games, Olympic games, and so on. What is common to them all?—Don't say: "There *must* be something common, or they would not be called 'games' "—but *look and see* whether there is anything common to all. —For if you look at them you will not see something that is common to *all*, but similarities, relationships, and a whole series of them at that.[6]

And only then, after explaining and discussing the analogy of games for a while, does Wittgenstein introduce the new analogy that interests us most, the one concerning the family: "I can think of no better expression to characterize these similarities than 'family resemblance'; for the various resemblances between members of a family: build, features, color of eyes, gait, temperament, etc. etc. overlap and crisscross in the same way. —And I shall say: 'games' form a family."[7]

Thus the wish to illuminate the nature of language leads Wittgenstein to the analogy of games, which, in turn, leads him to the analogy of the family, in order to illustrate the idea of a network of similarities.[8] Different kinds of language-use are compared to different kinds of games, which in turn are compared to members of a family, who resemble each other only partially. In all cases, the terms "language,"

6. Ludwig Wittgenstein, *Philosophical Investigation,* 31.

7. Ibid., 32.

8. One may mention another analogy introduced by Wittgenstein in this context, that of the thread made up of interwoven fibers "and the strength of the thread does not reside in the fact that some one fibre runs through its whole length" (ibid.).

"game," or "family" cannot and should not be defined against finite lists of necessary and sufficient conditions, simply because the diverse kinds of phenomena they designate do not have any one feature in common (as is stipulated by the very concept of a necessary condition).

Attempts to apply this fundamental statement of Wittgenstein's to literature will likely result in claims that different kinds of literature (i.e., genres) do not necessarily have anything in common.[9] In other words, "literature," like "language" and "game," may be a term that cannot be defined by a finite list of conditions. Note that I make no claim here about the internal structure (and hence the possibility or the impossibility of attaining a definition) of specific language games, and consequently of genres. One may even claim that the possibility of formulating a definition as far as specific language games are concerned is *implicitly assumed* rather than denied. Wittgenstein's target is the all-embracing term "language," not the specific types of actions that constitute language use.

According to this line of argument, a feasible way to apply Wittgenstein's concepts to the literary field would be as follows: "language" (denoting the multiplicity of diverse language uses), which is analogous to "game" (denoting the variety of specific games), should be seen as analogous to "literature" (referring to a complex of different genres). This, however, is not how literary scholars have applied Wittgenstein's concepts to the literary field. Instead, they have isolated one element—the family—from his network of analogies and, ignoring its function in the entire conceptual set, used it exclusively to establish the analogy frequently found in genre theory: between a "family" (designating some group of related individuals) and a "genre" (designating the various texts that are considered to be its members).

This is a possible reading of Wittgenstein's text, but it is by no means the most feasible or the most promising. I object to this formulation of the analogy on the grounds that whereas rigid concepts of genre are justifiably rejected, the alternative presented by the radical version of the family resemblance analogy seems to go too far in implying that genres are totally open and undelineated categories.

If all that is shared by members of a class is a partial network of similarities, how can we explain that we (as a community of speakers and readers) decide to delimit the field of phenomena as we do? In other words, why is there a relatively high consensus about the boundaries between different kinds of language use, or different kinds of literature, if what we have "objectively" is merely a continuum of loose networks of similarities?

9. Such a view can be found in John Reichert, *Making Sense of Literature*, 170.

If the concept of a definition consisting of a closed set of necessary and sufficient conditions is inadequate because it is too confined, the extreme alternative, based on a problematic application of Wittgenstein's concept, appears too open. The interesting point is that despite declarations concerning the adoption of Wittgenstein's concept of family resemblance in its radical version, some of its advocates find themselves, in their practical criticism, relying implicitly on concepts more closed than they would want to admit.

Morris Weitz is perhaps the critic who has contributed most consistently and elaborately to the application of Wittgenstein's notion to genre theory. In a genre, according to Weitz, each work will share only some characteristics with another, and it is virtually impossible to define genre in terms of necessary and sufficient conditions. Thus whether a text *N* is a novel is not a question of fact "but a decision as to whether the work under examination is similar in certain respects to other works, already called 'novels,' and consequently warrants the extension of the concept to cover the new case."[10]

This elusive situation where every new work reshapes and reshuffles the entire defining system, and consequently blocks the establishment of a definition, derives, according to Weitz, from the innovative nature of art. In a later book, Weitz refers to the impossibility of defining tragedy, because "its use must allow for the ever present possibility of new conditions. It is a simple historical fact that the concept, as we know and use it, has continuously accommodated new cases of tragedy and, more important, the new properties of these new cases."[11]

Definitions, Weitz believes, are not totally impossible in genre discussions. As long as we have "closed" the domain to which we refer (one specific period in one specific literature), definitions may be attempted, and a definition of Greek tragedy, let us say, is conceivable. But a definition of "tragedy"? According to Weitz, never. At one point, however, he states: "They [*Hamlet*'s representative critics] are unanimous on all the defining properties of a hero, his suffering and calamity; dramatic conflict involving important values; and the tragic effect. But there is little agreement on the cause of his suffering, and the particular response of the ideal spectator."[12]

From these formulations one can easily infer that a suffering hero and a "dramatic conflict involving important values" are (even in Weitz's reluctant presentation) necessary properties of tragedy set by all the

10. Morris Weitz, "The Role of Theory in Aesthetics," 32.
11. Morris Weitz, *The Opening Mind*, 103.
12. Morris Weitz, *Hamlet and the Philosophy of Literary Criticism*, 304.

diverse theories that he surveys. Now, these conditions may sound self-evident or trivial, but this is usually the fate of necessary conditions. It is only when one tries to add more substantial conditions that a definition is found to be truly enlightening and informative.[13]

Still, trivial or not, it seems that it is possible to find some necessary conditions for defining tragedy even according to Weitz's own presentation. And if this is the case, there is no reason to retreat to the much looser concept of family resemblance.

The point that there are some necessary conditions for tragedy may become clearer if we consider, from a different perspective, the many scholarly debates about the "true nature" of tragedy. No critic, for instance, suggests that the tragic hero is a buffoon; or that the tragic action consists of joyful and cheerful events; or that readers (or spectators) can feel no similarity between themselves and the tragic hero while experiencing the tragic effect. In other words, disputes about the "true nature" of tragedy, vehement and radical as they may be, are ultimately confined to some distinguishable area of human experience and artistic structure. And whereas there is serious debate over the exact lines of demarcation, from a distance these differences are diminished. In less metaphorical language, one may argue that by raising the level of abstraction one finds that most readers and critics do share some basic assumptions about tragedy. One might remind oneself in this context of the very basis for conceptualization about genres, namely, that "the definition of a genre works by a process of abstraction."[14] It is possible, of course, to capitalize on existing disagreements and present them as a conglomeration of incompatible, Babel-like critical approaches, as Weitz does, but I do not think that this would be a very faithful picture of how genres are actually written, read, and discussed.

The novel seems to offer an excellent case for the advocates of the concept of family resemblance. This move by some genre theorists seems natural because the novel, a relative newcomer to the generic repertoire, has always been characterized by its elusiveness and freedom from strict conventions.

Morris Weitz, for instance, immediately after introducing Wittgenstein's concept of family resemblance and its relevance to the theory of art, turns by way of illustration to the tradition of the novel. One may ask whether the term "novel" can be applied to new, modernistic works

13. For a discussion of the criteria that guide the formulation of definitions, see Irving M. Copi, *Introduction to Logic*, especially 154–58, and Raziel Abelson, "Definition," especially 322–23.

14. Thomas G. Rosenmeyer, *The Green Cabinet*, 3.

such as Dos Passos's *U.S.A.* or Woolf's *To the Lighthouse.* Weitz argues that to formulate the question in this form is misleading:

> What is at stake is no factual analysis concerning necessary and sufficient properties but a decision as to whether the work under examination is similar in certain respects to other works, already called "novels," and consequently warrants the extension of the concept to cover the new case. The new work is narrative, fictional, contains character delineation and dialogue but (say) it has no regular time-sequence in the plot or is interspersed with actual newspaper reports.[15]

The main objection to Weitz's argument here seems to be that instead of demonstrating that genuine genre definitions face difficulties whenever new, innovative works are produced, it shows us only that unrealistically restrictive and rigid definitions may lead us into a quandary when we try to accommodate new works. After all, who would seriously stipulate a "regular time-sequence in the plot" as part of a definition of the novel? Such a postulation would automatically exclude the bulk of the genre.

Robert Elliot follows the basic argument presented by Weitz and applies it to satire, claiming that satire is too evasive a genre to be defined in the traditional way, and that "there are no properties common to *all* the uses."[16] Yet, after pronouncing this Wittgensteinian principle in such unequivocal terms, Elliot adds a sentence that seems to undermine his whole argument: "Or, if I could find an essential property, it could be so general as to be useless for purposes of definition: 'All satire attacks something,' for example."[17]

This small addition, qualified and hesitant as it is, calls into question the concept of family resemblance in its truly radical interpretation. Because what is this condition that "all satire attacks something" but a classical example of a *necessary condition* in a definition?[18]

Note that I can heartily agree with Elliot that it is virtually impossible to supply a simple definition that will apply easily to all instances of satire. But this conviction need not dictate exuberant recourse to the

---

15. Weitz, "The Role of Theory," 31–32.
16. Robert C. Elliot, "The Definition of Satire," 22.
17. Ibid.
18. For another example of the explicit pronouncement of the family-resemblance approach, together with a tacit, almost unconscious, understanding that some necessary conditions (in the form of "minimal constraints") can be formulated after all, see Margolin, "The Concept of Genre," 141.

family-resemblance solution. There may be some viable middle position. Elliot himself, by pointing to the invective nature of satire, indicates such an alternative indirectly.

According to such an alternative view, one could speak of a necessary condition that applies to all satire, plus an additional cluster of character-istics that is dynamic and variable. These additional traits may change (not all of them at the same time) from one literary period to another, from one literature to another, and from one writer to another—or, even more common, they may switch their relative status in the hierarchy that defines the genre. This one necessary condition, the one "fiber" that runs throughout the whole thread (to stand Wittgenstein's analogy on its head), may also vary in its relative standing and should not necessarily be conceived as most important or central at all times (the invective may be sharp and central as in Juvenal, or subtle and marginal as in Horace).

In addition to the example of satire, Elliot takes a cue from Weitz in citing the novel as a prime instance of the application of the concept of family resemblance. But before reformulating Weitz's argument concern-ing the novel, Elliot makes a revealing remark: "Consider the novel for a moment (and consider the definition that E. M. Forster adopts, with comic despair, from M. Abel Chevalley: the novel is 'une fiction en prose d'une certain étendue.' Beyond this we cannot go, says Forster)."[19]

Again, as in his discussion of satire (and Weitz's discussion of tragedy), Elliot is actually offering—implicitly and unconsciously—a necessary condition for the definition of the novel, despite the fact that according to the family-resemblance concept there cannot be a necessary condition. The formulation that Elliot is quoting, in fact, might even be recast as three necessary conditions: (1) a novel has to be a work of fiction (as opposed, say, to history or to philosophy); (2) it should be written in prose (as opposed to verse);[20] and (3) a novel should be of considerable length (as opposed to a short story or a novella).

Stated in this way, Forster's definition seems less a function of "comic despair" and more a cautious and flexible formulation of certain basic, necessary features of the genre. It is also possible to add to these three elements a fourth one: (4) a novel should be a narrative text (as opposed to merely a description of a landscape, or a logical argument).

These conditions cannot be dismissed as mere truisms, because they

19. Elliot, "The Definition of Satire," 22.
20. There may be a few exceptions to this condition (e.g., Pushkin's *Eugene Onegin*, or Seth's *Golden Gate*). In the face of such counterexamples I can claim that, as far as the overwhelming majority of novels is concerned, the condition still applies, and that the novel in verse is a "marked" case. It is also evident that the prototypical members of the novel category are written in prose.

do have some informative value. To be sure, one should neither see these four conditions as necessary and sufficient for defining the novel (there may be texts that observe the four requirements and still are not considered novels), nor confuse these conditions with a comprehensive theory of the novel. Any serious theory should elaborate the exact meaning of each of the terms used in the formulation (how, for instance, to define "fiction" or "narrative"). Furthermore, a theory of the novel would examine how the four elements are related to one other and to other relevant levels of the novelistic text (e.g., point of view, expositional modes). But the crucial fact is that such theories will accept the above four characteristics as their point of departure. Thus even in the case of the novel, apparently the most elusive and protean of literary forms, the concept of family resemblance is found to be too open.

Instead of once and for all solving the conceptual difficulties involved in genre theory, proponents of the family-resemblance approach tend to create new problems and inconsistencies. These seem to stem from a radical, reductive interpretation of Wittgenstein's concept. Instead of demonstrating the rich network of relations that in fact exists between members of a "literary family," they have chosen to isolate the "negative" aspect of the family resemblance, namely, the statement that there is no single trait shared by all members. This reductive-radical commitment has led them to unrealistic and unconvincing claims about specific genres as well as to certain inconsistencies in argumentation.

If we embrace a more "positive" reading of Wittgenstein's concept, some useful implications may arise. Weitz himself, in a comprehensive defense of the use of "open concepts" in various areas of the human experience, points to different models of definition that are not based on a closed set of necessary and sufficient conditions, but nevertheless show different degrees of "openness": "The investigation of the logical grammar of certain concepts may reveal concepts with no necessary, no sufficient, and no disjunctive set of sufficient criteria; or concepts with a necessary criterion but no necessary and sufficient set of criteria; or concepts with no definitive set as well as no undebatable necessary criteria."[21]

I do not think that in the field of genre theory one has to embrace the most negative-radical model according to which the concept of tragedy, for instance, is open "in the precise sense that it has no necessary and sufficient conditions but only a disjunctive set of nonnecessary, nonsufficient conditions" and is "perennially flexible as well as perennially debatable."[22] Even if we grant that there is no necessary condition shared

21. Weitz, *The Opening Mind*, 34.
22. Ibid., 103.

by all tragedies, I think Weitz's own description suggests that the open concept of a disjunctive set of sufficient conditions may be applied to the history of tragedy, every historical phase having its special characteristics. Further, when we think of the heterogeneous field of literary genres, ranging from genres mainly characterized by formal structure (e.g., the sonnet), to genres more oriented to theme (e.g., the historical novel), there is no reason to assume that the family-resemblance approach, especially its negative-radical version, is appropriate for all, or for most of them. Admitting that a close, real definition is not available does not mean that we are left with a relativistic position. Even in using loose concepts, there are some things that are not vague and loose, as Max Black has argued: "In using a loose concept, I must know that there are instances that are indisputably 'clear' and must be able to recognize such cases; and I must also be able to recognize 'border line cases.' "[23]

There are, in short, some more fruitful and positive methodological positions, some of which are indicated in Weitz's own formulations (or his actual analyses), which also take into account the more stable aspect(s) of our "open" and "loose" concepts.

Such a positive model, based on the concept of family resemblance, has been developed by Eleanor Rosch in the field of cognitive psychology for studies in the internal structure of categories.[24] Although Rosch's work is primarily concerned with common categories of natural language, I would like to suggest that some of its principles are also applicable to the more complex area of literary genres. Rosch's research project offers a powerful model, combining the concept of family resemblance with that of a prototype. Her basic hypothesis is that "members of a category come to be viewed as prototypical of the category as a whole in proportion to the extent to which they bear a family resemblance to (have attributes which overlap those of) other members of the category. Conversely, items viewed as most prototypical of one category will be those with least family resemblance to or membership in other categories."[25]

The relevance of these principles to genre theory is obvious. Rosch's basic hypothesis seems as valid and illuminating in the field of literary genres as in that of common natural language categories. One of the major implications would lead to the perception of genres neither as rigid

23. Max Black, *Margins of Precision*, 12.

24. See Eleanor Rosch and Carolyn B. Mervis, "Family Resemblance: Studies in the Internal Structure of Categories," and Eleanor Rosch, "Principles of Categorization."

25. Rosch and Mervis, "Family Resemblance," 575.

and unified categories, nor as conglomerations of texts, randomly collected, sharing merely a loose network of similarities. Rather, literary
genres would be perceived as structured categories, with a "hard core"
consisting of prototypical members,[26] characterized by their relatively
high degree of resemblance to each other. Marie-Laure Ryan, in her
highly illuminating presentation of goals and perspectives in genre
theory, also emphasizes the important role of "typical" and "archtypi-
cal" members of genres in constituting our notion of a genre within the
framework of the family resemblance approach: "There would be highly
typical and less typical members of every genre. . . . This approach
invites us to think of genres as clubs imposing a certain number of
conditions for membership, but tolerating as quasi-members those individuals who can fulfill only some of the requirements, and who do not
seem to fit into any other club."[27]

Thus when we wish to describe tragedy, we should neither adopt the
rigid criterial approach, nor deny the existence of a structured "hard
core" in the "literary category," i.e., the genre, of tragedy. Instead, in
order to understand how "tragedy" functions in the literary system, we
should look for the prototypical members of the genre, namely, those
texts considered to be the most representative of tragedy, works such as
Oedipus Rex, King Lear, and *Phèdre,* which are perceived as prototypical
because they share many traits with each other (e.g., a tragic hero with
a *hamartia,* a structured plot that includes a relatively distinct *peripeteia*
and *anagnorisis,* etc.). The word "many," of course, is here relative:
Oedipus Rex and *King Lear* have more thematic and structural traits in
common than either (or the two of them) might share with works such
as Chekhov's *Cherry Orchard,* although it is possible to read the latter as
a tragedy, as Stanislavsky did in his interpretation of the play.[28]

By focusing on the prototypical cases of a genre, we should not, of
course, overlook or underestimate those texts that are not prototypical
of that particular generic tradition. The "marginality" of these texts
might sometimes be hailed as the source of aesthetic merit. What a
classicist might perceive as a fault may be considered an advantage by
modernist standards. But I am not concerned to condemn those "mar-

26. Sometimes there may be only one prototypical member, but that does not confirm
Hirsch's claim, in *Validity in Interpretation,* that "a type can be entirely represented in a
single instance" (50).

27. Ryan, "Introduction: On the Why, What and How of Generic Taxonomy," 118.

28. For an interesting analysis of the essential schema of tragedy that focuses on
prototypical tragedies but at the same time pays due attention to marginal and questionable
cases, see Dorothea Krook's *Elements of Tragedy.*

ginal" cases or to praise them. Rather, I simply wish to argue, in a
purely descriptive manner, that in our perception of generic categories
the prototypical cases play a major role.[29] Furthermore, the "prototypical
hypothesis" enables genre theory to break the conceptual deadlock
implied by the approach despairing of generalization on literary genres
that permeates modern criticism. This hypothesis opens up new empirical prospects for examining how the literary community actually perceives and uses generic categories, or, as Marie-Laure Ryan says: "to lay
out the implicit knowledge of the users of genres."[30] The implicit
knowledge involved in generic categories can be described also as having
a coordinative epistemic and social role, especially when dealing with
popular and media genres, as S. J. Schmidt, for instance, stresses in his
work on media genres.[31] The main point, however, is that generic
categories, both literary and those of the media, are part of a community's shared linguistic and cultural knowledge.

If dictionaries represent a great part of the tacit linguistic knowledge
of a community, including its knowledge of concepts of literary genres,
it is instructive to see that many definitions of generic terms mention
prototypical examples, or the names of authors of prototypical works.
When "satire" (or "satirical") is defined and illustrated in the *Random
House College Dictionary,* Swift is named; Fowler's *Dictionary of Modern
English Usage* mentions Pope; *Petit Larousse* refers to Horace, Juvenal, and
Boileau. It is this combination of certain typical traits with prototypical
members of the generic category that constitutes the core of our generic
concept. Dictionaries of common linguistic usage are, in that respect, a
good starting point for revealing the "implicit knowledge of users of
genres." Next, we can move to dictionaries and glossaries of literary
terms in which there is more room for elaboration. Here the principle of
combining a set of descriptive traits with reference to prototypical works
is even more central and conspicuous.[32] The list and variety of prototypical works cited will, of course, increase, but without shaking the "hard
core" of the generic concept. Moving to dictionaries of literary terms

29. An interesting and promising attempt to develop a "preference model" for genre
definition that takes into account gradient-necessary conditions, typicality conditions, and
gradient-typicality conditions, can be found in Schauber and Spolsky, *The Bounds of
Interpretation.*
30. Ryan, "Introduction: On the Why, What and How of Generic Taxonomy," 112. For
some useful empirical research on generic categories, see the special issue of *Poetics* on
"media genre" edited by S. J. Schmidt, and the essay by Margie Schuur and Gerard
Seegers, "The Perception of Book Categories by Adult Users of Dutch Public Libraries."
31. S. J. Schmidt, "Towards a Constructivist Theory of Media Genre."
32. See, for instance, "Satire" in Abrams's *Glossary of Literary Terms* and Joseph T.
Shipley's *Dictionary of World Literature.*

also brings us closer to those who participate more actively in shaping our concepts of literary genres, namely, critics, writers, scholars, teachers, students of literature, and other active members of the literary community. I would like to stress that the compiler's basic function in such dictionaries is mainly to pronounce and make explicit the implicit knowledge of the community of users of genres. He or she may sometimes also perform a more fundamental role by trying to modify the "hard core" of the generic concept by adding to it a work not usually considered a prototypical member of the genre. These attempts, however, are not very frequent, and not always successful. Critics may perform an important constitutive role in assigning literary status to verbal artifacts,[33] but within a given literary community of genre users, their role in describing generic categories is not so much constitutive as it is descriptive and explicatory.

In addition to the family-resemblance-prototype assumption, there may be another fruitful application of the concept of family resemblance to the study of literary genres. Wittgenstein's concept was evoked by Paul Alpers in a very interesting discussion of the literary tradition of the pastoral. The significant point in Alpers's article is his emphasis on a tacit "dialogue" between writers of pastoral throughout history. How the lives of shepherds were represented and how these representations were made to "stand for" human life in general underwent constant modification. Thus every pastoral can be regarded as "an interpretation or development or use of the representative anecdote of shepherds' lives."[34] In other words, we have a continual and intimate intertextual relationship between different phases of the genre. Some writers may take the previous phase as an admired model, some as a challenge, but in all cases we will have some kind of textual "ancestry." This brings us back to Wittgenstein's concept of family resemblance. Maurice Mandelbaum, in a critical account of Wittgenstein's concept, points out that in hailing the "openness" of the concept of family, Wittgenstein ignored one crucial "stable" element, namely that members of a family "are related through a common ancestry."[35]

Thus the very vehicle supposed to be the emblem of extremely loose relations between its members—the family—has a far stronger "glue" that binds its parts: common ancestry. This trait, unlike the visible physiognomic features that create only an elusive network of similarities, is shared by all members of the family.[36] As with the common ancestral

---

33. See C. J. Van Rees, "The Institutional Foundation of a Critic's Connoisseurship."

34. Paul Alpers, "What Is Pastoral?" 457.

35. Maurice Mandelbaum, "Family Resemblance and Generalization Concerning the Arts," 221.

36. Weitz, in an attempt to defend Wittgenstein's position, argues that Mandelbaum

bond that ties families, so with games; the common feature should not necessarily be sought on the apparent, but rather on some underlying level: an enjoyable activity, governed by constitutive rules, that has no material products.[37]

In any event, it is possible to see the implications of the concept of "common ancestry" for the theory of literary genres. Alpers's remark about the "line of descent" of the pastoral may be viewed as implying a common ancestry for all pastorals. The intertextual relationships among diverse writers can be traced back to the "founding father" of pastoral— Theocritus. Virgil, Theocritus's "heir," represents the first significant bifurcation of the genre into idyllic and more realistic versions, which then evolved and branched out further during the Renaissance and later during the romantic era. Every writer in this line carries on the textual heritage of the genre, or participates in its "gene pool" (to use a biological metaphor).

Further, the generic "line of descent" often tends to be structured around the figures of either a "founding father" or even more frequently two "parental" figures, representing certain basic generic options and directions: Theocritus and Virgil in pastoral, Homer and Virgil in epic poetry, Aristophanes and Plautus in comedy, Horace and Juvenal in satire, Petrarch and Shakespeare in the sonnet, and so forth. The "line of descent" then tends to display further bifurcation, but in most cases it is not too difficult to "trace" later, even modern, manifestations back to the primal figures.

Thus focusing solely on the conspicuous textual features of a literary genre may sometimes lead a theorist to despair of finding any common specific features. This despair is unjustified, for two reasons. First, as we have seen, many genres, even the most elusive, usually share at least one fundamental trait. This may sometimes be general or vague, but it still may provide us with vital information about the scope and possibilities of the genre.[38] Second, in addition to these fundamental characteristics,

---

fails to show that Wittgenstein's doctrine of family resemblance is incoherent (*The Opening Mind*, 56–57). It seems to me, however, that Mandelbaum only intended to show that Wittgenstein's doctrine is incomplete.

37. For defining games as activity governed by constitutive rules, see Searle, *Speech Acts* (especially chapter 2). I add the elements of enjoyment and of no material products to distinguish games from other institutional activities governed by constitutive rules, but which are not necessarily enjoyable and which have material products (e.g., economic institutions). For some interesting observations on the concepts of institutional fact and of constitutive and regulative rules and their applicability to the literary field, see Van Rees, "The Institutional Foundation," 190–93.

38. M. M. Bakhtin and P. M. Medvedev, in their *Formal Method in Literary Scholarship*, refer to such fundamental characteristics when they say that "every genre has its own orientation in life, with reference to its events, problems, etc." (131).

every writer who chooses to compose in a generic framework (and most writers do work in some generic framework, even if reluctantly) participates in the transmission of a textual heritage. In order to understand and to evaluate the writer's work we are expected to take into account the generic background against which he or she operates. It follows also that we can establish a "genealogical" line, i.e., the series of writers who have participated in shaping, reshaping, and transmitting the textual heritage established by the "parental figures" of the genre, including the dialectical relationship of "parents" and "children" in genre history.[39]

What is proposed here is a picture of the "genre family" consisting of individual writers who have contributed to the generic tradition. And as a family tree maps for us the diverse lines of descent of a family (to use Alpers's image), so does the "family tree" of a genre.

The determination of whether an individual is or is not part of a given family is a function of pedigree and of legal and cultural norms; similarly, the decision whether the works of a particular writer belong to a given genre is a function of direct influence and of how literary genres are perceived and divided in a specific period and literature. Demonstrating that a specific writer was influenced by a particular generic tradition is not enough. One should also show that this generic tradition is recognized as such by the reading public, as part of its "horizon of expectations." This latter aspect is concerned with the institutional nature of literature as a cultural activity. In order to determine whether a given work is perceived against a specific generic tradition by the reading public, one has to check various "clues" such as the work's title and the author's other works and reputation. In addition, some very important literary-institutional factors are involved in determining the generic "horizon of expectation" of the literary community: the work's publisher, how it is referred to by critics, presented by salespersons, and, when it becomes part of a curriculum, how it is grouped with other works.[40]

Showing an "influence" in and of itself is not enough. On the other hand, trying to "force" the works of a writer into a generic schema without being able to demonstrate any specific line of influence (no matter how intricate) may result in arbitrary groupings of texts. The

---

39. The "genealogical" line of genre can be described to some extent as operating in reverse, where the son—by choosing certain texts as models—"begets" his parents. This interesting idea is suggested by Jean-Marie Schaeffer, who describes, in "Literary Genres and Textual Genericity," 183, how "the synthetically generic text *constructs its own generic lineage*" (italics added).

40. The term "horizon of expectation" is borrowed from Jauss, *Toward an Aesthetic of Reception*.

term "influence" that I use here in referring to generic transmission has been discredited in literary theory, because it may lead to indiscriminate talk of ubiquitous "influences" and to focusing on the biography of the writer rather than on his work.[41] I think, however, that this traditional term conveys to us the intimate relationships that sometimes exist between the works of two writers, especially within a generic tradition, and, when used carefully, can be fruitful.[42] Being recognized as part of a genre is thus a function of a dialectical relationship between individual influence and reception by a literary community. This becomes especially striking when a new genre tries to establish itself as part of the audience's "generic world view." It took some time before the novel, for example, was accepted as a genre in its own right and not some sort of literary Aristotle's camel, a creature that does not fit into the existing generic schemata: Fielding's famous definition of the novel as "a comic epic poem in prose" is perhaps the best-known attempt to reconcile traditional labels with the new generic development.

To conclude my discussion, I want to stress that although I have criticized some hasty uses of the family-resemblance concept, I do not deny that it has had a positive role in modern genre theory. It has been a vital force of liberation from certain rigid and inflexible concepts of genre. After granting this important liberating function, however, one should seek a more balanced approach to the issue of describing literary genres. Such a desired model will neither confine itself to a closed set of necessary and sufficient conditions, nor shun the attempt to formulate certain salient characteristics that can be easily found in the prototypical members of a generic category. In addition, one has to recognize the plural nature of literary genres; some genres tend to be more homogeneous, others more heterogeneous, and thus the issue of "open-endedness" has a different status in each case.

Moreover, as we have seen, other aspects of the analogy—related to the idea of a generic heritage passing from "parents" to "children"— may be highly pertinent to genre theory. The rest of this chapter is therefore devoted to exploring various implications of this dialectical relationship of "parents" and "children."

41. For an astute criticism of the slippery use of this term in literary history, see the articles by Boris Ejxenbaum and Jurij Tynjanov and the articles coauthored by Tynjanov and Jakobson in *Readings in Russian Poetics*, ed. Ladislav Matejka and Krystyna Pomorska, especially 59, 76, and 79.
42. For a persuasive defense of the concept of "literary influence" see Claudio Guillén, *Literature as System*, 62.

THE FAMILY ANALOGY:
PARENT–CHILD RELATIONSHIPS AND BEYOND

Recent psychological and especially psychoanalytic forms of criticism are only minimally relevant to my study. The psychoanalytic readings of literary texts, or alternatively the literary readings of psychoanalytic texts, are only remotely related to genre theory, which is, after all, my main concern. But before I go on to present some implications of the family analogy that are relevant to genre theory, especially those associated with the concept of transmitting the generic heritage from "parents" to "children," I want to discuss one interesting, psychoanalytically oriented, critical effort that is very pertinent to my interests: Harold Bloom's *Anxiety of Influence*. Despite the fact that Bloom does not refer explicitly to the question of literary genres, with only a few modifications his perspective can easily be adapted to genre theory.

Since Christopher Norris summarizes Bloom's ideas both faithfully and well, it is worthwhile to quote him at some length:

> *The Anxiety of Influence* (1973) laid the ground-work of Bloom's revisionist poetic. There exists, he argued, a complex and fascinating tension between the 'strong' poets in any tradition—those with a powerful drive to preserve their own identity—and the predecessor poets whose influence they have to cope with and somehow turn to advantage. The poet suffers with peculiar anguish that guilt-ridden hatred of the father that Freud detected at the root of family relations. His will to expression is pursued through cunning forms of displacement, or defensive 'tropes', which at the same time disguise and elaborate the will to be self-begotten, to acknowledge no previous authority or influence. The strong poet has the courage to recognize his own belatedness *vis-à-vis* the tradition he inherits, and the strength to subvert it by 'troping' his predecessors.[43]

If we add "generic" to "tradition" in the above quotation, the relevance of these formulations to genre theory become apparent. According to Bloom's ideas, any new writer in a generic tradition is a "son" who regards the dominant writer in this genre as the "father" against whom the "son" has to assert his own identity.

My fundamental reservation, however, about Bloom's parental model

43. Christopher Norris, *Deconstruction: Theory and Practice,* 117.

is that his promising initial insight is lost in the lines he develops from it. It is very often unclear whether Bloom is speaking about the texts of a poet or about the poet's psyche. In many cases it seems that he is interested above all in the psyche, but the book is subtitled *A Theory of Poetry*. Any invocation of psychological analogies should be careful to refer to the poet's psyche only as far as it is manifested in the text, or is highly relevant to our understanding of the text. Hence my stress on the *poetic* personality of a writer, which might be seen as an extended metonymic way of talking about the texts themselves.

After proposing the parental model, and the principle that any poet "tropes" his or her precursor, Bloom provides us with six different types of "troping." But nowhere does he state the criteria to determine whether a given poem is, for example, a manifestation of *daemonization* and not *apophrades,* or any of the other four. Neither the quasi-psychological elaborations of the terms, nor the specific examples provided make the distinctions any clearer. It is even unclear whether the movement from one category to the next is determined by one and the same criterion.

Surveying Bloom's six types of "transformations," M. H. Abrams makes an ironic comment: "These amalgamated transformers are not only versatile enough to establish each of Bloom's new readings, but also antithetical enough to convert any possible counter-evidence into a confirmation of his own reading."[44]

On a different front, I also have some reservations about the dominant role Bloom's familial model gives to Freud's theory and to its most famous element: the Oedipus complex.[45] This restriction of focus to Freud's perception of the family goes hand in hand with an approach that depicts the writer, or any artist, as a fundamentally neurotic or infantile personality (at least as far as the creative aspects of his personality are concerned): "Freud humanely saw the Oedipus complex as only a phase in the development of character, to be superseded by the Überich (superego) as mock-rational censor. Yet no poet-as-poet completes such a development and still remains a poet."[46]

Thus the writer is described as a regressive type, trapped forever in his (poetic) Oedipal stage, trying desperately to exorcise the father. I think that this is misleading because it overemphasizes the negative role played by the "father" figure in his relationship with the "son,"[47] and also

44. M. H. Abrams, "How to Do Things with Texts," 290.
45. One might also mention Freud's predominantly male perspective as a limiting shortcoming of the model.
46. Harold Bloom, *The Anxiety of Influence: A Theory of Poetry,* 109–10.
47. For a more balanced view of the relationship between "father" poets and "son"

because it leaves no room for a writer to mature. Again, M. H. Abrams comments pointedly about this restrictive point of view:

> The poetic self remains forever fixed at the Oedipal stage of development; for Bloom explicitly denies to the poet "as poet" the Freudian mechanism of sublimation, which allows for the substitution, in satisfying our primordial desires, of higher for lower goals and so makes possible the growth from the infantile stage of total self-concern to the mature recognition of reciprocity with other selves.[48]

Thus one should look for a less restrictive, non-Oedipal model to examine the parent–child relationship within genre theory. Such a model has indirectly been suggested in a recent attempt to revaluate the very earliest genre theory. In his instructive discussion, Thomas Rosenmeyer has proposed that the ancients tacitly relied on a familial model when they came to describe the "inventory" of genres in their days: "Instead of genre criticism, the ancients practiced model criticism. Their allegiances and affiliations connect up, not with a mode or a kind, but with a father, a personal guide."[49]

This familial model, which focuses on the (poetic) relationships of father and son (but without a restrictive Oedipal orientation), facilitates a description of the dialectics of indebtedness and independence that is the hallmark of generic development: "The prestige of the father and the rivalries within the family account most satisfactorily for what stability there is in the formal and aesthetic continuities over the years, while also explaining the great variety of creative departures."[50]

Rosenmeyer's illuminating description helps to reveal the "deep metaphor" that guided the ancients' genre thinking (and thus to explain its scope and its basic reasoning). By exposing the familial model underlying this thinking, he succeeds in explaining how the seemingly systematic ancient classifications are in many respects incomplete and deficient; they were guided, not by logic, but rather by the familial analogy. By accepting the familial model as a legitimate conceptual framework for genre theory, and by distinguishing it from an attempt to provide a

---

poets, equally emphasizing the stimulating and positive effects of the poetic "father" figure on his "heir," see Christopher Ricks, "Allusion: The Poet as Heir."

48. Abrams, "How to Do Things with Texts," 292.

49. Rosenmeyer, "Ancient Literary Genres: A Mirage?" 81–82.

50. Ibid., 82.

systematic classification, we can both escape the ancients' inconsistencies and develop new insights into how the generic heritage is transmitted.

Every writer who seeks a place in the "family tree" of a given genre participates in the dialectics of imitation and rebellion, of affirmation and negation. To accomplish this, the writer must absorb a great deal from the parental figure but must also declare a distinct identity. In many cases this process, in which the new writer establishes an independent self in the generic family of writers, is marked by an *ambivalent* attitude toward the parental figure. This process might remind us of the stage of adolescence in family life: "[The adolescent's] feelings toward authority are loaded with ambivalence. His need of parental protection continues. His emotional dependence upon them is unresolved. Simultaneously, however, he has a strong need to live his own life, to demonstrate his self-sufficiency, and to make his own decisions."[51]

I suggest that this ambivalent attitude of a new writer trying to establish an independent place in the "generic family" is best found in the satirical and parodistic attitudes taken up by the new writer toward the "parents." Parodic and satiric manipulation of theme, character, and style of the "parent" figure's poetics expresses the "child's" need to define the self against the parental figure and to clear the way within the generic framework for the new poetics being offered. These parodic and satiric attitudes are thus most likely to appear when the new writer is taking the first steps in the process of establishing an independent new poetics.

I am interested here in parody and satire not in and of themselves, but only as a part of the ambivalent, transitional phase in the development of the genre. Thus, while trying to "get rid" of the parental figure, the parodic structures and satiric arrows are part of an overall artistic effort to set off for new horizons.[52]

GROWING UP IN AND THROUGH THE NOVEL

The novel is an appropriate genre for a demonstration of the family analogy because in their fictional worlds novelists can show characters that represent their (poetic) parental figures. These representations are in many cases distorted and satirical, being part of the dialectical relation-

---

51. Nathan W. Ackerman, *The Psychodynamics of Family Life,* 218.

52. The important role of parodistic structures in literary history has been stressed by Jurij Tynjanov and other formalists. See, for instance, Tynjanov's "Dostoevsky and Gogol: Theory of Parody."

ship of imitation and distortion, influence and independence, that marks the development of a genre. Jurij Tynjanov analyzes the satirical and parodistic elements in Dostoevsky's early, "adolescent" writings. These artistic attacks were directed against Dostoevsky's parental figure, Gogol, and were part of the young Dostoevsky's auto-emancipation. When Dostoevsky portrays Gogol in "The Friend of the Family" as a ridiculous character and parodies his ponderous rhetoric, he is taking an important step toward establishing his new poetics in the Russian novel. He is making his first declaration of independence and staking his claim to a separate "branch" of the "family tree" of the Russian novel.

So the first reason why the novel "fits" the family analogy is that it represents, in its elaborated and verisimilar fictional world, the "familial" tensions that play a crucial role in shaping the poetics of a writer. In other words, the familial tensions are often thematized (in the Russian Formalist sense): the novel sometimes brings the artistic "family" issues that are part of its mechanism of development into the world created in the novel.

There is one more reason why the family analogy seems pertinent to the novel—its ability to incorporate the artistic family story not only into the characters' world but also into their psychology.

An author can present a heroine, or a hero, entrapped in an infantile or adolescent phase (the blame for which can be put on an excessive reading of novels!), within a work that as a whole is liberated from such "adolescent" artistic models and succeeds in creating a new, mature model. In such cases, though, the character's inability to grow up and to overcome previous literary models that have shaped his or her attitude toward life is a symptom of the author's own struggle to achieve artistic maturity. Flaubert's *Madame Bovary,* for instance, is a case of an immature heroine entangled in her romantic, "adolescent" models, observed by a mature and realistic writer, who is also striving to liberate himself from romantic clichés.

As a matter of fact, one may go back to the first great novel, *Don Quixote,* and see how Cervantes rebels against his "parental" chivalric romances and wages his artistic war by following the painful psychological process of his hero's maturing. Thus we have an analogous process on the artistic and on the psychological levels: Don Quixote has to outgrow his childish daydreaming about chivalry, and *Don Quixote* is an attempt by Cervantes to throw off these same generic conventions in order to introduce a different, more realistic version of the genre.

By locating the process of growing up on the psychological level of the fictional character, the author chooses to supply a realistic motivation (in the Russian Formalist sense) for this artistic attitude. He thus achieves more rhetorical force for his new aesthetic values. In *Don Quixote,* making the knight face the mirror that he thinks to be reality is a slow and agonizing way of disillusioning the knight, and for us, the readers, it is a very effective artistic method for obliging us to examine our own concepts of reality. Needless to say, in this highly complex work, the knight's occasional crashing into the mirror only opens the question of where fiction ends and reality begins. The simple realistic interpretation is incorporated into a kaleidoscopic carnival of real, "real," and fictional authors, narrators, and characters that seems to shake up and put into question any simplistic opposition of fiction and reality.[53]

But rather than try to fit this highly complex novel into the Procrustean bed of schematic formulation about generic and psychological growth, I would like to have a closer look at a less ambitious and less complex novel that can demonstrate some of my points: Jane Austen's *Northanger Abbey.* I focus on this relatively minor work by Austen because in it we can detect a mechanism that operates in many other, more sophisticated novels, albeit more subtly. The heroine of this novel does not achieve real maturity, despite the fact that she grows up during it; and its author, despite her rejection of "parental" novelistic models, still has recourse to them and does not achieve full poetic independence.

Similar problems can be found, by the way, in many other novels, especially those of the nineteenth century, when the issue of the hero's growth became central in the development of the novel (the bildungsroman).

Jane Austen makes clear her ironic intentions, directed at certain popular novels of her time, from the very beginning of the book:

> No one who had ever seen Catherine Morland in her infancy would have supposed her born to be an heroine. Her situation in life, the character of her father and mother, her own person and disposition, were all equally against her. Her father was a clergyman, without being neglected, or poor, and a very respectable man, though his name was Richard—and he had never been handsome. He had a considerable independence, besides two good livings—and he was not in the least addicted to locking up his daughters.[54]

In this opening passage we have, on the one hand, the conventional expectations of what a heroine should be, based on Gothic and sentimen-

---

53. On these teasing and intriguing aspects of the novel, see the illuminating analysis in chapter 1 of Alter's *Partial Magic.*

54. Jane Austen, *Northanger Abbey,* in *The Novels of Jane Austen,* 13.

tal models; and, on the other, trivial reality, which this novel is presenting. The very choice of an ordinary girl for the role of the central
character is an act of aggression against the prevailing novelistic models,
and the comic tension between these models and "real life" is the
perennial ammunition in this war.

These opening sentences gain an additional dimension, moreover,
because the literary clichés they evoke can be interpreted (as we shall see)
as part of the mental world of the heroine, Catherine Morland. In other
words, all these conventions about what is appropriate to a heroine and
her "history" are part of Catherine's way of thinking. Such an interpretation might, of course, come only in retrospect. In the "first reading"
we understand Austen's irony as directed against the presuppositions
held by certain hypothetical readers. Later, when we learn to what extent
Catherine herself has been influenced by these literary conventions, we
can reinterpret the irony in this passage as directed also toward the
heroine herself, discovering the textual clues that encode these literary
clichés as well-disguised "quotations" of Catherine's mental speech.[55]

Thus, with very little change, we can recast some of these sentences as
an interior, unconscious monologue of Catherine's, deeply influenced
by the contemporary novels she is reading: "My situation in life, the
character of my father, my own person and disposition, are all equally
against me. . . ." Assuming that thoughts like these have crossed
Catherine's mind, we can understand better why later on she would try,
despite these "disadvantageous" opening circumstances, to believe that
she herself was a heroine of a Gothic novel and that Northanger Abbey
was a setting for horrid deeds.

The device of opening a novel with phrases that seem to represent the
author's point of view, but are later revealed to be representative of the
thoughts of one of the characters, is not rare in Jane Austen's works. The
opening sentence of *Pride and Prejudice* is an excellent example: "It is a
truth universally acknowledged, that a single man in possession of a
good fortune, must be in want of a wife." On the face of it this sentence
seems to be the author's; later on, though, we will find out that it
actually reflects Mrs. Bennet's thoughts, characterizing her husband-
hunting for her daughters. This reinterpretation of the first sentence
provides us with a better understanding of the characters and a better
integration of different elements of the text. These same arguments may
apply to the reading of the first sentences of *Northanger Abbey*.

Kenneth Moler, in his *Jane Austen's Art of Allusion*, quite rightly

55. For the subtle and complex ways in which a writer can combine, fuse, and share the
speech and thoughts of his characters, see Dorrit Cohn, *Transparent Minds*.

distinguishes between two kinds of satire: "In 'Quixotic' satire a character absorbs misconceptions from reading a certain kind of literature; in the second sort of satire characters are not necessarily deluded by, or even aware of the literature that they and their actions mock."[56]

He is less convincing, however, when he declares categorically that there is a very clear borderline between these two kinds of satire in *Northanger Abbey:* "Catherine Morland is treated as a mock heroine of the second type of satire consistently throughout *Northanger Abbey.* She is a 'female Quixote' when, after reading Mrs. Radcliffe, she imagines Northanger Abbey to be another Udolpho—and, in my opinion, *only* then."[57]

Were we to confine ourselves to the explicit level of the text, Moler's statement might be valid. The opening sentences are, formally, the author's, and only slightly later are we told that Catherine began reading Gothic and sentimental novels. But if we are aware of the complex and subtle ways in which a writer can combine authorial discourse with the words and thoughts of a character, and of the fact that the reading process has two directions—while progressing through the text, we also move back in order to modify, qualify, or reverse perceptions from earlier in our reading—then Moler's apparently clear borderline is called into question.[58]

Nevertheless, one should not unduly emphasize the importance of the fact that the literary models and clichés mocked at the beginning are part of Catherine's mind. The dominant tone of the first chapter is that of the author, and some of the descriptions there cannot be attributed to Catherine. It is difficult to imagine her characterizing herself with sentences such as "She never could learn or understand anything before she was taught, and sometimes not even then, for she was often inattentive, and occasionally stupid." The possibility of interpreting some of the opening passage as part of Catherine's thoughts brings more coherence to our reading, and demonstrates the intimate relationship that can be created between the author's discourse and her character's consciousness, despite the formal and ironic gap between them.

Recognizing Catherine's immaturity, I concede that she does go through a long and sometimes painful process of growing up. In the course of this process she learns to abandon the literary models of the

56. Kenneth L. Moler, *Jane Austen's Art of Allusion,* 17 n. 1.
57. Ibid.
58. For a detailed and systematic description of the process of reading, which includes the dialectics of reinterpreting earlier perceptions, see Benjamin Harshav (Hrushovsky), "Theory of the Literary Text and the Structure of Non-Narrative Fiction," and Menakhem Perry, "Literary Dynamics: How the Order of a Text Creates Its Meanings."

Gothic novels as infantile and inadequate to real life. Her fantasizing about General Tilney—perceiving him as an English villain in the manner of the Gothic novel; interpreting his behavior as an ominous sign of horrid criminal guilt—all this comes crashing down when confronted by the principles of common sense pronounced by his son Henry, Catherine's future husband and the author's surrogate in the work.

When Henry understands where Catherine's fantasies have carried her—to suspecting that his father, the General, has murdered his wife—he openly criticizes her and states the principles of sane, plausible interpretation:

> "If I understand you rightly, you had formed a surmise of such horror as I have hardly words to—Dear Miss Morland, consider the dreadful nature of the suspicions you have entertained. What have you been judging from? Remember the country and the age in which we live, remember that we are English, that we are Christians. Consult your own understanding, your own sense of the probable, your own observation of what is passing around you—Does our education prepare us for such atrocities? Do our laws connive at them? Could they be perpetrated without being known, in a country like this, where social and literary intercourse is on such a footing, where every man is surrounded by a neighbourhood of voluntary spies, and where roads and newspapers lay everything open? Dearest Miss Morland, what ideas have you been admitting?"[59]

Henry's arguments have an immediate and deep effect on Catherine's mind: "The visions of romance were over. Catherine was completely awakened. Henry's address, short as it had been, had more thoroughly opened her eyes to the extravagance of her late fancies than all their several disappointments had done. Most grievously was she humbled. Most bitterly did she cry."[60]

And after this deep emotional shake-up and disillusionment, Catherine accepts Henry's commonsense outlook and starts to reject the Gothic literary models as inadequate. At first it might seem that at this point she has reached mental maturity. She even tells herself how misleading and simplistic these models are when confronted with the complex and morally mixed picture of reality:

59. Austen, *Northanger Abbey*, 197–98.
60. Ibid., 199.

Charming as were all Mrs. Radcliffe's works, and charming even
as were the works of all her imitators, it was not in them perhaps
that human nature, at least in the midland counties of England,
was to be looked for. Of the Alps and Pyrenees, with their pine
forests and their vices, they might give a faithful delineation; and
Italy, Switzerland, and the South of France, might be as fruitful
in horrors as they were there represented. Catherine dared not
doubt beyond her own country, and even of that, if hard pressed,
would have yielded the northern and western extremities. But in
the central part of England there was surely some security for the
existence even of a wife not beloved, in the laws of the land, and
the manners of the age. Murder was not tolerated, servants were
not slaves, and neither poison nor sleeping potions to be procured,
like rhubarb, from every druggist. Among the Alps and Pyrenees,
perhaps, there were no mixed characters. There, such as were not
as spotless as an angel, might have the dispositions of a fiend. But
in England it was not so; among the English, she believed, in
their hearts and habits, there was a general though unequal
mixture of good and bad.[61]

A closer look at Catherine's "mature" line of reasoning reveals Austen's irony. As a matter of fact, at the very moment we might expect a
complete and deep reversal, a true *anagnorisis,* we can still easily detect
some old illusions.

First, Catherine seems to cling to one marginal and relatively insignificant remark made by Henry, her spiritual mentor, and to make it the
core of all her reasoning. When Henry declares, "Remember that we are
English," it is only a rhetorical cry aimed to shake up Catherine's mind,
which has been floating around amid foreign territories and exotic places
and characters. In Catherine's line of reasoning this distinction between
England (or, more precisely, only part of it) and other foreign places
becomes the central issue. Only in these close and familiar lands does
she dismiss Gothic plots as improbable, and only in England is human
nature a "mixture of good and bad." In all other foreign places, Gothic
plots and characters might still be considered a truthful and realistic
representation of events. As a matter of fact, the sharp opposition drawn
between England on the one hand and the Alps and the Pyrenees on the
other hand only reinforces the impression that the literary Gothic models
are not only logically possible but may well be a probable and "faithful
delineation" of human nature.

61. Ibid., 200.

Thus, instead of truly absorbing the principles that underlie Henry's arguments, Catherine is struck only by one of his rhetorical exclamations. Instead of exposing the absurdity and basic improbability underlying the literary models set forth by Ann Radcliffe and her imitators, Catherine confines her critical perspective to what she might have known from direct observation. One might say that she takes the empirical principles advocated by Henry to the point of absurdity, refraining from making any feasible inferences about human beings in foreign countries because she does not have a direct knowledge of them. Thus, with this unreasonable restriction, she ends up being very close to the position that she set forth to refute.

This mixture of rejection and belief is ironically interwoven into the first sentence of the last passage quoted above. Whereas the main sentence states the divorce from Mrs. Radcliffe's works as realistic representations of life ("it was not in them perhaps that human nature . . . was to be looked for"), the subordinate clause inserted there by the master-ironist Jane Austen—"at least in the middle counties of England"—undermines this whole attack. Moreover, the more she meditates on the subject, the more she provides reasons why the Gothic novels are after all realistic: at least for the foreign places they depict they very possibly may provide, in Catherine's thoughts, a faithful picture.

Leaving the heroine aside, my second argument is that Jane Austen, who successfully presents Catherine's immaturity with regard to the Gothic and sentimental novel, could not herself reach a totally independent, realistic, and probable literary model, and thus relies on a mechanical, improbable (and to some extent "Gothic") plot.

This artistic tension between the new and the "parental" models is conspicuous in the concluding chapters of the novel, when Austen makes General Tilney treat Catherine with improbable cruelty. His abrupt order to expel her from Northanger Abbey goes beyond any reasonable reaction of a would-be father-in-law who finds out that his hoped-for daughter-in-law is not as rich as he had previously thought her to be. As a matter of fact, in his outrageous behavior he more resembles a typical Gothic villain than a respectable English gentleman.

Furthermore, toward the end of the novel, Austen not only retreats to the use of conventional prevailing literary types (e.g., the inflexible father opposing his child's matrimonial choice), but also seems to abandon her commitment to realism altogether. This move becomes apparent when, in order to give the novel a happy ending, she looks for a quick and improbable way to pull our young couple out of their forced separation. With an amused and ironic tone (reminiscent of Fielding's addresses to the reader throughout *Tom Jones*), Austen undermines the serious realistic intentions that were carefully constituted earlier in the novel:

> The anxiety, which in this state of their attachment must be the portion of Henry and Catherine, and of all who loved either, as to its final event, can hardly extend, I fear, to the bosom of my readers, who will see in the tell-tale compression of the pages before them, that we are all hastening together to perfect felicity. The means by which their early marriage was effected can be the only doubt; what probable circumstance could work upon a temper like the General's? The circumstance which chiefly availed was the marriage of his daughter with a man of fortune.[62]

Note how the word "probable," which earlier in the novel referred to the hard core of Austen's artistic realistic convictions in whose name Gothic and sentimental literary models were criticized and rejected, is now being used tongue-in-cheek. It is as though Austen's realistic strategy has been forgotten and she is busy (to use Marvin Mudrick's expression) pulling a viscount out of her hat.[63] Later on, she would even dismiss the whole closure of the novel as a joke: "I leave it to be settled by whomsoever it may concern, whether the tendency of this work be altogether to recommend parental tyranny, or reward filial disobedience."[64]

These ironic metatextual comments foreground the issue of the new novelistic model set up previously in which the *probable* served as the measuring rod for judging events. The author does not sustain a coherent, realistic poetics, as the heroine does not totally absorb the commonsensical approach to life. Whereas Catherine is unaware of her lapse into the Gothic models, Jane Austen consciously calls our attention to the incongruity between the "parental" model and her own new poetics. The self-ironic commentary also reminds us of the ambivalent status of the novel: it exposes the inadequacy of the "parental" novelistic model, but it is still not totally independent itself.

The ending of *Northanger Abbey* has prompted certain critics (e.g., Moler, Mudrick) to fault Austen for raising realistic expectations only to frustrate them at the end. Others have tried to claim that, by presenting General Tilney as a typical Gothic villain, Austen wants to question all the principles of common sense.[65] I think that instead of adopting

---

62. Ibid., 250.
63. Marvin Mudrick, *Jane Austen: Irony as Defense and Discovery*, 58.
64. Austen, *Northanger Abbey*, 252.
65. This approach is taken, for instance, by Lionel Trilling in *Sincerity and Authenticity*.

evaluative language we should do better to understand the significance of this novel as part of an ambivalent phase in the development of Austen the novelist. Such a stage brings us the playfulness of parody, irony, and satire on "parental" models; it blazes the way to a new poetics, but it does not provide a totally independent, consistent poetics. If we do not stipulate such a consistency and are willing to accept the work as signifying an ambivalent stage in generic development, some of the evaluative arguments about the novel become irrelevant and we can concentrate on its indisputable merits.

A FINAL FAMILIAL THOUGHT

To conclude this chapter, I would like to hint at one more issue that can be related to the family analogy: that of the change of the status of genres in modernist literature. One might draw an analogy between the process of change that the modern family is undergoing and the process of change in the "literary family," the genre.[66]

The classic extended family, structured in a very hierarchical manner, with some revered ancestral figures, has been replaced by the nuclear family, loosely structured and prone to change, with little respect for or even awareness of any "founding fathers." The analogous process in the literary field is obvious. The rigid, hierarchical model of literary genres that prevailed for many centuries[67] has been replaced by the more flexible and elusive modern generic system. The modern Western concept of the family, which provides more individual autonomy and supports rebellion against the parental figures (as opposed to seeing them as revered models), is strikingly pertinent to the literary field, where the poetics of the individual writer have a highly autonomous status with regard to generic conventions.[68]

In stressing the central role played by the individual writer at the expense of the well-structured conservative genre, one should not jump

66. A survey of the process of change in the modern family can be found in the article by Clifford Kirkpatrick, "Family: Disorganization and Dissolution."

67. For a survey of the different hierarchies among literary genres (some of which are still part of contemporary literary consciousness), see chapter 12 in Fowler's *Kinds of Literature*.

68. Margolin, in "The Concept of Genre," 224, claims that the poetics of the individual writer and of the literary movement have replaced the literary genre as the organizing principle of modern literature. Although I agree with some of his observations, I think he underestimates the still continuing power of genres as an organizing principle in the literary field.

to the conclusion that all generic concepts, especially in modernist literature, are chimerical. Needless to say, one cannot accept the Crocean concept that any literary work exists *sui generis,* because when this notion is taken seriously it is at odds with our experience as writers and readers, who constantly group, connect, and relate literary works to one another.

We should remember that the loosening of family ties does not entail the disappearance of the family altogether, just a modification of it. Nathan Ackerman describes the elusive and ubiquitous nature of the family in terms that can be applied almost verbatim to the field of literary genres:

> The family is a paradoxical and elusive entity. It assumes many guises. It is the same everywhere; yet it is not the same anywhere. Throughout time it has remained the same; yet it has never remained the same. The steady transformation of family through time is the product of an unceasing process of evolution; the form of family molds itself to the conditions of life which dominate at a given time and place. On the contemporary scene, the family is changing its pattern at a remarkably rapid pace; it is accommodating in a striking way to the social crisis which is the mark of our period in history. There is nothing fixed or immutable about family, except that it is always with us.[69]

Even a confirmed bachelor has some family relationship, no matter how much he tries to present himself as a self-contained person. He may be autonomous, but is by no means autarchic. Similarly, no matter how fervently an author claims that his text is unique, it still has intimate links with existing types of literature, i.e., with literary genres.

In modern literature, too, genres still play a major role. First, we should not forget that the greater part of literature produced today, i.e., mostly "non-canonic" literature, is still written and read in accordance with relatively strict generic rules. One could claim that the more a genre appeals to a large audience, the more it is subject to conventional rules. Further, even in those areas of modern literature where it seems that generic rules are absent, the innovative areas of canonic literature, generic rules are still a vital part of the literary communicative situation. These generic conventions might be viewed as a challenge, or a horizon, against which the writer and his reader have to define themselves. The writer may stretch the generic rules, he may produce some unpredictable "match" between different existing conventions of existing literary

---

69. Ackerman, *The Psychodynamics of Family Life,* 15.

genres (or even between literary conventions and conventions taken from other media), but in order to understand the overall significance of his text, we should be aware of the generic system against which he is working. A writer does not create in a textual vacuum, and a rebellious child is still part of the family.

Chapter 4

Literary Genres
as Social Institutions

In the two previous chapters, the analogies used to illuminate literary genres—biological species and families—were taken from realms different in kind from the literary. The metaphors used in the next two chapters are from "closer to home." Social or cultural institutions, in their broadest sense, can be interpreted as including the literary domain among other cultural systems (e.g., economic, political, or educational). When we come to the fourth analogy, that of speech acts, the relationship between the two compared elements becomes even more intimate: in both literary genres and speech acts (such as ordering, asking, promising) we are dealing with the organizing principles of language use.

However, I would like to stress that my basic methodological assumption is that we are dealing with *analogical* relationships, not with a taxonomy of members of the same category. In other words, the literary genre is not merely a type of social institution; the latter term is used here in a metaphorical and not a literal sense.

The intimate relationship between various social and cultural institutions on the one hand, and literary "institutions" (i.e., genres) on the other, creates an interesting situation in that the same concepts are sometimes used in both fields. This chapter will focus on two such concepts that overlap the boundaries between social institutions and literary genres, between sociology and poetics: *convention* and *role*.

I would like to state at the outset that these two concepts seem to me most useful when discussing dramatic genres. The very distinction between "life" and "stage" is conceivable only as part of a communicative situation based on cultural conventions. The audience is supposed to know and tacitly accept that the figures and the scenery on the stage are not "real," but rather representative. This understanding is an example of one basic convention—on which I will shortly elaborate—that governs the production and reception of dramatic genres. Concerning roles, it seems that we can talk in similar ways about roles that constitute social institutions and those that define the internal structure of dramatic genres: in both cases we detect in the actions of real people and of characters in a drama certain patterns determined by their "roles," i.e., they both fulfill certain functions appropriate to the social or literary institutions in which they participate. A professor is expected to comply with certain patterns of action, and to interact with other role-players (e.g., students) according to the structure and functions of an educational institution. And in a like manner, a character in a comedy is expected to perform certain acts and to interact with other characters according to the structural principles of the literary "institution" of comedy. In the second part of this chapter I will focus on one such comedic role.

But before expanding on the relevance of the concept of convention to dramatic genres, and illustrating the applicability of the concept of role to the structure of dramatic comedy, let me first quote a passage that formulates the pertinence of the institutional perspective in general to genre theory. As a matter of fact, it was this passage from Wellek and Warren that, a few years ago, triggered this whole study by showing me the strong conceptual potentialities inherent in some kinds of analogical thinking about literary genres:

> The literary kind is an 'institution'—as Church, University, or State is an institution. It exists not as an animal exists or even as a building, chapel, library, or capital, but as an institution exists. One can work through, express oneself through, existing institutions, create new ones, or get on, so far as possible, without sharing in politics or rituals; one can also join, but then reshape, institutions.[1]

Warren, the author of this chapter on literary genres in *Theory of Literature*, synthesizes two statements here. One is that of Norman Pearson, presenting literary forms "as institutional imperatives which both coerce and are in turn coerced by the writer,"[2] and the other, by

---

1. Wellek and Warren, *Theory of Literature*, 226.
2. Norman Holmes Pearson, "Literary Forms and Types: or, A Defense of Polonius," 70.

Harry Levin, describing literature in general as an institution that "cherishes a unique phase of human experience and controls a special body of precedents and devices."[3]

Warren's powerful insight was to apply Levin's institutional formulations to the field of literary genres, as already suggested by Pearson. In this passage Warren also suggests an important distinction between the "material" aspects of a phenomenon (e.g., a building, or the printed book, as a material object) and the "institutional" aspect that makes the phenomenon culturally meaningful. This distinction is related to the distinction between "brute facts" and "institutional facts" that has been elaborated in modern studies in the philosophy of language.[4] Whereas the statement "It rains in Spain" refers to a "brute fact," the statement "Kasparov won the chess game" refers to an "institutional fact" the meaning of which is determined by a set of institutional rules (in this case, the rules of chess) that assign cultural meaning to the movements of carved wooden pieces. This distinction may help us to see the difference between, for example, circumcision as a surgical act and as a ritual, institutional act in a particular culture.

The institutional perspective in literature has been stressed by some structuralist theorists. Jonathan Culler, for instance, points out that "actions are meaningful only with respect to a set of institutional conventions."[5] Later he refers to "the conventions of poetry as an institution."[6] This institutional approach to genres has also been advocated by Fredric Jameson, who adds a sociocultural dimension to the structuralist-semiotic usage of the term: "Genres are essentially literary *institutions,* or social contracts between a writer and a specific public, whose function is to specify the proper use of a particular cultural artifact."[7]

Immediately after this, Jameson remarks that the concept of institutionalized generic rules, together with many other institutions, "falls casualty to the gradual penetration of a market system and a money economy."[8] But despite this sociological (neo-Marxist) contention about the changing status of generic rules, it seems that their diminishing power would not deprive them of their institutional nature; it would only make them socially passé.

3. Harry Levin, "Literature as an Institution," 552.

4. See, for instance, Searle's *Speech Acts.*

5. Jonathan Culler, *Structuralist Poetics,* 5.

6. Ibid., 69.

7. Fredric Jameson, "Magical Narratives: On the Dialectical Use of Genre Criticism," in *The Political Unconscious,* 106.

8. Ibid., 107.

Perhaps the most interesting application of the institutional perspective to literary genre is Michael Globinsky's "The Literary Genre and the Problems of Historical Poetics."[9] Globinsky uses the distinction between social structure and social conjuncture introduced by the French sociologists George Gurevitch and Henri Lefebvre. Various conjunctures (in the form of literary movements) operate on and modify the literary genre described as the basic structure. These sociological concepts also prompt Globinsky to analyze various processes of structuring and destructuring in the history of a genre and of the relationship between genres.

To apply an institutional perspective to literary genres does not mean that I have committed myself to a static view of them. Some connotations of "institution" may be stability, conformity, and fixed patterns of behavior, but modern sociology has exposed the inadequacy of a static concept of institutions. Shmuel Eisenstadt, for instance, states that "the possibility of innovation and change is not something external or accidental to any institutional system. It is given in the very nature of the process of institutionalization and in the working of institutional systems."[10]

Later on he enumerates some common forms of innovation in institutions. Some of these might easily be adapted to the literary field and to the patterns of innovation of literary "institutions":

> Some groups may be greatly opposed to the very premises of the institutionalization of a given system. . . . Others may share these values and accept the norms to a greater degree but may look on themselves as the more truthful repositories of these same values. . . . Others may develop new interpretations of existing values and strive for a change in the very bases of the institutional order.[11]

It seems that we can see in the first type any *avant-garde* literary movement that challenges the very order and constitution of literary genres; the second type may be found in traditionalist writers who claim to be more faithful to the generic rules; whereas the third type can be seen in "reformers" who push generic rules one step further by reinterpreting them. But whatever our interpretation of the forms of innovation in the social-institutional dimension may be, we can be sure that taking

9. Michael Globinsky, "The Literary Genre and the Problems of Historical Poetics," 19–25.
10. Shmuel N. Eisenstadt, "Social Institutions," 418.
11. Ibid., 418–19.

the institutional perspective does not commit us to a conservative or static position.

CONVENTIONS IN THE THEATER:
THE SEMIOTIC CONNECTION

I would like to start by introducing a definition of social convention that seems to me acceptable both on its own merits and because of its potential implications for literary and dramatic theory. Margaret Gilbert's definition, which will be my point of departure, relates the concept of convention to those of the social norm and *quasi-agreement:*

> The account of convention we have arrived at can be stated, in a somewhat cumbersome fashion, without using the technical term *quasi-agreement:* roughly, there is a social convention in a group when and only when it is common knowledge in that group that most people think that one ought to do such-and-such in a certain context, and that one ought to do this because it is common knowledge that most people believe that one ought to do this.[12]

One important feature of this account of convention is that it does not entail, as Margaret Gilbert notes later on, any actual conformity to the convention. In other words, a convention is not primarily based on statistical grounds; people may rebel against prevailing conventions or ignore them, yet we can still speak of these prevailing conventions as long as people believe that some specific "oughtness" is part of the cultural scene in which they operate. This feature is particularly pertinent to the artistic field, where in our post-romantic era the very notion of conformity may make some people shudder.

One should, nevertheless, qualify this concept so far as artistic conventions are concerned. With or without romanticism, there is always a latent demand for innovation from the artist. This demand may be a very modest one in traditionalism and may be overt and powerful in modernism, but in both cases the artist is expected to manipulate the existing conventions and to carry them (at least) one step further. This ambiguous status of the artistic convention applies to both the writer and the reader. From the writer's perspective, the generic convention is a model to follow but also a challenge to overcome. In a complementary way, the

---

12. Margaret Gilbert, "Notes on the Concept of a Social Convention," 245.

reader demands compliance with the established generic conventions so that he can integrate the new text, but at the same time he expects the writer to manipulate these established conventions so that the new text is more than a tedious repetition of the generic tradition.

A similar approach to generic conventions, relating them to the concept of the quasi-agreement, or the quasi-contract, was introduced by Jonathan Culler:

> The function of genre conventions is essentially to establish a contract between writer and reader so as to make certain relevant expectations operative and thus to permit intelligibility: "it is essentially a matter of making the text as *perceptible* as possible; one can see what role this conception gives to the notions of genre and model: that of archetypes, of partly abstract models which serve as guide to the reader" (Genot, "L'écriture libératrice", p. 49). A statement will be taken differently if found in an ode and in a comedy. The reader attends to characters in a different way if he is reading a tragedy or if he is reading a comedy which he expects to end in multiple marriage.[13]

Another peculiar feature of the concept of social norms or conventions makes it highly pertinent to the literary field: its dual descriptive and prescriptive nature. A concept of scientific discourse should be, of course, descriptive. The concept of social convention, therefore, would be descriptive in sociological discourse—i.e., from "outside" the social system—but prescriptive from "within" the system. To say that wearing a swimsuit while conducting a graduate seminar violates a convention of the academic world is to make a descriptive statement. For the instructor, however, this convention takes the form of an obligation, a tacit demand, a quasi-agreement, in the form of "you had *better* wear professionally suitable clothes while teaching."[14] It does not follow, of course, that every professor dresses formally, but the convention nevertheless stands.

In an analogous way, we can speak of statements such as "comedies have happy endings" as descriptive when stated from "outside" the system. When, however, a playwright wishes to write a comedy, the statement becomes tacitly prescriptive, with the implication: "You had better write a happy ending for this piece of yours, if you want it to be a comedy." This dual nature of statements about generic rules can be

---

13. Culler, *Structuralist Poetics*, 147.

14. For this duality—descriptive and prescriptive—in the nature of statements about institutional facts, see John Searle's "Deriving 'Ought' from 'Is,' " in *Speech Acts*, 175–98.

traced back to Aristotle's *Poetics*, the first serious attempt to discuss literary genres systematically. According to this interpretation of the *Poetics*, to *describe* catharsis and how it is produced also serves to guide writers of tragedies.[15]

Whereas some degree of the conventional is to be found in any literary work and in any literary genre, I shall focus here on the theatrical genres, because the very distinction between life and stage presupposes a convention that makes the action on stage culturally meaningful. Moreover, the fact that in the gathering at the theater dramatic and social conventions seem to interact intimately, makes the relevance of the concept of convention even more apparent.[16]

Every social institution has its specific conventions. Every system of social institutions has a minimal set of conventions shared by the specific institutions. The university may have its ritual for awarding students their earned degrees. High schools may differ from the university in their specific conventions to mark graduation. All educational institutions, however, share the basic convention of marking graduation (perhaps as a remnant of initiation rituals). In a similar way, one may talk about the specific conventions of the dramatic genres of tragedy, comedy, melodrama, and farce (among others), but also about certain conventions shared by all dramatic genres. In this part of the chapter I want to focus on the convention that makes possible the successful performance of every play, of every dramatic genre, the *semiotic convention* that underlies the dramatic performance.

The semiotic perspective on theatrical art was developed by the "Prague School" during the thirties and forties. Jindrich Honzl's formulations on this subject are representative of this school's emphasis on the theatrical *sign*:

> Everything that makes up reality on the stage—the playwright's text, the actor's acting, the stage lighting—all these things in every case stand for other things. In other words, dramatic performance is a set of signs. . . . It has already been maintained that although the stage is usually a construction, it is not its constructional nature that makes it a stage but the fact that it *represents* dramatic place. The same can be said about the actors:

---

15. For a discussion of the basic methodological assumptions of the *Poetics* and the status of this treatise as part of "the productive sciences" in Aristotle's philosophical framework, see "The Poetic Method of Aristotle: Its Powers and Limitations" by Elder Olson in his anthology, *Aristotle's Poetics and English Literature*.

16. The importance of conventions in drama is emphasized by Harry Levin in his "Notes on Convention," 67.

the actor is usually a person who speaks and moves about the
stage. However, the fundamental nature of an actor does not
consist in the fact that he is a person speaking and moving about
the stage but that he *represents someone, that he signifies a role in a
play.*[17]

Following these formulations, I take representation to be the innermost convention of the theatrical genres. In order to examine this basic
convention more closely, it will be helpful to look at two cases that
constitute a violation of it. Paradoxically, as with any social convention,
we are made aware of its meaning or even of its very existence, when it
is violated. Then, and sometimes only then, what was unconsciously
learned and practiced becomes conscious and conspicuous. A professor
entering a graduate seminar wearing a swimsuit (to revert to my earlier
example) would, by violating the convention, make it the center of our
attention.

My first example of a violation of the semiotic convention of the
theatrical situation is the puppet show scene in *Don Quixote*. The boy,
Master Pedro's assistant, is narrating the typical chivalric adventures of
Sir Gaiferos, who is trying to rescue his beloved Melisendra from the
Moors. When it seems that our heroes are on the threshold of freedom,
the Moors start to chase the fleeing couple:

> "See what a numerous and resplendent cavalcade rides out of the
> city in pursuit of the pair of Christian lovers! How many trumpets
> sound, how many clarions blow, how many drums and kettle-
> drums beat! I am afraid they will catch them and bring them back
> tied to their own horse's tail. That would be a dreadful specta-
> cle."[18]

Hearing these dreadful prospects awaiting the fleeing couple, Don
Quixote initiates one of the most famous scenes in world literature:

> Now seeing this pack of Moors and hearing such an alarm, Don
> Quixote thought it only right to help the fugitives. So, rising to
> his feet, he cried aloud: "Never while I live shall I permit an
> outrage to be done in my presence on so famous a knight and so
> bold a lover as Sir Gaiferos! Stop, sow-born rabble! Neither follow
> nor molest him, or you must do battle with me."

17. Jindrich Honzl, "Dynamics of the Sign in the Theater," 74–75.
18. Miguel de Cervantes Saavedra, *The Adventures of Don Quixote*, 641.

Matching his actions to his words, he unsheathed his sword, and at a single bound planted himself in front of the show. Then with swift and unparalleled fury he began to rain blows upon the puppet-heathenry, knocking down some, beheading others, maiming one, and destroying another; and, among other thrusts, he delivered one down-stroke that would have sliced off Master Pedro's head as easily as if it had been made of marzipan, had he not ducked and crouched and made himself small.[19]

Quixote's behavior epitomizes the confusion between dramatic *illusion* and *delusion*. The comic and pathetic effect is heightened by the fact that the dramatic illusion is created only by a puppet show, not even in a play with human actors.[20] This fact, by the way, reminds us of the semiotic principle of the dramatic show according to which there should be a *represented action*; the question of how this action is represented is secondary.[21] Don Quixote, in other words, missed the semiotic, representational principle of the dramatic situation by confusing the puppets with the characters for which they stood. Any represented action, in order to be dramatically successful, should involve the audience in the action represented and arouse in it feelings appropriate to the situation represented.[22] The audience, however, should never forget that these feelings are related only to a *represented* action, not real events. This *quasi-agreement* is broken by Don Quixote; hence his reaction.

Needless to say, this scene is an excellent example of Quixote's inability to distinguish between art and life. From a broader perspective, it may also exemplify the intricate relationship between art and life as a major theme of *Don Quixote*.[23]

Using semiotic terminology, Quixote's intervention in the play can be described as his overlooking the signifier and treating it as if it were the

19. Ibid.

20. One might wonder whether such audience intervention would have had the same comic effect in a different play. How about, for instance, a spectator trying to stop a scene in which an actor plucks off a fowl's head on stage in some experimental "brutal" theater? Such an example illustrates that theatrical conventions may sometimes be in actual, serious conflict with other, ethical norms.

21. See in Honzl, "Dynamics of the Sign," some interesting observations on this issue. Honzl points out, for instance, that in radio drama the action is represented by sound alone.

22. The mode of representation may also evoke various feelings that are an important part of the audience's overall aesthetic experience. Compared to the effects created by the represented action, however, these effects are secondary.

23. For some illuminating comments about this aspect of the scene, see Alter, *Partial Magic*, 11–13.

signified, i.e., ignoring the status of the play as a sign. Quixote is carried away by the process of signification. He leaves the signifier behind. He has been absorbed by the represented action and forgets that it is (only) represented.

The case of Don Quixote at the puppet show exemplifies one important type of deviation from the semiotic convention underlying the dramatic situation. My next example illustrates another significant violation of this essential semiotic principle. It is the mirror-image of Quixote's, and is taken from another great novel, *War and Peace*. Tolstoy is describing Natasha's first visit to the opera, and how she perceives things:

> The middle of the stage consisted of flat boards; by the sides stood painted pictures representing trees, and at the back a linen cloth was stretched down to the floor boards. Maidens in red bodices and white skirts sat on the middle of the stage. One, very fat, in a white silk dress, sat apart on a narrow bench to which a green pasteboard box was glued from behind. They were all singing something. When they had finished, the maiden in white approached the prompter's box. A man in silk with tight-fitting pants on his fat legs approached her with a plume and began to sing and spread his arms in dismay. The man in the tight pants finished his song alone; then the girl sang. After that both remained silent as the music resounded; and the man, obviously waiting to begin singing his part with her again, began to run his fingers over the hand of the girl in the white dress. They finished their song together, and everyone in the theater began to clap and shout. But the men and women on stage, who represented lovers, started to bow, smiling and raising their hands.
>
> In the second act there were pictures representing monuments and openings in the linen cloth representing the moonlight, and they raised lamp shades on a frame. As the musicians started to play the bass horn and counter-bass, a large number of people in black mantles poured onto the stage from right and left. The people, with something like daggers in their hands, started to wave their arms. Then still more people came running out and began to drag away the maiden who had been wearing a white dress but who now wore one of sky blue. They did not drag her off immediately, but sang with her for a long time before dragging her away. Three times they struck on something metallic behind the side scenes, and everyone got down on his knees and

began to chant a prayer. Several times all of this activity was interrupted by enthusiastic shouts from the spectators.[24]

Victor Shklovsky cites this passage as an example of Tolstoy's use of the technique of defamiliarization, which to him is the hallmark of the literary art. For Shklovsky it is particularly important to demonstrate this estranging effect not only in avant-garde writers (where one might expect strange and novel devices) but in the heart of realistic writing; and Tolstoy, it seems, provides an abundance of examples.

My own purpose is not to see this opera scene as an example of the constitutive technique of literature, but rather as another example of the breach of the conventional "contract" of the dramatic situation. Natasha, visiting the opera house for the first time and in a state of emotional upheaval, is indeed a poor spectator. From time to time she tries to make sense of what she sees ("the men and women on stage, who represented lovers") but usually she perceives things as if too clearly, without being able to understand their function in the represented action. Her shaky psychological state prevents her from responding to the semiotic convention that governs the theatrical situation.[25] Natasha's confused state of mind provides Tolstoy with the realistic motivation for this distorted presentation of opera. Behind this motivation one might also detect Tolstoy's criticism of opera as an art form in which the superficial prevails and in which the appeal of the signifier is so strong that the signified is forgotten.

Natasha's distorted perception of the represented action differs, however, from the kind of distortion we saw in Quixote's case. Quixote was carried away by the signified; Natasha is "stuck" on the level of the signifiers without being able to integrate these signs into a meaningful action. She sees the signifiers and feels that something should be signified; sometimes she dimly glimpses that something, but all in all, she cannot integrate it into a coherent represented action. Quixote is fascinated with the signified, Natasha with the signifiers. In both cases, the breaking of the semiotic convention stems from the distorted psychological state of the respective character who cannot comply with the accepted (tacit) agreement.

This basic semiotic convention, which requires that we integrate the signs into coherent action without forgetting that they are only signs, can also be extended to some nondramatic genres. As a matter of fact,

24. Quoted in Victor Shklovsky, "Art as Technique," 16.
25. A precedent for Tolstoy's treatment of opera can be found in Flaubert's description of Charles with Emma at the opera in *Madame Bovary*.

some neo-Aristotelian theorists try to apply this representational approach to all literary genres. Different literary genres differ in their object of representation, but all may be seen as having the dual (semiotic) representational structure.[26]

Even without accepting such conceptual extension, we can easily apply the concept of convention as defined earlier to more specific artistic quasi-agreements that govern the communicative situation between a writer and his audience. Again, the dramatic genres are a very good example, precisely because they invite us to see the performance on stage as a "piece of life." Speaking in verse, singing instead of speaking (in opera), and the soliloquy illustrate the role of conventions (i.e., quasi-agreements between writer and audience) in dramatic genres. The division of the play into scenes and acts is also a convention that applies to dramatic genres, this time at the level of structuring text and performance.

As with Don Quixote and Natasha, such a convention is foregrounded when it is violated. Deviations from some prevailing conventions may fulfill an artistic goal, as a challenge to the existing artistic norms; or a thematic goal, as part of the author's statement about life and art; or as a means to present the psyche of a character more vividly or realistically. In most cases all three factors will be involved in an artistic decision to deviate from some prevailing convention, as the examples from Cervantes and Tolstoy illustrate.

Before closing this part of the chapter, I will adduce two brief illustrative examples of a breach of the generic contract in two nondramatic genres, so that the broad implications of the concept of literary and generic convention will become apparent. When Samuel Beckett's narrator tells us in *Watt* about "Sam's other married daughter Kate aged twenty-one years, a fine girl but a bleeder[1]," he adds a footnote: "(1) Haemophilia is, like enlargement of the prostate, an exclusively male disorder. But not in this work."[27]

Beckett's footnote bewilders the reader. The basic convention that links words to the world has been shaken. This example from Beckett's novel is more radical than certain typical cases of "unreliable narrator."[28] In those cases the text itself exposes the narrator's bias or incompetence. Here, however, the introduction of a footnote—an "external" channel of communication with the reader—as well as the content of this footnote,

---

26. See, for instance, Elder Olson, *On Value Judgments in the Arts and Other Essays,* and Barbara Herrnstein Smith, *On the Margins of Discourse.*

27. Quoted by Richard Ohmann in "Speech, Action, and Style," 244–45.

28. For this term see Wayne C. Booth, *The Rhetoric of Fiction,* 158–59.

undermine the confidence the reader should have in the text. Readers find themselves in an almost impossible situation where they start to wonder whether the very words in the novel can be trusted. They have the footnote—but what about all the other words and sentences? Are they trustworthy? How is one supposed to know? To be obliged to suspect some of the narrator's words is the reader's typical dilemma with an unreliable narrator; that *all* the narrator's words are suspect is a breach of contract between writer and reader. Beckett wishes to shake up certain ideas readers have concerning things they view as self-evident about the world and about novels. Aside from these thematic intentions, violating the convention produces a comic effect that is almost a standard by-product of every violation of convention, either social or literary.

Indeed, authors may violate literary conventions simply to achieve this comic effect, as is the case in many parodies and burlesques that expose generic conventions as ridiculous and "unnatural." Often, however, conventions are deliberately violated not with a comic but with a bitter satirical intent. The parodic effect of Swift's "Modest Proposal" is secondary to the moral issues it raises. Swift's text is especially interesting because it creates a delicate balance during its first few paragraphs between observing the conventions of a serious proposal and planting clues that foreshadow its radical deviation into satire. Swift's intentions become clear when he starts to describe, in detail, how children can be eaten: "I have been assured by a very knowing American of my Ackuaint-ance in London, that a young healthy child, well nursed is at a year old a most delicious, nourishing, and wholesome food, whether stewed, roasted, baked, or broiled, and I make no doubt that it will equally serve in a fricassee or ragout."[29]

The subtle and sophisticated way in which Swift breaks the quasi-agreement that unites writers and readers of serious proposals is amusing. But it is the breaking of the *moral* conventions, which dictate what means are appropriate to deal with social and economic problems, that is emphasized here. Still, despite the overt breaking of both generic and moral conventions, readers succeed in establishing a context that will make sense out of this apparently abominable proposal. They succeed in doing so because they know that the writer is a competent satirist, manipulating various conventions to achieve certain reasonable goals, and not a delirious psychopath.[30]

29. Jonathan Swift, *Gulliver's Travels and Other Writings*, 441.

30. For a step-by-step analysis of the process of reading "Modest Proposal," and how the literary and moral conventions are broken and reestablished, see Wayne C. Booth, *A Rhetoric of Irony*, 105–19.

In the second part of this chapter I will focus on a concept that has not received enough critical attention, at least not from the point of view that I stress here: the concept of *role* as a junction of certain sociological and literary perspectives on literary genres.

LIFE IS BUT A STAGE, THE STAGE IS BUT LIFE

The concept of "role" has been exported from drama to sociological discourse, and there it has been integrated into discussions of social institutions.[31] Thus its first usage was a literary one, and it became part of sociological discussion only through analogical expansion. My aim here is to bring this important concept back home to the literary field, enriched by the sociological perspective.

Every social institution can be characterized by its goals, the means by which these goals are achieved, and the institutional roles that assign certain modes of behavior to persons.[32] According to this model the university, for example, can be best described and analyzed as an institution with the goals of promoting and conducting study and research in various branches of advanced learning, achieved by means that include face-to-face teaching, tutorials, laboratories, and field re-search, by individuals assigned to the roles of student, teacher, or administrator.

When Asa Kasher defines institutional role as "a cluster of require-ments which a person has to fulfill in order to operate in a certain way *within a certain institution*,"[33] the intimate connection between describing institutional roles and describing the other aspects of the institution becomes apparent. In other words, in order to understand what a professor is, one cannot avoid describing certain goals and means of the university. To explicate the concept of a graduate secretary requires an understanding of what a graduate student is, what graduate school is, what its goals are, and how these goals are reached, among other things.

This *interdependence* of the three levels is also true if we take another level as our point of departure: understanding the goals of the university

31. Both Theodore R. Sabrin and Ralph H. Turner open their discussions of "Role" in the *International Encyclopedia of Social Science* with a reference to this conceptual borrowing. An interesting sociological usage of the dramatic concept of performance has been developed by Erving Goffman in *The Presentation of Self in Everyday Life*.

32. Emphasis on the concept of institutional role in analyzing social institutions can be found in many sociological writings, especially those of Talcott Parsons.

33. Asa Kasher, "What Is a Theory of Use?" 111.

entails understanding the various institutional roles that the university assigns to people in order that these goals be met. Each level may serve as a different angle from which we describe the institution as a whole. But no matter where we start or what our focus may be, the basic features of the institution recur in each description.

For this study, I am focusing on the dramatic genre of comedy as it was shaped in Rome by Plautus and Terence—both because it has a basically stable plot structure despite its otherwise varied nature, and because I believe the concept of role to be especially relevant to dramatic genres. The lifelike situations, the exchanges and interactions between characters, the minimal (explicit) interventions of an author or a narrator (in the form of stage directions) all contribute to the relevance of the concept "role."[34] In other words, if I want to present a genre as a system of interacting roles, like a social institution, the dramatic genres lend themselves most readily to such a perspective.

By analogy to the three levels of institutional analysis, I propose to analyze comedy as a literary "institution" that has its specific goals, its specific means to achieve these goals, and certain characteristic *generic roles*. The goal every comedy works toward is the happy ending, usually in the form of the union of the young couple. This goal is reached through a combination of intrigue and coincidence. The central roles are those of the young lovers, the blocking figure who tries to stop them on their way to the happy ending, and whoever is responsible for clearing the way, i.e., overcoming the role of the blocking figure.

Thus we can talk, for instance, about the characters of Philocomasium and Pleusicles in Plautus's *Swaggering Soldier (Miles Gloriosus)* who perform the *roles* of the loving young couple. Not only are the roles of the young couple in *Miles Gloriosus* a constitutive part of this specific play, but they are also essential to a central version of the tradition of comedy as a dramatic genre. Further, it is impossible to give an account of the roles of the loving young couple in comedy without being familiar with the relationships these roles have with other complementary roles, and consequently with the goals and means of this genre. To understand the characters' generic roles, we have to make an abstraction from the actual performance of the characters, just as we need to make abstractions from the behavior of people when we wish to describe their institutional roles. This abstraction involves ignoring those aspects of behavior which are

34. I use the term "role" here in a sense other than its common theatrical reference to a specific character in a specific play, e.g., the role of Hamlet in *Hamlet*. I want to suggest saving the term for the level of the literary genre. Thus, the *character* Hamlet fulfills *the role of the tragic hero* in *Hamlet*, and the role of the tragic hero is defined in relation to tragedy, as a social role is defined in relation to the institution of which it is part.

not relevant to the goals and means of the social institution and those aspects of (the characters') performance which are not related to the goals and means of the generic, literary "institution."

Very important in this context is the realization that none of these elements—the goals, means, or generic roles of comedy—is properly perceived in isolation. The role of the loving young couple in comedy is interwoven into a structured plot where it holds a position complementary to other roles. These other roles, through their interactions, constitute the plot of intrigue and coincidence typical of comedy. The ultimate goal of this plot, in turn, is to achieve the happy ending, which is the hallmark of comedy as a genre.

The principle that institutional roles should not be perceived in isolation has been formulated in discussions of the sociological concept of role and can be applied also to generic uses. Ralph Turner points to this aspect of social role as defining itself with and against other roles: "To the extent to which roles are incorporated into an organizational setting, each tends to develop as a pattern of adaptation to multiple alter roles. The teacher role must incorporate tenable adaptations to pupils, parents, other teachers, and principals, as well as to less salient alters."[35]

Talcott Parsons, who contributed perhaps more than anybody else to establishing the institutional perspective in modern sociology, also talks about the interrelations and complementarity of roles, as opposed to their mere conglomeration:

> A social system must possess a minimum degree of integration: there must be, that is, a sufficient complementarity of roles and clusters of roles for collective and private goals to be effectively pursued. Although conflict can exist within a social system and, in fact, always does, there are limits beyond which it cannot go and still permit a social system to exist. By definition the complementarity of expectations which is associated with the complementarity of roles is destroyed by conflict. Consequently, when conflict becomes so far reaching as to negate the complementarity of expectations, there the social system has ceased to exist. Hence, for conflict among individuals and groups to be kept within bounds, the roles and role clusters must be brought into appropriately complementary relations with one another.[36]

This stress on complementarity and cooperation among social roles for the benefit of the social institution should be qualified when discuss-

35. Turner, "Role: Sociological Aspects," 555.
36. Talcott Parsons, *On Institutions and Social Evolution*, 119–20.

ing literary genres. Because of the representational nature of dramatic literature, there are *two levels* on which we can refer to questions of conflict, role expectations, and complementarity. On the level of the represented action roles are not always complementary. In most (if not all) cases, conflicts between different characters are not resolved through agreement. There are winners and there are losers who may be removed from the world of the stage. As a matter of fact, almost all dramatic genres presuppose a conflict between different roles, and they differ in what the conflict is about and how (and when) to resolve it.

In comedy the conflict between the young lovers and the blocking figure(s) (the *alazon*) is resolved through the victory of the former over the latter (often with assistance of a trickster figure, or *eiron*). The blocking figure can, willingly or reluctantly, accept the happy ending and participate in the nuptial celebration, or he may leave the stage grumbling to himself. Further, whereas in social institutions we need some stability and reliability of expectations, the dynamics of the comic plot are based on violations and manipulations of expectations through cunning and disguise. The action is typically propelled and the happy ending achieved through deceiving at least one character.

But the moment we shift our perspective from within the fictional world to the communicative situation of playwright and audience, the principle of maintaining complementarity of roles and expectations seems to apply. Viewing the represented situation from outside, the different roles do participate in achieving a common goal, i.e., in bringing the comic plot forward to the happy ending. This dual logic or perspective makes the blocking figure (unnecessary from the perspective of the young lovers) an essential figure (from the perspective of the comic plot). Although the blocking figure fails to achieve his goal on the represented level, he succeeds in performing his role on the level of the comic genre. Similarly, the blocking figure, or *alazon,* and his opponent, the *eiron,* are not pursuing any common goal on the first level, but they are working in harmony to achieve the goals shared by the writer and readers (or audience) of comedies. In short, enemies on the stage are cooperating partners so far as the generic structure is concerned.

According to the schema I propose here, the concept of role is inseparable from that of genre. In relating these two concepts I avoid a pointless debate about whether a character can, or should, be perceived only in terms of its function in the plot. This debate has been carried on heatedly for the last twenty years between certain structuralists, on the one hand, and almost everybody else, on the other.[37] The arguments

37. For a critical presentation of the structuralist view of character as a mere function of the plot see Culler, *Structuralist Poetics,* 230–38; Seymour Chatman, *Story and Discourse,*

against the structuralist approach sometimes point out that what constitutes a character cannot be exhausted by its structural role in the play (or
narrative). Many of the character's traits, superfluous from the narrow
point of view of plot structure, help to create the realistic effect.[38] Still,
when we abstract the "skeleton" of a certain play (i.e., the basic pattern
of actions shared by some generic tradition), we can talk of the agents
who carry out these actions (i.e., the roles), without doing an injustice
to the individuality and realistic nature of specific characters.

To say, for instance, that the tradition of comedy requires two young
lovers and an *alazon* who tries, ultimately in vain, to disrupt their love,
does not diminish the rich and realistic nature of any character in any
specific play.[39] On the contrary, realizing that a certain character fulfills
a certain (generic) role enables us to appreciate more fully its individuality and uniqueness by comparing it to previous manifestations of this
same role in other plays. Pointing out that a text is part of a generic
tradition can sometimes highlight the originality of its writer; by the
same token, describing a certain character as fulfilling a generic role may
emphasize that character's individuality by underscoring how specifically
it fulfills that role.

Thus the concept of role is inseparable from the plot-scheme of a
narrative genre. The analysis of texts in terms of plot and agents (or
actants) has mostly been applied by structuralists to narrative fiction. In
principle, it is fruitful to apply the concept of role to any literary genre
with a relatively schematic and stable narrative structure, plot-schema,
and set of roles. It is not surprising that Vladimir Propp chose the
folktale for his classical structuralist analysis, since it has a high degree
of schematization and repetition of plot structures.[40] When some of his
followers tried to apply the same analytical strategy to the versatile and
complex genre of the novel, their attempts became problematic and
unsatisfactory.

As I noted earlier, focusing on a single role in the tradition of comedy

---

107–45; Shlomith Rimmon-Kenan, *Narrative Fiction*, 36–40; Baruch Hochman, *Character in
Literature*, 13–27; and Robert Alter, *The Pleasures of Reading in an Ideological Age*, 49–76.

38. See Roland Barthes's article "L'effet de réel," 84–89.

39. In describing comedy's structure in terms of the interrelations between certain basic,
functional roles, I am greatly indebted to Frye's analysis of comedy in *Anatomy of Criticism*,
especially 163–76. The role of the blocking figure might be seen as a manifestation of a
more general constitutive element of comedy, the "deadlock," as opposed to the "riot."
Zvi Jagendorf proposes, in *The Happy End of Comedy*, to see these two elements as the
basic forces that the comic plot should reconcile in order to achieve a happy ending. I
prefer, however, not to reach such a high level of abstraction because these two abstract
elements might also apply to works other than comedies.

40. Vladimir Propp, *The Morphology of the Folktale*.

provides a rich view of the tradition itself, since each specific role gains its meaning from its relationship to the other roles, and ultimately it is the structure of their interrelations that constitutes the genre. Consequently, to focus on the role of the blocking figure in comedy—to which we will turn shortly—means, *ipsio definitio*, to elucidate indirectly the structure of comedy.

THE ROLE OF THE BLOCKING FIGURE: THE *ALAZON*

If any comedy of the type in which I am interested here has a loving young couple who strive to unite, it also has the role of the blocking figure who tries, in vain, to obstruct them, *and* someone who helps to pave their way. This schema, in fact, along with the principle of disguise and blurred identities, is flexible enough to include many examples of famous comedies shaped by, and later modeled after, the New Comedy. Yet, it is narrow enough to exclude even other types of comedies (for instance, the Old Comedy with its satirical overtones, its farcical elements, and its lack of interest in young lovers) and to arouse some specific expectations in the audience about the developments on stage. Not least among them is the expectation that the blocking figure be himself blocked and that the young couple prevail in a happy ending.

My first example of the role of the blocking figure is Pyrgopolynices from Plautus's *Miles Gloriosus*. This swaggering soldier is one of the "types" first developed in the New Comedy and later adapted in innumerable works.[41] He has abducted Philocomasium (Pleusicles' beloved) from her home town and made her his concubine. The plot consists of the efforts of Pyrgopolynices' slave Palaestrio, who was once owned by and who is still loyal to Pleusicles, to rescue her from Pyrgopolynices' clutches and to bring about the happy reunion of Philocomasium and Pleusicles.

---

41. For a survey of the types of New Comedy see the comprehensive book by George E. Duckworth, *The Nature of Roman Comedy*, especially chapter 9; and the more concise work by R. L. Hunter, *The New Comedy of Greece and Rome*, especially chapters 3 and 4. The basic disadvantage of these otherwise erudite and enlightening presentations is that they set up a typology of characters, or "types," not according to the function that the characters play in the comic structure but rather according to certain preexisting social and cultural criteria (fathers and sons, women and men, social professions, etc.). In so doing, they fail to identify an important means of relating the heterogeneous "comic types" to the relatively homogeneous abstract roles dictated by the structure of comedy.

Who is this swaggering individual and why does he fail to perform his blocking function? The answer is given as early as the opening lines of the play, in which Pyrgopolynices is portrayed as pompous and conceited, who will jump at any flattery:

> PYRGOPOLYNICES: My shield, there—have it burnished brighter than the bright splendour of the sun on any summer's day. Next time I have occasion to use it in the press of battle, it must flash defiance into the eyes of the opposing foe. My sword, too, I see, is pining for attention; poor chap, he's quite disheartened and cast down, hanging idly at my side so long; he's simply itching to get at an enemy and carve him into little pieces. . . . Where's Artotrogus?
> ARTOTROGUS: Here, at his master's heels, close to his hero, his brave, his blessed, his royal, his doughty warrior—whose valour Mars himself could hardly challenge to outshine.
> P. [reminiscent]: Ay—what of the man whose life I saved on the Curculionean field, where the enemy was led by Bumbomachides Clytomestoridysarchides, a grandson of Neptune?
> A.: I remember it well. I remember his golden armour, and how you scattered his legions with a puff of breath, like a wind sweeping up leaves or lifting the thatch from a roof.
> P. [modestly]: It was nothing much, after all.
> A.: Oh, to be sure, nothing to the many more famous deeds you did—[aside] or never did. [He comes down, leaving the Captain attending to his men.] If anyone ever saw a bigger liar or more conceited braggart than this one, he can have me for keeps. . . . The only thing to be said for him is, his cook makes a marvelous olive salad . . .[42]

We learn also that his real interest and expertise is not in the battlefield about which we hear this absurd bragging, but in "conquering" women.

In the light of this reputation, Pyrgopolynices' address to his sword, an unambivalent phallic symbol ("poor chap, he's quite disheartened and cast down, hanging idly at my side so long"), can be interpreted ironically when we learn that because of Palaestrio's maneuvers he is as frustrated by inactivity in the sexual field as on the battlefield, and that his "sword" is indeed idle.

Pyrgopolynices' self-deception and his enslavement to his own fantasies, military and sexual alike, make him a perfect alazon,[43] and his

---

42. Plautus, "The Swaggering Soldier," in The Pot of Gold and Other Plays, 153–54.
43. Plautus himself tells us that "In the Greek this play is entitled Alazon—The Braggart; which in Latin we have translated by Gloriosus" (ibid., 156).

efforts to block the loving couple are doomed. Yet even such an incompetent and ridiculous figure can pose a threat. It is an essential part of the comic plot that a threat be posed before the final happy ending is achieved. Palaestrio formulates this structural requirement of the comic plot in a charming metaphor. Whereas Palaestrio's remark refers to the specific situation in the particular play, I think Plautus is also making a general remark about the plot structure of comedy:

> Ah but know, when you've climbed out of a deep well nearly to the top, that's the time when there's the most danger of your falling down to the bottom again.[44]

And indeed, just when the trick is about to succeed, when the two lovers are united and prepare to depart under the watchful eyes of Pyrgopolynices, who has been led to believe that the man who accompanies Philocomasium is but a boatman (though in truth he is Pleusicles, her lover), then his suspicions are aroused and a tense moment ensues:

> PYRGOPOLYNICES [suspiciously]: I don't see why they need have their heads so close together. Hey you, boatman, take your lips away from hers, confound you! . . .
> PYRGOPOLYNICES: What is going on there?
> PALAESTRIO: She'd just fainted, that's all. [Aside to Pleusicles] Look out, or we shall be giving the game away if we're not careful.[45]

But this lasts for only a moment, after which Pyrgopolynices' suspicions quiet and the expected and well-orchestrated happy ending arrives—though not before Pyrgopolynices loses some of his fortune and gets beaten up by a slave. Then Pyrgopolynices makes the bitter discovery of the plot against him:

> Fool, fool that I am! Now I see what an ass they've made of me; and it was Palaestrio, the double-dyed villain, that lured me into the trap.[46]

This revelation does not lead him to an outburst of anger, nor to a deep contemplation of his life and values, but rather to a chagrined acceptance of the situation, accompanied by a general moral:

44. Ibid., 199.
45. Ibid., 207–8.
46. Ibid., 212.

Well, it was a fair catch, and justice has been done. Serve all
lechers so, and lechery would grow less rife; the sinners would
have more fear and mend their ways.[47]

Before I move on to the second example of the role of the blocking
figure, I would like to point out an interesting connection between this
role and the paternal figure in comedy. One may say that the *alazon* has
a paternal figure as its shadow, as if there were a latent association
between the two, compelling the playwright to either confirm or reject
this tacit connection. This latent association is probably related to some
deep cultural assumption in accordance with which the loving young
couple must, on their way to self-fulfillment, overcome the authoritative
figure representative of the older generation: the father. Comedy, while
acknowledging this underlying cultural attitude, does not take it for
granted but rather uses it in many cases to play with the audience's
expectations; the assumption is there to be questioned, but not necessarily followed.

In *Miles Gloriosus,* for example, Palaestrio's accomplice is an elderly
neighbor, Periplectomenus. When Palaestrio introduces this accomplice
to Pleusicles, the young lover, the latter's reaction reveals his cultural
expectations of the older generation:

That you, at your age, should be involved in a juvenile escapade
of this sort; that I should be asking you to lend your efforts to
save my face, to help me in my love affair; that you should be
engaged in the sort of business which a man of your age should
turn his back on, not encourage.[48]

Periplectomenus gives Pleusicles a long answer to his query, part of
which is that he chose not to have children, i.e., that he is not a father.
From this we can perhaps infer that, had he been a father, possibly he
would have played the blocking figure as is generally expected of a
parental character. In any case, Plautus found it important to contest the
almost automatic identification of the role of the blocking figure with
the older generation.

In Molière's *L'Ecole des femmes* the role of the blocking figure is enacted
by Arnolphe, an elderly guardian who is young Horace's rival. When
Oronte, Horace's father, appears on the stage toward the end of the play,
Arnolphe tries to exert his influence over Oronte so that the latter will

47. Ibid.
48. Ibid., 176.

exercise his authority as father and marry Horace off to a prearranged marriage:

> Your son has set his heart
> Against this marriage from the very start.
> He even begged me to defend his side;
> But here's all the advice I can provide:
> Do not put off these nuptials, but rather
> Exercise the authority of a father.
> Young people must be shown that we know best;
> Indulgence is against their interest.[49]

Oronte seems to adopt Arnolphe's attitude:

> I quite agree with everything you say
> About this match; I warrant he'll obey.[50]

But just when it seems that Arnolphe, who succeeds in enlisting Oronte on his side, is going to prevail, Molière pulls the rabbit out of his hat (something we could, of course, have anticipated)—the enforced marriage is none other than the desired union of the young couple. We find out that the object of Horace's love and the intended bride of the prearranged match are one and the same. Thus younger and older generations can participate in the communal celebration of the marriage—all but Arnolphe, who is unable to take the blow sportingly and leaves the stage with an "Ouf!"

One interesting characteristic of Molière's play is the fact that Arnolphe fears he may play the role that he eventually does play, that of the failed blocking figure, the *alazon, and* the old cuckold.

In the opening scene Arnolphe discusses with his friend Chrysalde his plan to marry Agnes, the young girl he has brought up. After recounting several examples of husbands tricked by their wives, Arnolphe concludes:

> In short, when all around lies comedy,
> May I not laugh at all these things I see?[51]

Arnolphe may be using the term "comedie" here in the sense of "play-acting, performance," but by using this specific term Molière refers us

---

49. Molière, "The School for Wives," in *Tartuffe and Other Plays,* 164–65.
50. Ibid., 165.
51. Ibid., 102.

to the literary tradition of comedy. Thus Molière makes us aware of the relationship between this comedy and the genre of comedy and between Arnolphe and the *alazon*. Against the too-familiar schemes and plots of comedy (in the literary and nonliterary senses of the word), Arnolphe has decided to issue a challenge:

> The one who catches *me* is not born yet.
> I know each cunning trick that women use
> Upon their docile men, each subtle ruse,
> And how they exercise their sleight-of-hand.
> And so against this mishap I have planned.
> My guarantee against such accident
> Is marriage to a perfect innocent.[52]

Arnolphe here poses a challenge not only directly to the reality he knows, but also indirectly, on a metadiscursive level, to the tradition of comedy. Needless to say, it is a lost cause. It is true that there is no comparison between the sophistication of Molière's Arnolphe and the stupidity of Plautus's Pyrgopolynices. Still, with all his sophistication, Arnolphe is only a marionette jerked by the comic strings toward his inevitable failure. No matter how tricky his maneuvers may be (and some of them are truly ingenious), as long as he plays the blocking role in a comedy he may complicate matters, but he cannot change the outcome.

Apart from the surprising coincidence (Agnes is the lost child of Oronte's friend) that completely overthrows Arnolphe's plans, he himself is prone to conceit and self-deception, qualities that qualify him for the title of *alazon* despite his short-term cleverness. This is manifested when he changes his name from Seigneur Alphonse to the pompous Monsieur de La Souche (it is not by chance that the name has some phallic connotations). After trying unsuccessfully to argue with him about this whim, Chrysalde, the sensible friend, concludes: "My lord, he is completely daft, I swear!"[53]

The biggest irony is that Arnolphe uses the term "comedie" when he first speaks to Horace, the young lover who will play the role of the young successful lover in this comedy:

> As regards pleasures, every man his own.
> And for gallants (for thus I think they're known)

52. Ibid., 103.
53. Ibid., 107.

This town offers delights beyond compare.
The women here are ripe for an affair:
Blonde or brunette, all are exceeding kind,
And all their husbands suitably resigned.
It is sport for a prince; and what I see
Is an unfailing source of comedy.
Already you have smitten one, I'll bet.
Haven't you had some such adventure yet?
Good looks achieve much more than purses do,
And cuckolds owe their horns to such as you.[54]

Almost all the elements of the comedy are here, except that Arnolphe does not realize that he himself will become "an unfailing source of comedy." And it is this partial blindness that makes Arnolphe a perfect candidate for the role of the unsuccessful blocking figure. Arnolphe refers to reality when he uses the term "comedie"; Molière—smiling behind his back—is referring to the literary tradition of comedy and to the role Arnolphe plays in this tradition.

L'Ecole des femmes lacks a trickster character, an *eiron*, the go-between, usually a servant, who introduces the two lovers. In Plautus's *Miles Gloriosus* we had the charming and clever Palaestrio who orchestrated the whole chain of events. In Molière we have only a faint remnant of such a character. When Horace confesses to Arnolphe how he has established contact with Agnes, unaware that his "friend" is actually his keenest enemy, he refers vaguely to such a go-between:

I hope I am not imposing on a friend.
I've only foes inside; their eyes are keen;
And maid and servant, whom I just have seen,
No matter what cajoleries I try,
Keep me away with a suspicious eye.
I used to have, for such things, an old woman
Whose gifts, to tell the truth, were superhuman.
It helped at first to have her on my side;
But just four days ago the poor thing died.[55]

The character is dead, but not its role. If we perceive comedy as *a system of interrelated roles,* which consists of two young lovers, the blocking figure, and the one who schemes in order to overcome the

54. Ibid., 113.
55. Ibid., 137–38.

obstacle, then *L'Ecole des femmes* is still typical. Paradoxically, the role of the intriguer is performed by the character who performs the role of the blocking figure, Arnolphe. It is he who manipulates the young lovers, plays with identities and disguises; but, because of his faults and short-sightedness (as well as some fortunate circumstances), all his plotting only helps to bring about the union of Horace and Agnes.

Thus the institutional perspective on comedy, with its emphasis on generic roles, enables us to see how specific characters in a specific comedy perform and embody these roles. As long as we can detect the four basic roles (the boy, the girl, the *alazon,* and the *eiron*), no matter how they are manifested, and as long as the interaction of these four roles brings about a happy ending—we have a comedy.

SOME VARIATIONS ON THE ROLE OF THE BLOCKING FIGURE

One should note that there is no need to assume a simple identity between character and role: not only can the same character perform two roles (as in the case of Arnolphe), but also the same role, or roles, can be performed by more than one character. This is the case with Marivaux's *Le Jeu de l'amour et du hazard,* in which, as in many other comedies, we have two pairs of loving couples: Dorante and Silvia, the "official" major loving couple, and their "low," comic, mirror image in the characters of Arlequin and Lisette. The latter couple, who play only a supporting function in the major plot, nonetheless attract our attention, partly because their vivid conversation and pungent language are more engaging than the melancholy and sober appearance of their masters. The result is a double structure in which the two couples parody each other and their juxtaposition helps to heighten the comic effect.

But the real drama is with the "high" couple, Dorante and Silvia. As far as Arlequin and Lisette are concerned, there is little suspense about the outcome of their love affair. Disguised or not, Arlequin will find his way to the closest bottle of wine, and both of them will probably find their way to the closest bedroom. With Dorante and Silvia things are much more complicated, not only because of social norms that hinder them from without, but also because of internal impediment. Thus, one can describe the situation as an internalization (or psychologization) of the role of the blocking figure by the young lovers themselves.

Why, in the first place, do they have to internalize the role of the blocking figure? Isn't there an authoritative father in Marivaux's play?

Silvia's father (as well as her brother) is there, but he is a liberal parent. After we hear Silvia expressing her apprehensions about her intended marriage, Orgon, her father, relieves her of her anxiety:

> Come, come, there is no need for all this. My dear child, you know how much I love you. Dorante comes to marry you. On my last visit to the provinces, I arranged this match with his father who is an old companion and friend of mine. But we agreed that there should be a condition—that you and he should please each other. We also agreed that you should have complete freedom to decide. I forbid your mere obedience or respect for my choice. If Dorante does not suit you, you have only to say. He will go. If you do not suit him, he will do the same.[56]

This type of father is at odds with the typical figure to which the French audience had been accustomed since Molière, and should be seen as one element in Marivaux's modification of the genre. Being a liberal father, however, does not mean that Orgon is not in charge. In fact he sometimes appears almost as an omnipotent puppeteer to whom his daughter and Dorante are mere marionettes. Orgon knows that Dorante will come to his house disguised as his own valet so that he may independently observe his intended bride. When Silvia proposes the same idea, i.e., to disguise herself as her maid, he sees in it only an additional source for amusement. He sets the stage, he observes and knows everything, and he is in a position to manipulate the young couple's feelings (and sometimes he takes advantage of these privileges). At one point, for instance, when Silvia is repelled by the figure of Arlequin, whom she thinks to be Dorante, and is attracted to the real Dorante, under the disguise of a valet, these latter feelings terrify her and she asks her father to call the game off. Suddenly, Orgon's reaction becomes tough and almost tyrannical:

> SILVIA: I am tired of the part I have to play. And would have unmasked a long time ago if I were not afraid of displeasing my father.
> ORGON: That's just what I came to warn you about: don't you dare displease me. I was indulgent enough to allow you this disguise. Now you must, if you please, be gracious enough not to judge Dorante too quickly. I want you to see if this revulsion that you have been made to feel is justified.[57]

56. Marivaux, "The Game of Love and Chance," in *Up From the Country / Infidelities / The Game of Love and Chance*, 320–21.
57. Ibid., 345.

Still, despite this tone, Orgon is basically interested in promoting the expected match. Here he forbids her unmasking because he wants to see his daughter struggle a bit more with her pride as her love for Dorante, who is disguised as a valet, develops. In the long run, this is supposed to strengthen her love for the real Dorante, as the happy ending ultimately assures us. Thus, despite his apparent harshness, Orgon is still acting to promote the young couple's union, although in an unusual way.

But if my assumption that a comedy requires an *alazon* is correct, and if the liberal father is reluctant to play this role, who will? The assumption that in a given literary "institution," i.e., genre, a role is not lost but rather is carried on by a different character, is closely connected to the sociological observation that

> if one actor changes roles, there is a tendency for another actor to make a compensatory change of roles in order to maintain the original role structure. [This] has been referred to as role appropriation by Perry, Silber, and Bloch (1956), who noted that in some families, when the parent became disorganized and assumed a childlike role of dependence in a disaster situation, a child suddenly blossomed into responsibility and helped to supply family leadership.[58]

As I suggested earlier, the answer to the question of who plays the role of the blocking figure is to be found within the young lovers themselves. It is Silvia's self-esteem against which she has to fight in order to admit that she has fallen in love with a valet. And it is a bitter fight indeed. After Lisette, Silvia's chambermaid, insinuates that Silvia has developed some affection for Dorante's valet (the disguised Dorante), Silvia is shaken and vexed. Her indignation, needless to say, only betrays her true emotions:

> I still tremble because of what I heard her say. In their thoughts our servants treat us with nothing but impudence. Oh, how they degrade us! I do not know how I shall ever recover, and I dare not think of what she said! It frightens me still. A valet! A valet! What a strange turn of events! I must put out of my mind the idea with which that wretch blackened it. Here is Bourguignon [the disguised Dorante]. Here is the object for which I rush into frenzies. But it is not his fault, poor boy, and I should not take it out on him.[59]

---

58. Turner, "Role: Sociological Aspects," 554.
59. Marivaux, "The Game of Love and Chance," 340.

The sudden change from anger to tenderness ("poor boy") is another indication of Silvia's true feelings revealed in ways she cannot control.

Dorante, for his part, also has some barriers to overcome, because he believes the woman with whom he has fallen in love to be only a chambermaid. But his decision and course of action are relatively straightforward. After he reveals his true identity to Silvia and expresses his love for her, she asks him: "Is your inclination for me that serious? Do you love me so much?"[60] To which Dorante responds with a passionate answer that rejects all the social obstacles which might have blocked the union of the two lovers:

> Further—to the point of renouncing all my engagements if I am not to be allowed to link my fate to yours. And so the only joy I can still hope to have is to think that you do not hate me.[61]

Despite the social differences, Dorante has made up his mind. The path leading to the happy ending has been cleared; Silvia has only to follow Dorante, to reveal her own identity and announce her affection for him. But here on the threshold of the happy ending, in accordance with the structural principle typical of comedy, we face a hindrance. Its source is Silvia herself, who decides not to reveal her true identity to Dorante. She wants to test his love further, to see whether he is willing to sacrifice everything for her, even to become a rival to her brother, whom she presents as another admirer.

At this point the postponement of the happy ending has nothing to do with society or morality, it is simply Silvia's pride wishing to get full satisfaction after the torments she herself has gone through. This strategy almost topples them to the bottom of the well (to use Palaestrio's image). Dorante, depressed to hear that Silvia has what he believes to be another lover, too anxious to ask her about it directly, and discouraged by her seemingly cool attitude, is prepared to leave. Silvia, suspecting that his leaving is a sign that he is going to give up the whole affair, is alarmed:

> If he leaves, I don't love him any more, I will never marry him. . . . But he's stopped; he's hesitating, he's looking to see if I am looking; I couldn't call him back, not . . . I would not know how to. And yet it would be very strange if he did leave after all that I have done. Ah, there, it's all over now. He is going.[62]

60. Ibid., 349.
61. Ibid.
62. Ibid., 362.

But of course Dorante does not leave. The blocking figure, whether a specific character or a force within the young lover's heart, can only delay the happy ending of comedy. Now, and only after this temporary suspension, has the time come to reveal all the true identities, to remove the obstacles that Silvia, in the role of the blocking figure, has set up, and to celebrate the marriages of masters and servants alike in the communal spirit of comedy.

The interrelation of roles in the university, for example, compels a professor to perform his teaching functions. A professor may, of course, tell jokes; a good professor may also intermittently change roles with his students and be the one who learns from them. Ultimately, however, the professor must *teach* if he is to continue to be considered part of the institution of the university. Analogically, the interrelation of roles in comedy assigns to the blocking figure the specific function of suspending, not of reversing the comic plot. Thus, no matter what obstacles the blocking figure puts forth, as long as we have the basic comic plot, those obstacles will be only temporary ones.

Beaumarchais's *Le Mariage de Figaro* is another interesting example of how the *alazon* can be manifested in a comedy. One should note that in *Le Barbier de Seville* Beaumarchais brought to new perfection the typical role of the lustful old guardian in the character of Bartholo (partly modeled on Molière's Arnolphe in *L'Ecole des femmes*), and that of the trickster *(eiron)* in the personage of Figaro. In *Le Mariage de Figaro* we still have the role of the blocking figure (the Count), the young lovers (Figaro and Suzanne), and the trickster (Figaro). At some point Figaro, following some of his predecessors, boasts about his abilities as a trickster:

> FIGARO: Will you leave it to me?
> SUZANNE: Since it's a question of intrigue we can.
> FIGARO: Two, three, four threads at once—tangled and crossed into the bargain! I'm a courtier born . . .[63]

Ironically enough, most of this arch-trickster's schemes are spoiled, and most of the time he is either busy trying to make sense out of events, or extricating himself from unexpected complications.

But aside from the basic similarity and the fact that in *Le Mariage* we meet some characters whose "history" we know from *Le Barbier*, there are some new elements that make the situation much more complex and multilayered than in *Le Barbier*.

63. Beaumarchais, *The Barber of Seville and The Marriage of Figaro*, 133.

First, there is an interesting change of roles in the process of moving from one play to the other. The Count who in *Le Barbier* plays the young lover becomes in *Le Mariage* the blocking figure to a different couple—again, an indication that there is no identity between role and character, neither within one play nor when we have a series of plays in which the same characters appear. This change of role on the part of the Count is indirectly mentioned by Suzanne, who tries to convince him to waive his "Droit du seigneur":

> Since your Lordship rescued your own wife from the Doctor and married her for love—since you abolished at her instance a certain horrible privilege . . . [64]

The analogy between the two basic situations of the two plays is thus established within *Le Mariage de Figaro* itself, but this argument, designed to evoke nostalgia in the Count, does not help the young couple. Remembering the help provided to him by Figaro the trickster in *Le Barbier* makes the Count only more cautious in his plans.

Another difference between the two plays is that the objective of the blocking figure has shifted. He does not want to prevent the marriage altogether (although he tries to push in this direction too, with the aid of Marceline); he "only" wishes to exercise "the right of the master," to have Suzanne before her marriage, and preferably later too as a mistress. But as far as the abstract scheme of comedy is concerned, and in terms of Figaro's concerns, this is not a significant difference.

In addition, in *Le Mariage* we actually have two pairs of lovers rather than one. Although Figaro and Suzanne are at the center of the plot, the Count and the Countess still hold an important place in the play. They are already married, to be sure; but there is something that keeps them apart, and they, like Figaro and Suzanne, have to achieve their union so that the comic scheme will be accomplished. What separates the older lovers is the same trouble that keeps Figaro and his beloved apart, namely the Count's pursuit of other women, especially Suzanne. By playing the *alazon* to the young lovers, the Count is also the blocking figure for himself and the Countess, of course without being aware of it. In pursuing Suzanne he blocks *himself* from realizing his true love.

The problem with the noble couple is not any external force prohibiting them from consummating their love (as had been the situation in *Le Barbier*), but rather the internal forces of married life, the lack of excitement and novelty, that sense of tedious repetition that can smother

64. Ibid., 119.

any spontaneous spark of love. At one point early in the play, the Countess tries to pinpoint the problem: "Ah, I have loved him too dearly! I have wearied him with my solicitude and tired him with my love."[65] The Count does not know where his true feelings lie and why his love for the Countess has faded, and the Countess, though aware of the problem, has no solutions. Both of them have to go through the process of self-discovery that will ultimately bring them together. Ironically, the path that the Count is taking, thinking it will lead him away from the Countess (i.e., the overtures he makes to Suzanne), brings him into her arms.

After a twisted and complicated course of action consisting of disguises, schemes, and games of "hide-and-seek,"[66] the Count thinks he is going to a discreet rendezvous with Suzanne. This precious moment comes only after some misdirected kisses and punches have been exchanged in the darkness of the garden, so when the Count meets the woman whom he takes to be Suzanne he wastes no time. He starts kissing and embracing . . . the Countess, dressed up as Suzanne. Some ironies ensue:

> THE COUNT [*takes her hand*]: What a lovely skin! Would the Countess had such a hand!
>
> THE COUNTESS [*aside*]: How little you know!
>
> THE COUNT: Or an arm so firm and rounded! Or such pretty fingers!
>
> THE COUNTESS [*counterfeiting Suzanne's voice*]: Is this how love . . .
>
> THE COUNT: Love is no more than the story of one's heart; pleasure is the reality that brings me to your feet . . .
>
> THE COUNTESS: Don't you love her any more?
>
> THE COUNT: Very much—but three years of marriage makes it seem so respectable.
>
> THE COUNTESS: What did you seek in her?
>
> THE COUNT: What I find in you, my beautiful one.[67]

The eyes of the blocking figure are, as usual, blocked. When everyone reveals his true identity, the Count realizes where his true feelings lie, and that while trying to play the blocking figure to Figaro and Suzanne he was blocking his own relationship with the Countess. His failure becomes his success.

65. Ibid., 130.

66. In an astute analysis of the play, Walter E. Rex, in "*Figaro*'s Games," relates the plot to the concept of children's plays, and to the concept of games in general.

67. Beaumarchais, *The Barber of Seville and The Marriage of Figaro*, 205.

In the examples of Marivaux and Beaumarchais we have seen how writers find new ways to portray the role of the blocking figure. Beginning with the pompous and ridiculous *alazon*, the role eventually becomes but one component in the shaping of a complex character. The "type" has become a more rounded and individualized personage.[68] Instead of complete failure inflicted by the trickster, we have a seeming failure that is actually a triumph for the blocking figure himself. The blocking of the other's path turns out to be a self-blocking, and the failure of this blocking is in turn a self-revelation and victory.

Note that the basic function of the blocking figure has not changed, despite its long evolution and its varied manifestations. It is this, in the form of a ridiculous *alazon* or in the form of a mental force within the loving figure, that provides the suspense in the comic plot. It is this that threatens the success of the young lovers and whose failure makes their union possible.

The university, for instance, as an institution of education, has changed dramatically during the last eight hundred years. How professors (and students) dress, how they conduct themselves in class, the material of instruction—everything has altered drastically. Yet, if we but perceive this institution of learning as a cluster of interrelated roles, we understand that the university of the twelfth century and the one we know today are "the same": the basic structure of interelated roles has been preserved. An examination of, for example, the role of "professor" in the university over a long period will give us a sense both of continuity and of change in the institution of the university throughout history. Analogically, perceiving the tradition of comedy through the perspective of a set of interrelated roles enables us to see both what connects each play to the tradition and what makes it a particular and innovative work of art.

---

68. Elder Olson in *The Theory of Comedy*, 85, points out this process in the history of comedy, though from a different perspective than mine here. For some general observations on why a character is perceived as "type" or "individual," see my "Types of Characters, Characteristics of Types."

Chapter 5

Literary Genres as Speech Acts

If the twentieth century can be called the century of linguistics, marking the enormous influence of this discipline on the humanities and social sciences, then the seventies may be subtitled the decade of pragmatics. Whereas the fifties and sixties were dominated by developments in syntax and semantics (notably Chomsky's generative grammar), the seventies witnessed the emergence of a Cinderella, pragmatics, complete with glass slipper—speech-act theory.[1]

Linguistics seems to be the success story of the humanities, not only because it has achieved a high degree of sophistication and accuracy in its methods, theories, and descriptions, but also because concepts developed within it appear fruitful outside the boundaries of linguistics proper (for example, such notions as *langue* and *parole*, synchrony and diachrony, competence and performance, etc).[2] One could almost say that any important theoretical development in linguistics (or in the philosophy of language) will be found in some neighboring discipline soon afterwards. Thus we should not be surprised that Teun Van Dijk's *Some Aspects of Text Grammar* proposed a Chomskian model for literary texts. Then, when both linguistics and the philosophy of language focused on the

1. Notably in Searle's *Speech Acts*. For the differences between syntax, semantics, and pragmatics, see the excellent and critical survey in John Lyons's *Semantics,* 114–19.

2. See, for instance, the survey by Terence Hawkes, *Structuralism and Semiotics,* especially 19–58 and 123–50. Culler's *Structuralist Poetics* is an influential description of attempts to use linguistic concepts and theories in literary theory.

relationships between context and language, Marie Louise Pratt took the
cue and in her *Toward a Speech Act Theory of Literary Discourse* proposed
the application of certain developments in the philosophy of language
(especially those associated with the works of Searle and Grice) to the
literary arena.

These theoretical efforts are by no means merely an attempt to imitate
a successful colleague. They stem from the deep, and often correct,
conviction that some of the theories developed in linguistics and in the
philosophy of language can contribute new insights to literary theory.
Language, after all, is not the monopoly of linguistics, and some
problems of language extend to neighboring disciplines that also deal
with human communication.

Pragmatics, perhaps even more than any other field of linguistics or
philosophy of language, offered (or seemed to offer) some promising
perspectives. After some futile efforts to define literature in phonetic,
syntactical, or semantic terms, literary scholars turned to pragmatics,
attracted by its resort to contextual factors in defining meaning. Pratt
formulates these considerations clearly:

> In sum, speech act theory provides a way of talking about
> utterances not only in terms of their surface grammatical proper-
> ties but also in terms of the context in which they are made, the
> intentions, attitudes, and expectations of the participants, the
> relationships existing between participants, and generally, the
> unspoken rules and conventions that are understood to be in play
> when an utterance is made and received. There are enormous
> advantages to talking about literature in this way, too, for literary
> works, like all communicative activities, are context-dependent.
> Literature itself is a speech context. And as with any utterance,
> the way people produce and understand literary works depends
> enormously on unspoken, culturally-shared knowledge of the
> rules, conventions, and expectations that are in play when lan-
> guage is used in that context. Just as a definition of explaining,
> thanking, or persuading must include the unspoken contextual
> information on which the participants are relying, so must a
> definition of literature.[3]

The next step in this argument is to draw an analogy between these
various types of speech acts and literary genres: "One of the most
obvious kinds of contextual information we bring to bear in confronting

---

3. Marie Louise Pratt, *Toward a Speech Act Theory of Literary Discourse*, 86.

a literary work is our knowledge of its genre . . . genres and subgenres can to a great extent be defined as systems of appropriateness conditions."[4]

Pratt is perhaps the most elaborate and consistent advocate for the application of speech-act theory to criticism, but she is not the only one to point in this direction.[5] The direction is in turn part of a broader perspective, not necessarily confined to recent developments in linguistics or the philosophy of language, which draws an analogy between speech acts and literary genres. However, close examination shows that the application of the speech-act perspective to literature actually confounds two theoretical frameworks with different assumptions and goals. The first describes literary genres as complex forms of ordinary speech acts; the second, as imitations of speech acts.[6] I will discuss these further before turning to the texts, and I will propose my own views only after discussing the concrete examples.

LITERARY GENRES AS SPEECH ACTS

The first theoretical perspective—mostly, but not always, associated with new developments in pragmatics—is shown clearly in Elizabeth Bruss's *Autobiographical Acts*. After asserting the relevance of speech-act theory to literary discourse, and drawing the basic analogy between speech acts and genres (see quotation in my opening chapter), she goes on to propose her own analysis of one particular literary genre—autobiography.

Bruss's definition of autobiography roughly follows Searle's model for analyzing speech acts,[7] and it would be instructive here to quote the three rules she formulates:

4. Ibid. Note, by the way, that Sandy Petrey, in *Speech Acts and Literary Theory*, 76–77, describes Pratt's application of speech-act theory to literary genres as one of her most fruitful methodological moves.

5. See, for example, Bruss (1976), Lejeune (1975), Petrey (1990), Schauber and Spolsky (1986), Stierle (1972), Traugott (1973), and also Altieri (1975), though with a different stress. Shoshana Felman's *Literary Speech Act*, despite its promising title, has little to offer to the approach I describe here, because her use of the concept of "speech act" involves some metaphysical and psychoanalytical meanings that go beyond this study. For criticism of the application of speech-act theory to the literary field, see Margolis (1979) and Fish (1980).

6. In presenting the two approaches, I follow the division suggested by Ora Segal in "The Theory of Speech Acts and Its Applicability to Literature." See also Richard Ohmann's "Speech Acts and the Definition of Literature."

7. Searle's model consists of different rules applying to different levels of the speech

Rule 1. An autobiographer undertakes a dual role. He is the source of the subject matter and the source for the structure to be found in his text. (a) The author claims individual responsibility for the creation and arrangement of his text. (b) The individual who is exemplified in the organization of the text is purported to share the identity of an individual to whom reference is made via the subject matter of the text. (c) The existence of this individual, independent of the text itself, is assumed to be susceptible to appropriate public verification procedures.

Rule 2. Information and events reported in connection with the autobiographer are asserted to have been, to be, or to have potential for being the case. (a) Under existing conditions, a claim is made for the truth-value of what the autobiography reports. . . . (b) The audience is expected to accept these reports as true, and is free to "check up" on them or attempt to discredit them.

Rule 3. Whether or not what is reported can be discredited, whether or not it can be reformulated in some more generally acceptable way from another point of view, the autobiographer purports to believe in what he asserts.[8]

One may challenge some of these statements. I question what seems to be an overemphasis on the truth-value of the autobiography. Some of Bruss's formulations on this point evoke more a courtroom than the writing and reading of an autobiography. Sometimes the intriguing aspects of an autobiography consist precisely in the tension between its allegations and what we happen to know from other sources to be true. In most cases of autobiography, we are interested in the writer's attempt to produce a coherent self-portrait, rather than in corroborating his or her statements by digging into archives. These elaborated rules seem more suited to simple spoken versions of "autobiography"—to speech acts in which the speakers tell us about themselves and about their lives. Every written autobiography has in it much more than simple utterances of the form "I was/did X." All those aspects of literary autobiographies

---

act: a "propositional content," "preparatory conditions," a "sincerity rule," and finally an "essential rule," which includes all the others. Thus a request, for example, will be analyzed as follows: The proposition content is some future act (A) of the hearer (H). The preparatory conditions are (1) that H be able to do A and the speaker (S) believes that H is able to do A, and (2) that it not be obvious to S or to H that H would do A in the natural course of events of his own accord. The sincerity rule states that S wants H to do A. The essential rule tells us that this speech act counts as an attempt to get H to do A. For further discussion of examples, see Searle, *Speech Acts*, 54–71.

8. Elizabeth W. Bruss, *Autobiographical Acts: The Changing of Literary Genre*, 10–11.

which make them worth reading are, according to Bruss's analysis, only optional "extras." I think this is a very limiting description of the genre.

Pratt tries to prove that literary genres can be analyzed as speech acts are analyzed, and that in some cases the "literary act"—that is, the specific genre—has intimate affinities with its "original" spoken counterpart.[9] A central chapter in her book is devoted to showing how the novel basically shares rules, modes, and techniques with real-life cases of storytelling ("natural narratives"). Following William Labov's analysis (in *Language in the Inner City*) of the rules that govern such storytelling, Pratt argues that these same rules also apply in the novel:

> Literary and natural narrative are formally and functionally very much alike. Put another way, all the problems of coherence, chronology, causality, foregrounding, plausibility, selection of detail, tense, point of view, and emotional intensity exist for the natural narrator just as they do for the novelist, and they are confronted and solved (with greater or lesser success) by speakers of the language every day.[10]

In my view, Pratt's arguments are sometimes shaky, especially when she tries to reduce complex phenomena in novel-writing to simple "natural-narrative" principles, or when she tries to dismiss certain conventions peculiar to the novel (such as the omniscient narrator) as a mere reproduction of the same phenomena in natural narrative. She herself admits that the most fundamental convention of human communication—the "cooperative principle" formulated by Paul Grice—is constantly violated in modern novelistic practice. In the face of such phenomena, Pratt introduces the linguistic opposition of *marked* versus *unmarked* cases, where the latter designates the neutral term of two units in contrast (e.g., the formally unmarked *boy* and the marked *boys*, unmarked *lion* and marked *lioness*) and postulates an "unmarked" case of the novel in which some strict rules of real-world narrative display are followed.[11] As in Bruss's analysis of autobiography, this seems a reductive approach that overlooks the most interesting aspects of the literary work.

9. Note that in this context a "literary act" is an act that produces a literary text, not an act that is *represented* in a literary work.

10. Pratt, *Toward a Speech Act Theory of Literary Discourse*, 66–67.

11. The tendency to postulate "unmarked" cases is also evident in Pratt's description of the "unmarked" novel, as contrasted with the "marked" short story, in her "The Short Story: The Long and The Short of It." The "preference model," suggested by Schauber and Spolsky in *The Bounds of Interpretation*, seems more promising than the binary opposition of "marked" versus "unmarked" cases.

Pratt sums up the novel as a conjunction of two sets of rules: the essential rules, which govern acts of narrative display, and the stylistic rules, which govern any written text. How would she deal with Benjamin's interior monologue in *The Sound and the Fury?* Well, of course, it should be treated as a "marked" case because it violates both the first and the second set of rules. But then where are we to draw the line between "marked" and "unmarked" cases? Taking the "classical" novel of the nineteenth century as our "unmarked" case, as Pratt suggests, leaves us with only *one version* of this multifaceted genre.

Todorov, in a short and illuminating article "The Origin of Genres," identifies three basic relationships that may exist between a speech act and a literary genre:

> Either the genre (such as the ballad) codifies discursive properties, just as any other speech act would; or the genre coincides with a speech act that also has a nonliterary existence, such as prayer; or, finally, it derives from a speech act via a certain number of transformations or amplifications, as would be the case with the novel, beginning with the action of recounting.[12]

There is a slight difference between Pratt's treatment of the novel and Todorov's perspective. Whereas Pratt gives us a picture of the same narrative principle operating in different domains (oral utterance, written segments), Todorov suggests that the principles underlying a speech act may be changed (through a set of "transformations") on the way to establishing a literary genre.

To support his perspective, Todorov cites two examples. The first, taken from the Luba culture in Zaire, consists of a comparison between the speech act of an invitation and the literary genre of "invitation," which exists in that particular culture. The second example, taken from more familiar material, is a comparison of the act of recounting some marvelous event with the literary genre of the "fantastic." In both cases, Todorov shows how a set of transformations (such as narrativization, specification, repetition, variation, thematic proliferation) operates on the basic speech-act rules to produce the more complex literary genre. Todorov's main point here is to demonstrate the principle that in the third type of relationship, in which a speech act becomes a literary genre through a series of transformations, "one goes from a simple act to a complex act."[13]

12. Tzvetan Todorov, "The Origin of Genres," 165–66.
13. Ibid., 165. This formulation may remind us of another theory of genres: André Jolles, in his *Formes simples*, proposes that literary genres can be traced back to basic types

The most important point from my perspective is that Todorov, despite the transformational process he describes, treats literary genres and speech acts as members of the same category. A literary genre may be a much more complex phenomenon than a speech act, but both are basically "codification[s] of discursive properties," playing similar roles in human communication. It is a difference of degree, not of kind.

Regarding the basic approach, which stresses the resemblance between speech acts and literary genres, one may cite works that are not related to the specific conceptual framework developed in the philosophy of language, such as E. D. Hirsch's *Validity in Interpretation*. To Hirsch the concept of historical genres has a dubious epistemological status. He considers genres to be heuristic and provisional only, because in his view they do not describe anything in the real world. To Hirsch, the only valid concept would be the "intrinsic genre" that encapsulates the work's meaning. Although this concept of "intrinsic genre" seems too narrow for my purposes, and although I attach more significance to the broad concept of historical genres, let me put my objections aside and see to what Hirsch compares the "traditional genre concepts": "To be able to speak or understand speech, a person must have recourse to a genre idea, and if the utterance is not a mere formula, he usually must have recourse to a genre that is broader than the intrinsic genre. *The genre 'command' names a type of use* that the speaker has learned from previous uses, and he knows that what he says must have significant elements in common with these past uses."[14]

Thus, despite the differences between Hirsch's methods and theoretical framework and the ones we saw earlier, despite even the slight significance that he assigns to the concept of (regular, not intrinsic) genre, he too draws the basic analogy on which we focus in this chapter: the analogy between the structure and communicative function of a type of language use and those of a literary genre. Although we recognize some discrepancies, or even major differences, between the various theorists who propose this analogy, all of those whom we have considered so far share the view that speech acts and literary genres belong fundamentally to the same category of "language use" and should be treated with the

---

of language use. Stierle, in "L'Histoire comme example," for instance, refers to Jolles's work as a source of inspiration for such a perspective. Contemporary theorists, however, are very skeptical and critical of attempts to pin down some ultimate nine (or ten, or twelve) "simple forms" from which all complex forms can be said to have evolved. The tacit equation of older with simpler is another assumption rejected in modern theories. Traces of this questionable proposition are still found in Todorov's opposition of "simple " and "complex."

14. Hirsch, *Validity in Interpretation*, 109 (italics added).

same theoretical tools. Literary genres may of course differ in various aspects from speech acts—they are usually written and more complex than their spoken counterparts—but from the point of view of pragmatics, they are simply another, basic, genuine manifestation of language use. It is this underlying assumption that our second group of thinkers challenges.

LITERARY GENRES AS IMITATIONS OF SPEECH ACTS

Monroe C. Beardsley, in his *Possibility of Criticism,* proposes an analysis of meaning that emphasizes not abstract "propositions" but rather the illocutionary act a speaker performs. He defines the meaning of a sentence as that sentence's illocutionary-act potential. The conditions set on the performance of such an illocutionary act resemble those formulated by Searle for performing a speech act. This should not surprise us, because both Searle and Beardsley perceive themselves as followers of Austin's pioneering *How to Do Things with Words.*[15] After advocating this approach to the problem of meaning, Beardsley refers to the intimate connection between a poem and an illocutionary act.

But here, where it appears that Beardsley finds himself closest to the first approach we presented above, he also manifestly deviates from it. From the point of view of the first approach, a literary genre is but another kind of speech act, though in a written form. To Beardsley, a poem (of the literary kind on which he is focusing) "is *an imitation* of a compound illocutionary act."[16]

One could still claim that the term "imitation" suggests a conspicuous network of similarities between a poem and an illocutionary (speech) act. However, according to the approach that defines a poem as an imitation of an illocutionary act, the literary genre is no longer merely another kind of speech act among many. The imitative approach emphasizes the fact that an imitation of a speech act only looks like, but is not, a genuine one. It is something with its own internal logic and rules, and these should be related to the *artistic demands of imitation* rather than to the requirements imposed on the performance of a speech act. To put this differently, when we encounter a string of words in a literary text, it

15. According to Petrey, in his *Speech Acts and Literary Theory,* 59–69, there is a major difference between Austin's social perspective on speech acts and Searle's focus on the individual (intentional) performance of speech acts. We should note, however, that Searle's formulations of speech acts rules refer to *institutionalized,* not private, intentions.

16. Monroe C. Beardsley, *The Possibility of Criticism,* 58 (italics added).

does not have the illocutionary force it usually carries in a nonliterary context.

A poem may be used as a regular illocutionary act, but in such a case it will not be used *as a poem*. Or, as Beardsley humorously formulates the distinction, "A poem can, of course, be used in performing an illocutionary act—it may, for example, be enclosed in a box of candy or accompanied by a letter endorsing its sentiments. But the writing of a poem, as such, is not an illocutionary act, it is the creation of a fictional character performing a fictional illocutionary act."[17]

Barbara Herrnstein Smith, in her *On the Margins of Discourse*, alludes to Beardsley's statement that the "make-believe" nature of poetic usage is to be found in the "creation of a fictional character performing a fictional illocutionary act." According to her, "What is central to the concept of the poem as a fictive utterance is not that the speaker is a 'character' distinct from the poet, or that the audience purportedly addressed, the emotions expressed, and the events alluded to are fictional, but that *the speaking, addressing, expressing and alluding are themselves fictive verbal acts.*"[18]

It is thus possible to find some points of disagreement between the two, but they basically share the conviction that literary art is not a genuine, "natural" kind of illocutionary act. Despite his emphasis on the "fictive character," Beardsley does not restrict his argument to a small part of poetry (such as lyric poetry with a distinct voice), but rather expands it to include all kinds of poetry (poetry in the broad sense)— even didactic poetry in which the speaker seems to be a mouthpiece for the author who is performing a real illocutionary act of assertion: "Didactic poems are not to be taken as the verbal residues of real illocutionary acts. What makes them didactic is not, I think, that they are arguments rather than 'expressions of emotions' (whatever that may be), but that they *imitate* arguments rather than pleadings, laments, or cries of joy."[19]

This statement also implicitly suggests a way of distinguishing between different literary genres—namely, by classifying them according to the type of illocutionary act that they imitate. This point is made explicit in Smith's discussion: "The various genres of literary art—for example, tales, classical odes, and lyrics—can often be distinguished from each other according to what types of natural discourse they represent: here, respectively, anecdotal reports of past events, public speeches, and more or less private or personal utterance."[20]

17. Ibid., 59.
18. Smith, *On the Margins of Discourse*, 28.
19. Beardsley, *The Possibility of Criticism*, 59–60.
20. Smith, *On the Margins of Discourse*, 30.

The scope of the analysis has been broadened by Smith to include not only distinct types of poetry, but also poetry "in the broad sense bequeathed by Aristotle, i.e., to refer to the general class of verbal artworks."[21] Further, if poetry (now in the restricted sense) is characterized as representing various kinds of spoken, natural discourse, prose fiction would be analyzed as a representation of various kinds of inscribed, natural discourse: "Novels, for example, a distinctively post-Gutenberg genre, have typically been representations of chronicles, journals, letters, memoirs, and biographies."[22]

All these things (letters, memoirs, etc.) are seen as written, *natural discourse*. Whereas both written and spoken varieties of natural discourse derive their meaning from the context in which they are uttered (or composed), a poem, by virtue of cultural conventions, is "severed" from these contextual considerations and interpreted as an autonomous text. To underscore the distinction between the act of *composing* a poem and the speech act that the poem *represents,* Smith refers to dramatic poetry: "We must distinguish between the poet's act of composing the poem and the verbal act that the poem represents, just as we would distinguish William Shakespeare's act in composing *Hamlet* and the acts of the Prince of Denmark represented in the play."[23]

This reference to dramatic poetry is not accidental. The intent of Smith's theoretical perspective is to demonstrate how the notion of "imitation," which is central in dramatic form, is also pertinent to other forms and genres of literature.

Another important distinction Smith makes is that between a transcription of a natural spoken discourse (e.g., a transcription of a telephone call), a natural written discourse (e.g., a letter), and poetry, which is a *representation* (rather than a transcription) of a spoken discourse. It might be helpful, before we go on, to summarize Smith's distinctions in the following table:

	Natural Discourse	**Represented Discourse**
Spoken	Typical speech acts such as promising or asking	Prototypically various poetic genres such as the ode or the lyric
Written	*Inscribed* acts, such as letters or memoirs *Transcriptions* of speech acts originally spoken	Various forms of prose fiction

21. Ibid., 14.
22. Ibid., 30.
23. Ibid., 33.

Despite the various possible divisions and subdivisions within the categories of spoken and written natural discourse, the crucial distinction is between natural and represented (mimetic, "artistic") discourse. Each of these has its own rules and requirements, and its own conventions of understanding and interpretation. When Smith mentions Aristotle, she is not just appealing to authority. Her theoretical framework, highly original in many respects, nevertheless owes much to the critical tradition known as the neo-Aristotelian or "Chicago" school.

Elder Olson, one of its major figures, stresses the mimetic quality of poetry, in the broader as well as the narrower sense of the term. In an attempt to stretch Aristotle's concepts to cover poetry (in the narrow sense), he asks the typical Aristotelian question: What does it imitate? If the epic and tragedy imitate a system of actions, what does poetry imitate? Key to his answer is the speech act. In "An Outline of Poetic Theory," he distinguishes between four kinds of action that can be imitated in poetry. Referring to lyric poetry, he describes the represented character as one who "commits some verbal act (threatening, persuading, beseeching) upon someone existing only as the object of his action (Marvell's 'To His Coy Mistress')."[24]

In a later article, "The Lyric," Olson refines his distinctions within lyric poetry, but still holds that a major part of the genre consists of poetry that imitates verbal acts: "There is a lyric poem of the verbal act. There may be many verbal acts: of persuading, beseeching, commanding, informing, betraying, and so on. But we have an *act*."[25]

Although Smith's theoretical framework differs in certain ways from Olson's neo-Aristotelian approach, both of them introduce the concept of imitated speech acts into their views of poetry. They also share an emphasis on the process of inferring this speech-act situation as a major part of understanding and interpreting a poem.[26]

Richard Ohmann articulates this latter principle in his "Speech, Action, and Style": "A work of literature is also a series of hypothetical acts, grounded in the conventions for verbal action that we have all thoroughly learned. . . . [T]he reader, using his elaborate knowledge of the rules for illocutionary acts, constructs the hypothetical speakers and circumstances—the fictional world—that will make sense of the given acts. This performance is what we know as mimesis."[27]

Ohmann maintains that, in addition to this principle, styles of illocu-

---

24. Olson, *On Value Judgments in the Arts and Other Essays*, 282.
25. Ibid., 216.
26. Ibid., 127–28, 145–46, and Smith, *On the Margins of Discourse*, 24–39.
27. Ohmann, "Speech, Action, and Style," 254. For an elaborated attempt to define literature along these lines, see Ohmann, "Speech Acts and the Definition of Literature."

tionary action may help "to determine the most fundamental literary types."[28] Thus comedy could be characterized by repetitive series of speech acts (such as questions and assertions); tragedy, by a wide variety of illocutionary acts. Ohmann points to the relevance of speech-act theory to the classification of literary genres, a point we have also encountered in the writings of Beardsley, Smith, and Olson.

It is worth pointing out that both Austin, the philosopher who introduced the notion of speech acts into philosophy and linguistics, and Searle, who has contributed so much to the development and popularity of speech-act theory in literary criticism, adopted the basic view that I label here "imitative." When Austin refers to language uses such as joking or writing a poem, he characterizes them as "not serious" kinds of usage: "Language in such circumstances is in special ways—intelligibly—used not seriously, but in ways *parasitic* upon its normal use—ways which fall under the doctrine of the *etiolations* of language."[29]

And Searle, in "The Logical Status of Fictional Discourse," seems to take the cue from Austin's approach and discusses fictionality in terms of imitative activity. One of his aims is to refute the approach that assigns different illocutionary acts to different literary genres:

> According to this answer, Miss Murdoch or any other writer of novels is not performing the illocutionary act of making an assertion but the illocutionary act of telling a story or writing a novel. On this theory, newspaper accounts contain one class of illocutionary acts (statements, assertions, descriptions, explanations) and fictional literature contains another class of illocutionary acts (writing stories, novels, poems, plays, etc.). The writer or speaker of fiction has his own repertoire of illocutionary acts which are on all fours with, but in addition to, the standard illocutionary acts of asking questions, making requests, making promises, giving descriptions, and so on. I believe that this analysis is incorrect.[30]

After trying to substantiate his objection to the above view, Searle proposes his alternative. According to him, the writer of a novel does not perform a separate illocutionary act of "writing a novel," but is

28. Ohmann, "Speech, Action, and Style," 252.

29. J. L. Austin, *How to Do Things with Words*, 22.

30. John R. Searle, "The Logical Status of Fictional Discourse," 63–64. Searle's attempt to evolve a definition of *realistic* literature from his definition of fiction is very problematic, as Menachem Brinker has demonstrated in his *Representation and Meaning in the Fictional Work*, 55–70.

rather "pretending, one could say, to make an assertion, or acting as if she were making an assertion, or going through the motions of making an assertion, or *imitating the making of an assertion.*"[31] Writing fictional literature thus consists basically of imitating preexisting speech acts.

My purpose in this section has been to show the basic relevance of the notion of speech acts to that of literary genres, and to propose a distinction between the two main approaches to the issue: the one, describing literary genres as complex, written, but genuine speech acts, and the other, emphasizing that literary genres artistically imitate or represent, but are not genuine, speech acts. Although it would have been possible to classify the various approaches and thinkers in some other ways, the criterion I have chosen seems central from the point of view of literary theory.

Along with my presentation of these two basic attitudes, I have expressed some reservations about unsatisfactory formulations of the first approach, which mechanically applies speech-act theory to literary genres. Although the second approach seems more promising, because it acknowledges the peculiar communicative situation of literature, it nevertheless calls for certain modifications. Before spelling out these modifications, however, I would like to look at some concrete examples of poetry.

This focus on a generic tradition of poetry is not self-evident. An alternative view, stating that "in practical criticism with a speech-act orientation, pride of place is held by drama," has recently been advocated by Sandy Petrey.[32] Petrey argues that speech-act theory (with a strong Austinian emphasis) has the most relevance to practical drama criticism because there speech and action fuse. He supports this claim with a sensitive analysis of the illocutionary force of speech in various specific scenes. I should note, however, two reservations: (1) Although it is sometimes difficult to separate speech from action in drama, we should still acknowledge the latter's privileged, more fundamental status. To begin with, characters in drama express themselves in nonverbal ways (movements, gestures, silences) that are sometimes no less significant than speech. Then too, speech in drama is *a means* of expressing and conveying dramatic action, and in that sense is (logically) subordinated to action. We can conceive of a play's plot without referring to any specific speech acts, but we cannot think of the significance of a speech act within a play without referring to its plot. Here, Aristotle's subordination of *lexis* (as well as *ethos* and *dianoia*) to *mythos* is as pertinent and

---

31. Searle, "The Logical Status of Fictional Discourse," 65 (italics added).
32. In his rigorous study *Speech Acts and Literary Theory*, 86.

valid as ever. (2) In the analysis of dramatic speeches, practical criticism can indeed benefit from the speech-act perspective, but as far as genre theory is concerned, I would hesitate to describe dramatic genres as speech-act theory's most relevant, applicable domain, despite the apparent unity of speech and action. Speech-act theory seems relevant to dramatic genres in two, relatively restricted, ways. First, certain dramatic genres manifest specific tendencies for using certain types of speech acts, as Ohmann has suggested. And second, the interchange occurring in dramatic dialogues can be usefully explicated in terms of illocutionary forces (e.g., is Iago posing a question, making an insinuation, or inciting Othello when he says: "Did Michael Cassio, when you wooed my lady, Know of your love?").[33] But not much beyond that.

Thus I believe we should leave drama and look at some other generic traditions to discover where speech-act theory is most applicable. And here I think Smith's insight about the intimate, imitative linkage between speech acts and genres of poetry (in the restricted sense) is the most fruitful one.

CARPE DIEM OR VIVAMUS ATQUE AMEMUS

After so much theoretical discussion of the analogies between literary genres and speech acts, it might be useful to look at some specific texts. First, I will present a generic tradition associated with the *carpe diem* motif. After tracing some highlights of this subgenre throughout literary history, it will be easier to see how one can apply the speech-act model to certain literary genres. By proposing a schematic analysis of this subgenre based on the speech-act model, I will also make clear the limitations of such a model.

One should begin by distinguishing between *carpe diem* as an isolated motif[34] and the term's generic sense: in which reference to the brevity of life and exhortation to enjoy life in the context of love serve the organizing principles of a poem. This section will thus be devoted to examining

33. Shakespeare, *Othello*, act 3, sc. 3. In fact, Paul H. Grice's model of "implicatures" that emerge from the interrelations of words and contexts, as introduced in his "Logic and Conversation," seems even more pertinent than speech-act theory to the analysis of dramatic interchange.

34. It is treated as a motif in the excellent discussion by Fredelle Bruser, "Comus and the Rose Song," who presents Milton's *Comus* as a synthesis of the motif's corporal and spiritual traditions. This perspective is echoed in "Carpe diem," in Alex Preminger's *Princeton Encyclopedia of Poetry and Poetics*, 103–4.

some prime paradigmatic instances of this literary tradition. I will start *ab ovo*, with Asklepiades:

> You're saving it? What for? In the underworld
> you'll acquire no one to enjoy you, girl.
> Lovemaking's for the living. Past Styx we shall
> as bones and urn-meal, virgin, sprawl.[35]

It would be useful to consider this short poem as a schema of potentialities on which later writers will elaborate. The most important thing, however, is that all the essential elements that constitute the literary genre are already present here in an encapsulated form. We have (1) the reference to the inevitability of death, (2) the call to abandon chastity, (3) an attempt to deduce (2) from (1), and finally, the element that justifies the introduction of the *carpe diem* subgenre in this chapter, (4) the fact that the speaker is *addressing* his speech to the object of his effort of persuasion.

Needless to say, the argument presented by the speaker need not be logical. The main point is that it should be successful. The question at the beginning—"You're saving it? What for?"—(to which, theoretically, several answers are possible) is thus shown to be purely rhetorical by the very fact that there is no answer attached. The desired answer is clear: there is no valid reason to insist on retaining one's virginity.

The rhetorical power of the argument (or, better, pseudo-argument) is reinforced by creating a symmetrical opposition between the "underworld" on the one hand and "lovemaking's for the living" on the other. The impression of a compact and coherent argument is also due to the chiastic structure of the poem. After the initial challenge ("What for?") comes the reminder of death ("underworld"); then, in contrast, of love ("to enjoy you"). Follows swift reference to the theme of love ("lovemaking"), which leads to a brief elaboration of the theme of death ("bones and urn-meal"). The poem's structure can thus be represented as a rhetorical question followed by the chiastic sequence death-love-love-death.

The speaker's rhetorical strategy does not rely on subtlety; instead, one gets the impression that his aim is to stun his addressee (or let us rather call them the tempter and the tempted). This is done by the direct, even brutal reference to death, which is expanded later on. In this light, the ending of the poem seems to be its appropriate closure, because the

---

35. Asklepiades, in *The Greek Anthology, A Selection in Modern Verse Translations*, ed. Peter Jay, 58.

tempter is interested in numbing the tempted's capacity for rational response so that she will be lured to the "inevitable" conclusion—that is, abandoning her maidenhead. It is the realistic picture of death ("bones and urn-meal") that seems likely to be the most effective instrument in this process of "numbing." In an ingenious move, the speaker has introduced into this horrible picture of death an element—"we shall sprawl"—that can be interpreted sexually. The impression created by the previous lines has not totally faded away. And when we read "we shall . . . sprawl," the erotic overtones of the poem are still fresh—which is, after all, the tempter's intention.

My next sample is Catullus's *Carmina* 5 ("*Vivamus . . . atque amemus*"):

> Let us live, my Lesbia, and love,
> And value at one farthing all the talk
> Of crabbed old men.
> Suns may set and rise again.
> For us, when the short light has once set,
> Remains to be slept the sleep of one unbroken night.
> Give me a thousand kisses, then a hundred,
> Then another thousand, then a second hundred,
> Then yet another thousand, then a hundred.
> Then, when we have made up many thousands,
> We will confuse our counting, that we may not know the reckoning,
> Nor any malicious person blight them with evil eye,
> When he knows that our kisses are so many.[36]

One should first note the four essential elements: (1) the reference to the brevity of life, here through the allusion to sunsets; (2) the call to plunge into love, which opens the poem; (3) the fact that the argument is not made explicit, but rather implicitly built up through the very contrast between ongoing life and the mortality of the speaker and his addressee; and (4) the specific situation of all this rhetorical machinery, in which the speaker addresses his beloved.

In addition to these constitutive elements, which justify the juxtaposing of the two poems, Catullus introduces other elements that are not mere concretizations of the *amemus* schema. The most conspicuous of these is the whole dimension of social and cultural attitudes toward chastity and promiscuity. The representatives of the negative social attitude appear in strategic places: at the beginning, just after the first hortatory call, and at the end of the poem. In this respect, the speaker is

---

36. Catullus, *The Poems of Gaius Valerius Catullus*, 7–9.

fighting on two fronts: against inexorable time and also against social mores and censures. In order to overcome the former (by persuading Lesbia), he must first overcome the latter, the social barriers, which here take the form of moral strictures.

The first aspect of the elaborated rhetorical goal is conveyed by the image of the sun: the contrast between its never-ending natural cycle and the finite character of human life. Notice, by the way, how some of the terms referring (euphemistically) to death also belong to the semantic field of love (such as "sleep" and "night"), just as did the phrase "we shall sprawl," which we saw in Asklepiades' poem.

The speaker deals with the second issue—of social strictures—by the way in which he represents the social code, or more specifically by the characters he has chosen to represent it. They are unsympathetic ("crabbed old men"), and their pompous self-importance can be deflated by the speaker and Lesbia ("and value at one farthing . . ."). The whole moral issue thus turns out to be a humorous game in which the severe representatives of the social code become objects of laughter. The most effective rhetoric, however, comes toward the end of the poem, the argument being that virtually all moralistic prohibitions are actually a distorted and barely adequate disguise of bitter, impotent envy. Here, as in any successful persuasion, the desired effect is achieved not through explicit and logical argumentation, but rather through implication and insinuation.

The last thing to be observed is the difference between the strategies Catullus and Asklepiades deploy to achieve their common goal of numbing the addressee's reason and prudence. Asklepiades uses shock treatment by displaying vivid images of death, whereas Catullus sets out the bait of love. The quantitative balance that Asklepiades' poem sets up between the two poles, love and death, is shifted; most of Catullus's poem is dedicated to the evocation of the lovelier end of the spectrum. Moreover, it is not a detached presentation of love's charm; by asking Lesbia to bestow her kisses upon him, the speaker demonstrates the effects of love in his very speech.

Despite the formulaic numbers the speaker uses, the constant repetition and frequent embedding of subordinate clauses indicate how much he is carried away by his own words, and we get a very concrete and impassioned speech. These repetitions, which indicate the speaker's growing enthusiasm, are not uttered by a drunken libertine but by a calculating lover who wishes to entice his addressee to a similar enthusiasm for love. Note that Catullus's constant repetition of numbers may be perceived also as simulating a childish, preschool mentality. Thus Catullus is inducing Lesbia to participate in a seemingly innocent numbers game, of which the ultimate goal is not childish at all. Catullus pursues his object, rhetorically, from both ends: either Lesbia will succumb to his growing enthusiasm for (adult) love, or she will let herself be lured into a "childish" game.

The fact that Catullus's playful enthusiasm is calculated does not mean that it is insincere, but rather that it is, besides being genuine, an intentional rhetorical device. Actually, a speaker who hopes to persuade must strike a delicate balance between an authentic expression of his feelings and an intentional, calculated manipulation of rhetorical devices. Too much of the former leads to a sentimental outburst of entreaty, too much of the latter conveys an impression of coldblooded manipulation. Either would produce a very poor *amemus* poem.

Catullus, at any rate, succeeds in maintaining the tension between his roles of calculating seducer and ardent lover. In the following example the uncontrolled passion is restrained and other aspects of the genre are brought to the fore. It is Ronsard's famous "Mignonne, allons voir si la rose":

My sweet, let us go and see if the rose
Which this morning opened
Its crimson robe to the sun
Has not lost this evening
The folds of its crimson dress
And its color like yours.

Ah! See how in so short a time,
My sweet, it has, ah me, shed
Its beauties upon the ground!
O truly stony-hearted nature,
Since such a flower lasts only
From the morning till the evening.

So, if you will heed me, sweet,
While your young years bloom
In this freshest newness,
Gather, gather your youth;
As with this flower, age
Will wither your beauty.[37]

37. Ronsard, in *The Penguin Book of French Verse, Sixteenth to Eighteenth Centuries*, ed. and trans. Geoffrey Brereton, 51.

The delicate balance between the poem's gallant, almost Platonic terminology and its erotic insinuations is perhaps its most distinctive quality.[38]

The first stanza sets up the central simile of the poem: the comparison of the woman to the rose. But the ties between the two are not created merely through an overt simile at the beginning of the poem (something like "My sweet, you are like a rose," etc.). Rather, the first juxtaposition of the two is made when the rose, not the addressee, is presented as the subject of the discourse: "the rose / Which this morning opened / Its crimson robe to the sun." Here an element (the robe) taken from the domain of the subject of the poem (the woman) is used metaphorically to describe the rose, thus creating a temporary inversion of the normal hierarchy between the poem's subject and the vehicle used to address it. This temporary confusion contributes to establishing the intimate ties, even fusion, between the two entities—an impression the speaker, of course, is eager to establish.

Later the real hierarchy between subject and vehicle is set forth, but it has some interesting qualities. Formally it is an overt simile that states the ground for the comparison:[39] the addressee is like the rose in color ("its color like yours"), and since the color has been specified earlier ("crimson"), this might be considered a simple, determined, "closed" simile. But a formally "closed" simile may turn out to be a generator of suggestions and implications—just as when a stone is thrown into the water and hits the surface at one specific point, the beauty it creates arises from the growing concentric circles surrounding the single point of impact.

Here, some of the most suggestive erotic connotations are generated by that simple, "innocent" simile. Let us remember that, in the first place, the rose's petals were compared to a woman's robe, and that this comparison was introduced while describing the *opened* petals. Because of the temporary intentional confusion between subject and vehicle discussed above, and the introduction of the new element (the crimson color), it seems plausible to imagine, at least at a very covert and latent level, images of an opened robe and what may be hidden beneath it.

Besides the delicate balance between the erotic and the Platonic, the

38. Robert Mezey's translation, from Jon Stallworthy's anthology *The Penguin Book of Love Poetry*, 77, distorts that balance by underlining the erotic dimension of the poem: for instance, "votre beauté" becomes in Mezey's translation "your virginity" and the call "cueillez, cueillez votre jeunesse" is translated into the explicit demand "gather me."

39. For a concise and illuminating discussion of simile and metaphor and how they are understood and interpreted, see Geoffrey N. Leech, *A Linguistic Guide to English Poetry*, 151–57.

most important element that Ronsard brings into the tradition of the *amemus* here is the whole dynamic dimension of the speech-situation. The speaker is not just uttering some preconceived ideas and arguments in order to persuade his addressee; rather, his argument comes into existence through the very process of formulating it. In other words, things are happening during the uttering of the speech.

The dramatic aspect of the speech-situation is intensified by the speaker's expressive interjections ("Las! voyez. . . . Las! las!"). The dynamic element is, first, a physical change that occurs in the immediate context in which the utterance is made: "Ah! See how . . . it has, ah me, shed / Its beauties upon the ground." We can imagine the two approaching the rose, followed by the surprised reaction with which the second stanza opens, and we should assume at least some minimal change of time and place ("let us go" implying the change in place).

The crucial fact here is not that the speaker is describing to his addressee some change that has occurred in the world independently of the speech-situation. Rather, we are led to believe that the change occurs in the immediate proximity and during the very moment the speaker is addressing his beloved. Furthermore, this change in the immediate external circumstances triggers a change in the speaker's mind; we can see how this change affects him, and a moment later his tone and entire attitude have been altered. He is no longer the calm, self-assured speaker who invites his beloved to walk in the garden while he delivers an erotic message concealed in some of his descriptions. In the second stanza we see a surprised, shaken person who expresses in a *style coupé* a series of exclamations and protests. The change can also be described in terms of the speech acts that organize the two stanzas: cordial invitation in the first, sorrowful surprise in the second.

The change from the second stanza to the third is less dramatic than that from the first to the second, but nevertheless a dynamic element exists there too. If the elements that define the speech-situation are the speaker and his addressee, the relevant objects in the context, the medium of communication, and the type of speech act conveyed,[40] then something in the last element at least has been changed. We can imagine the speaker recovering, and trying through an intuitive insight to use the surprising experience he has just had in the best possible way. He does this by incorporating it into a "coherent" argument known to us from Asklepiades: since life is short, let us love.

---

40. Leech, *A Linguistic Guide*, 187–88, points out these four elements, though he does not refer to the fourth one in terms of speech acts but rather in a more general and elusive way as "the function of the communication."

In Ronsard's poem this old argument is revived through the dramatization of the line of thinking that produces such an argument, and through the analogy of the rose, which is enlisted as "evidence" to support the argument.

Ronsard was not the first to use this dynamic element in the speech-situation. We can in fact trace it back, though on a much lesser scale, to Horace, who is the first to use the famous expression *carpe diem*. His use of it, however, is not an instance of the specific subgenre in which I am interested since the poem in which it appears has nothing to do with the situation between lovers. Still, it is closely affiliated with our case and probably influenced the specific generic line, Ronsard in particular.[41] After advising his addressee (Leuconoe) to filter his wines and to "cut short far-reaching hopes," Horace remarks that "while we speak, envious time has sped." This acute realization, occurring at the very moment of speaking *(dum loquimur)*, brings him to formulate his memorable phrase: *carpe diem quam minimum credula postero* (Reap the harvest of today, putting as little trust as may be in the morrow!).[42] Thus what might have been merely a philosophical bromide is animated through Horace's reference to the speech-situation.

Ronsard, then, was not the first to introduce the dynamic element of the speech-situation into the *carpe diem* tradition, but, in contrast to Horace's brief remark, Ronsard incorporated it into the *amemus* tradition in a much more elaborate and sophisticated way. What was a relatively marginal remark in Horace becomes the center of Ronsard's ode.

After Ronsard, one could take an example from Robert Herrick: perhaps his "To the Virgins, to Make Much of Time," which is a simplified echo of the tradition, or the elaborate and complex "Corinna's Going A-Maying," which subtly conceals an erotic message in a cheerful quasi-pagan framework.[43] Instead, however, I think it would be more fruitful to turn to another masterpiece of the *amemus* tradition, perhaps even the culmination of some of its motifs: Marvell's "To His Coy Mistress."

> Had we but world enough, and time,
> This coyness, Lady, were no crime.

41. Paul Laumonier, in his comprehensive monograph *Ronsard poète lyrique*, especially 382–91, places this ode within the rich literary tradition of *carpe diem* and more specifically the *carpe florem*. He traces these traditions back to many Greco-Roman and Renaissance sources, highlighting the originality of Ronsard's use of them.

42. Horace, *The Odes and Epodes*, 32–33.

43. Although Cleanth Brooks, in *The Well Wrought Urn*, 54–64, shows the rich network of meanings created in the poem, he ignores its interesting erotic dimension.

We would sit down, and think which way
To walk, and pass our long love's day.
Thou by the Indian Ganges' side
Shouldst rubies find; I by the tide
Of Humber would complain. I would
Love you ten years before the flood:
And you should, if you please, refuse
Till the conversion of the Jews.
My vegetable love should grow
Vaster than empires, and more slow.
An hundred years should go to praise
Thine eyes, and on thy forehead gaze.
Two hundred to adore each breast:
But thirty thousand to the rest.
An age at least to every part,
And the last age should show your heart:
For, Lady, you deserve this state;
Nor would I love at lower rate.

But at my back I always hear
Time's winged chariot hurrying near:
And yonder all before us lie
Deserts of vast eternity.
Thy beauty shall no more be found;
Nor, in the marble vault, shall sound
My echoing song: then worms shall try
That long-preserved virginity:
And your quaint honour turn to dust;
And into ashes all my lust.
The grave's a fine and private place
But none, I think, do there embrace.

Now, therefore, while the youthful hue
Sits on thy skin like morning dew,
And while thy willing soul transpires
At every pore with instant fires,
Now let us sport us while we may;
And now, like amorous birds of prey,
Rather at once our time devour,
Than languish in his slow-chapped power.
Let us roll all our strength, and all
Our sweetness, up into one ball:
And tear our pleasures with rough strife,

Thorough the iron gates of life.
Thus, though we cannot make our sun
Stand still, yet we will make him run.[44]

Marvell's poem resembles Ronsard's "Mignonne" in its triadic structure. Whereas the first stanza evokes images of a calm, unhurried amorous situation, the second presents the cruel face of inexorable time, and the third draws the "inevitable" conclusion: let us make love, here and now. It also contains the inner movement of the speech situation, which enables us to "see" how the speaker's attitude changes in the course of articulating his thoughts.

In Marvell's poem, however, the dynamic element within the speech-situation is less dramatic than in Ronsard's. This is not only because it is not accompanied by emotional exclamations, but also because there is no concrete object that has been changed in the immediate context. The only thing that changes is the mind of the speaker, who refers to the grim reality after being absorbed in dreamlike fantasizing about the limitlessness of "world and time."

Thus the dynamic element is still present, but in a lower key. Needless to say, Marvell has not produced a mere watered-down version of Ronsard's dramatic power; he contributes other, equally interesting factors to the *amemus* tradition. First, we have the playful syllogism. We have seen how in every *amemus* poem there is some kind of argument. Marvell creates a syllogism with the first two stanzas as the premises and the last as the conclusion. The first opens with a hypothetical statement that may be roughly paraphrased as follows: If we had all the time in the world, I could have expressed my love at leisure. The second states that time is very limited. The conclusion is presented as if logically deduced ("therefore"!): We must love here and now. This possible paraphrase, aside from diminishing Marvell's marvelous poetic achievement, also exposes the invalidity of the syllogism, which was camouflaged by the speaker's rhetoric. As a matter of fact, after we have the "skeleton" of the two first premises, one can imagine a more justifiable conclusion (something like "Therefore, I will express my love in a more brief and condensed manner") than the one Marvell chose.[45]

But Marvell, of course, is not interested in such an anemic proposition, and he prepared his desired conclusion from the very beginning by planting the idea that coyness is a crime. "Syllogism," a straightforward

---

44. Andrew Marvell, *The Complete Poems*, 50–51.
45. One might also mention the fact that moving from a *factual* statement (about time) to a *recommendation* is very problematic in logic.

technical term in logic, may also suggest a subtle and deceitful way of misleading someone. Marvell's argument, which uses the outward form of logic, has no real validity. But Marvell the poet is interested in rhetoric and not in logic. If logical formulae will achieve the desired goal, he will make the most of them.

Besides the "tricky" uses of the logical form, Marvell's poem excels in the playful suggestion of erotic meanings. The description of the beloved's body in the first stanza seems to move downward from the top (eyes and forehead, then breasts), but instead of continuing with specifics, he retreats to the general and vague expression "But thirty thousand to the rest." The next couplet involves, again, an erotic insinuation: "An age at least to every part, / and the last age should show your . . ." At this point in the reading one might claim that some possibilities will arise in the reader's mind, first among them not necessarily the heart, with which Marvell concludes the couplet, smiling again at our titillation.

If we accept such playful associations as a legitimate and even desirable part of the reading process, the second stanza offers us even wilder possibilities. For instance, the use of "quaint" may remind us of "cunt,"[46] and there is the image of worms trying the addressee's virginity. This image, while functioning as part of the required "shock treatment," also has some interesting connotations of *penetrating* virginity. These smuggled sexual images culminate toward the end of the poem with the phallic picture of a sweet ball breaking through a gate (lines 41–44).

One other enchanting quality of Marvell's poem is the refined ironic tone of the speaker, which defies a single unequivocal reading. Is the speaker, for instance, truly absorbed in the imaginative series of hyperboles in the first stanza? Does he really believe in the double extolling (of his lady and of himself) at the end of the first stanza? Whereas the first line is an explicit tribute addressed to his lady ("For, Lady, you deserve this state"), the last line of the stanza ("Nor would I love at lower rate") suggests ironic self-praise: I have high standards, I do not bestow my admiration on everyone. It seems to me that these questions about the tone of the poem are hard to answer, and that this is one of the factors contributing to its complexity. One may also note the surprising inversion of the motif of the sun that occurs at the end. In Catullus's poem the sun's motion was a threat and the source of anxiety, whereas here the speaker wants to join the sun's motion and to dominate it in erotic exaltation—and to overcome it, paradoxically, not by arresting it but by spurring it on.

---

46. This possibility is raised in Kermode and Hollander, *The Oxford Anthology of English Literature*, 1148.

These elements, together with some others we have not discussed, make Marvell's poem one of the major achievements of the *amemus* tradition. One could argue that after the seventeenth century this tradition disappeared as a central and interesting factor in the literary scene. The eighteenth century cultivated new models and sensibilities that pushed the *amemus* aside. Still, generic traditions do not vanish into thin air. Sometimes some of their elements interweave with elements of other genres. Sometimes these new hybrids "found" a new generic line, sometimes they only indicate the end of a clear line of generic succession. Prior's "While Blooming Youth" is an example of the latter possibility. It represents an attempt to interweave elements from the *amemus* tradition with other elements. Consider some lines which seem to be taken verbatim from the *amemus* tradition:

> While blooming Youth, and gay delight
> Sit on thy rosy Cheek confest . . .
> Take Heed, my Dear, Youth flies apace:
> As well as Cupid, Time is blind:
> Soon must those Glories of thy Face
> The Fate of vulgar Beauty find . . .
> Haste, Celia, haste, while Youth invites:
> Obey kind Cupid's present Voice;
> Fill ev'ry Sense with soft Delights
> And give thy Soul a loose to Joys.[47]

One could easily add some brief transitional lines to make the above a typical *amemus* poem. But Prior uses elements of the *amemus* to other ends. Instead of promoting the idea that immediate lovemaking will counteract time's cruelty, Prior's speaker advocates the ideals of "Kindness and Constancy" and paints a harmonious picture (à la Baucis and Philemon) of living, loving, and growing old together:

> So shall I court thy dearest Truth;
> When Beauty ceases to engage:
> So thinking on thy charming Youth,
> I'll love it o'er again in Age:
> So Time it self our Raptures shall improve;
> While still We wake to Joy, and live to Love.[48]

47. Geoffrey Tillotson et al., eds., *Eighteenth-Century English Literature*, 223.
48. Ibid., 224.

It is very easy to recognize elements of the *amemus* in Prior's poem, but this is exactly my argument. Here we are dealing only with isolated *elements* that have become servants of other masters, i.e., their organizing principle is no longer that of the *amemus*.

Another belated appearance of the *amemus* tradition, which uses elements of the established tradition but carries them in totally new directions, is Keats's "This Living Hand":

> This living hand, now warm and capable
> Of earnest grasping, would, if it were cold
> And in the icy silence of the tomb,
> So haunt thy days and chill thy dreaming nights
> That thou wouldst wish thine own heart dry of blood,
> So in my veins red life might stream again,
> And thou be conscience-calm'd. See here it is—
> I hold it towards you.[49]

Keats's poem seems to deviate from the great line of the *amemus* tradition in that in it the hierarchies are almost totally reversed. In the *amemus*, horrifying pictures of death were used only to persuade the addressee to prize the joys of love: here they are dominant. It is apparent that there is no perspective of joyous love here, and it is revealing that even when speaking of death the speaker does not portray a shared death. Either the speaker is dead and his beloved is alive ("haunt thy days and chill thy dreaming nights") or the other way around ("thine own heart dry of blood / So in my veins red life might stream again"). Moreover, the only real moment of connection between the two seems to take place "in the icy silence of the tomb"—but it is a deadly touch. Moreover, in the typical *amemus* the lovers succeed, through their love, in "catching" the day, in putting a halt to time's devouring clutches. In Keat's poem, on the other hand, the lover succeeds in catching his beloved's hand, but it is a deadly grasp, epitomizing time's victory, not its defeat. By realizing the metaphor of "catching," Keats produces a totally reversed effect.

Someone unaware of the *amemus* tradition could read the poem as an expression of Keats's view that love is impossible, and of the romantics' fascination with morbid pictures of love.[50] Actually, one could claim that any rewriting of an *amemus* poem from a romantic point of view would

---

49. John Keats, *Complete Poems*, 384.
50. Mario Praz's *Romantic Agony* gives an illuminating presentation of this aspect of the romantic movement.

result either in a gloomy depiction of the impossibility of real, corporal love, or in a morbid description of scenes from the grave. In any case the true epicurean spirit of the *amemus* is no longer present. Still, the situation of the lover addressing his beloved in an attempt to achieve some kind of unity may remind one of the literary tradition of the *amemus*. But evoking this tradition only sharpens the contrast between the traditional elements and the new sensibility.

Moving on to the twentieth century, we may find some echoes of the *amemus* tradition, but often these echoes only underscore the distance between the traditional framework and the new sensibilities developed in modern poetics. T. S. Eliot's "The Love Song of J. Alfred Prufrock" is a good example of this breach. The speaker in the poem is making a pointed allusion to Marvell's "To His Coy Mistress" and to the entire *amemus* tradition associated with Marvell's poem. The allusion is made, first by creating a speaker who contemplates the possibility of addressing a woman; through constant reference to the question of whether there is "enough time"; and, at one point, by evoking the concluding image of Marvell's poem:

> And would it have been worth it, after all . . .
> To have squeezed the universe into a ball.[51]

When we compare the typical stand of the speaker in Marvell, or in any *amemus* poem, to the speaker in Eliot's poem the extent to which the latter has divorced itself from the former becomes clear. Eliot's speaker is caught in his inner monologue, intimidated by the very presence of women, and trapped in images of sickness and death, as the opening lines indicate:

> Let us go then, you and I,
> When the evening is spread out against the sky
> Like a patient etherized upon a table;[52]

The irony is that the "you" addressed here and elsewhere in the poem is probably not a woman at all but rather a part or aspect of an inner monologue of the speaker who ponders whether to dare address a woman. For such a speaker it is inconceivable to participate in any social discourse ("In the room the women come and go / Talking of Michelangelo"), let alone to gallantly address a woman. Thus, the literary

51. T. S. Eliot, *Collected Poems, 1909–1962*, 3.
52. Ibid.

allusion sharpens the *contrast* between the respective texts. Eliot's poem indirectly expresses its rejection of the idea that lovemaking is a viable answer to the inexorability of time, which is the central presupposition of the *amemus* subgenre.

I think there are two reasons for this rejection, both rooted in the modern world view and sensibilities. First, the sense of humanity's transitory state in the universe has become too deep to be soothed by physical love; the modern poet cannot cure his angst by making love. And lovemaking, in its turn, has ceased to unequivocally signify a liberating act of union. Second, as part of the questioning of traditional norms, hierarchies, and values, the figure of the dominating male who tries to coax a woman toward lovemaking has lost much of its viability. In Eliot, we find something radically different from the idea of the chaste woman confronted by an ambitious, self-satisfied suitor. What we get instead is a realistic picture of an intimidated man, desperately trying to overcome his fears and ultimately caught in his own unfulfilled desires.

THE *AMEMUS,* SPEECH ACTS, AND LITERARY GENRES

This rapid analysis of a few prime examples of the *amemus* tradition, and of some of its echoes in modern literature, does not pretend to provide a full interpretation of these complex and beautiful poems. My sole purpose has been to examine the elements that constitute the genre, as well as certain other elements that give variety to the tradition. The elements I consider essential are thematic (reference to the brevity of life, an exhortation to love, and an attempt to deduce the second from the first) and rhetorical (a speaker addressing the object of his love-persuasion, using some syllogistic devices).

The genre's variety is expressed on the prosodic level (among others): Asklepiades used the meter named after him (an extension of the Glyconic);[53] Catullus wrote his poem in hendecasyllables;[54] Ronsard wrote in octameter and used rhymed stanzas (a-a-b-c-c-b, etc.); and Marvell used the popular iambic tetrameter organized in couplets. There are also different ways of symbolically filling out the schema, the most conspicuous of which are the two basic symbols given for the fleetingness of time: Catullus and Marvell use the sun (though Marvell gives a twist

---

53. On Asklepiadean meter, see Paul Harvey, ed., *The Oxford Companion to Classical Literature,* 270.

54. Ibid., 271.

to the conventional symbol); and Ronsard, although he does refer to the sun and its movement, focuses on the rose, which is linked to a rich tradition in Latin, Italian, and French literature.[55] One may add the basic rhetorical strategies used in the process of persuasion ("shock treatment," the enticements of love, sophisticated syllogism, etc.), or the degree of dynamism introduced into the speech-situation, or the type of erotic sensibility the poems express.

These factors, and others, contribute to the sense of rich diversity that exists within the framework of the constitutive rules. This small survey can demonstrate that generic rules do not confine the author, but rather provide him or her with a context in which to express individual talent. By the same token, the generic rules are colored by the special qualities of the language, culture, and period in which the particular work is written.

We have also seen how, at some point in the generic tradition, the integrative set of rules starts to disintegrate. We have seen how, when this happens, sometimes generic elements are incorporated into other frameworks (as in Prior's poem); sometimes the *amemus* tradition is invoked only in order to present a reversed, macabre version of it (as in Keats) or to create a contrast between its premises and the new, modernist sensibility (Eliot). Needless to say, in some cases it is hard for us to tell whether the generic tradition is still operating or whether we are witnessing a different kind of phenomenon. One could claim, for instance, that Prior's and Keats's poems are still part of the *amemus* subgenre; however, I hope my presentation has shown that these poems, even if so considered, should not be seen as typical or paradigmatic instances.

Having made these general observations on the *amemus* tradition, it is time to go back to the theoretical issue with which I began this chapter: the relevance of the concept of speech acts to the theory of genre. First, I will propose an analysis of the *amemus* according to the model provided by speech-act theory:

1. The "propositional content" contains a reference to a future act of love (A) between the male speaker (S) and the female hearer (H).
2. The "preparatory conditions" are that S believes the following: (a) that both S and H are able to engage in A; (b) that H has

---

55. For an instructive discussion of the tradition of the rose motif in Greco-Roman and Renaissance literature, see John Symonds's "The Pathos of the Rose in Poetry"; and Laumonier, *Ronsard poète lyrique*, 382–91.

some inhibitions that have to be overcome; (c) that time is limited; and (d) that A is the best way to react to the constraints of time.

3. The "sincerity condition" is that S is really interested in A.

4. The "essential condition" states that S's utterance counts as an attempt to get H to do A.

It may be possible to improve some of the specific formulations in this proposal, but it captures the main features of an *amemus*. One should note, though, that these rules are not laws. A speaker may violate some of them for various reasons. In fact, rules become conspicuous precisely in those cases in which they are not followed. By formulating the rules, one can distinguish more clearly between different kinds of nonconformity.

If the speaker, after presenting himself as a typical speaker of an *amemus*, asks his hearer to go to the zoo with him (where the term "zoo" is understood literally), we have no *amemus* since the "propositional content" is not present. By the same token, a reference to a past act of love shared by S and H leads in a different poetical direction.

An *amemus* in which S declared his impotence would be very bizarre (or funny), as would be an *amemus* in which S addressed an animal, or even the dead soul of his beloved—because it would violate "preparatory condition" 2a. Addressing a prostitute in an *amemus* would seem strange because of condition 2b. Were the speaker to state that he and his hearer do indeed have "world enough and time," it would violate condition 2c and result in a different sort of poem. A speaker who, after raising the classical *amemus* points, recommended a devoted religious life as a response to the fleetingness of time might perhaps create a beautiful poem, but, having violated condition 2d, it would be a very strange *amemus*. Finally, if S concluded his poem with the line "But as for me, Lesbia, I am not really interested in your kisses," he would be violating at least conditions 3 and 4, thus undermining some fundamental elements of an *amemus*.

Some of these violations would completely exclude the utterance from the *amemus* category, while others would result in creating a tension or a contrast with this specific literary tradition. It is precisely the above set of rules that helps us to explain how specific poems may be related to the tradition or deviate from it (and if so, how and to what extent). In other words, these rules are intended to reflect the *paradigmatic* instances of this particular subgenre. One has to be aware that formulating generic rules, and then choosing paradigmatic texts that exemplify those rules, involves a certain circularity. But as long as this "hermeneutic circle" succeeds—in describing conspicuous patterns of similarity between the texts, and in demonstrating that these generic characteristics have been real factors in literary history, shaping how writers cope with a subject and building expectations in readers—then it should not be regarded as a "vicious circle."

Thus my proposed analysis based on speech-act theory turns out to be more than a mere intellectual exercise. It is in fact a useful way of describing the rules underlying the *amemus*. Now if the model for analyzing speech acts is found to be useful in looking at the *amemus*, can we draw some general inference from it? Tempting as it may be, I doubt it. We cannot infer, from a single case, general statements about the relevance of speech-act theory to *all* literary genres.

We can, however, draw a limited inference, namely, that cases exist to which the speech-act model is pertinent; it is pertinent to those cases in which *the organizing principle of the text can be described in terms of a distinct communicative situation*. It may thus be very relevant to some small forms of lyrical poetry (subgenres), or to a limited number of narrative forms (the confession, for instance); but to many other literary forms and genres it will be irrelevant. One may of course describe drama as the exchange of speech acts between characters, but it seems to me futile to talk of tragedy, for example, in terms of a speech act. By the same token, attempts to describe the novel as a kind of elaborated speech act will provide little insight, precisely because it is hard to define the specifics of the communicative situation that constitutes a novel, or that constitutes the relationships between the narrator and his addressee. The reason for this is, of course, the richness and diversity of the novel's tradition.

Thus when Pratt tries to describe the novel in terms of a speech act,[56] she ends up either with characteristics that seem vague and trivial ("the narrative utterance's . . . relevance is tellability"), or else unjustifiably confines herself to one particular phase of the novel's history, namely the classical nineteenth-century period (her "unmarked case")—and even then, her description is unsatisfactory in many respects. Pratt's problematical attempt is symptomatic, and its weaknesses attest to the fault inherent in any theoretical attempt to impose the concept of speech acts on the heterogeneous field of literature. The speech-act model may be pertinent to the analysis of some literary genres, but it is by no means an adequate basis for a general theory of genres.

Having restricted the scope of the relevance of speech acts, we still have some interesting issues to consider. First, in those cases to which the concept of a speech act is pertinent, do we face some kind of genuine

---

56. See Pratt, *Toward a Speech Act Theory of Literary Discourse*, especially 201–10.

speech act or an imitation of a speech act? These two basic approaches were presented in the first section of this chapter, and it is now time for me to formulate my own attitude toward them.

The *amemus* tradition seems to fit nicely into the mimetic perspectives, especially as articulated by Smith: the poet is representing a speech situation of exhortation to love. Note, by the way, that I refer to a distinct speech situation, without postulating that the poet must create a speaker who is distinct from himself (a "persona"). Such views have been advanced by various advocates of the "New Criticism"[57] and in recent discussions of "dramatic monologue."[58] I find this preeminence given to the poet-speaker relationship an unnecessary restriction. We may experience the *amemus* as a kind of dramatic monologue, without assuming that the poems' speakers differ (in their attitudes, feelings, convictions, etc.) from Asklepiades, Catullus, Ronsard, or Marvell.

What makes us experience these poems as a kind of dramatic monologue, or as imitations of speech acts, is the obvious *difference between the addressee and the reader,* not that between the poet and the speaker. Thus my proposal to take *the entire speech situation* as a point of departure has clear advantages, since it does not force us to make superfluous assumptions, and it enables us to see the relationship between two similar phenomena: the difference existing between the poet and the speaker, and that (its "reflection") existing between the addressee and the reader.

The *amemus* therefore seems to corroborate the view that, whenever the concept of a speech act is involved in our description of a generic tradition, we have a case of a *represented* speech act. Whereas this claim is in accordance with Smith's formulations on the subject, her insistence on the fact that *all* poems are representations of speech acts seems an unnecessary and unjustified generalization.

One might question such a generalization by looking at a poem that totally differs in tone and in subject matter from the *amemus* poems we were reading: Sergei Esenin's beautiful and touching suicide-poem:

> Goodbye, my friend, goodbye.
> My dear, you are in my heart.

57. See, for instance, Cleanth Brooks and Robert Penn Warren's discussion on tone in *Understanding Poetry,* 112–15.

58. Alan Sinfield, for example, defines the term in its broad sense as "a poem in the first person spoken by, or almost entirely by, someone who is indicated not to be the poet" (*Dramatic Monologue,* 8). Robert Langbaum's *Poetry of Experience,* though interested in the dramatic monologue's complex effect rather than in its formalistic definitions, also regards the poet-speaker relationship as the touchstone of the poem.

Predestined separation
Promises a future meeting

Goodbye, my friend, without handshakes and words,
Do not grieve and sadden your brow,—
In this life there's nothing new in dying,
But nor, of course, is living any newer.[59]

I would like to claim that the effectiveness of this poem stems precisely from our awareness of the concrete historical situation in which it was written—on the eve of Esenin's suicide. Furthermore, the poem can be described as a genuine speech act (of the type of a "departure" or a "farewell") *addressed from the poet to his reader*. Any attempt to describe the poem as an imitation of a departure denies the relevance of the circumstances of its composition to its interpretation. Such a reading, "severed" from the circumstances of composition, as proposed by Smith, would not do justice to how we actually experience and interpret the poem.[60]

There is thus no reason to postulate a representation of speech acts in all poetry as Smith does. Introducing the concept of imitation or representation is justified only where there is a discrepancy between the elements that constitute the communicative situation of poet-reader and the communicative situation evoked by the poem. This is the case when there is reason to differentiate between the poet and the speaker, or between the addressee and the reader, or when the poet refers to the specific situation of composition, different from the communicative situation of poet-reader (for example, Wordsworth's "Composed upon Westminister Bridge"). Needless to say, we can find very many poems in which it is feasible and fruitful to make the distinction and to describe the poem as a represented speech act. I can even concede that this is the case in most poems in which a speech act is involved. But still, recognizing the majority does not entail ignoring a minority or postulating the majority situation as a precondition for every poem.

To sum up, my basic attitude is to caution against impetuous generalizations; the concept of a speech act is relevant only to some forms and genres of literature; and when it is relevant, in most (but not necessarily all) cases we have a represented speech act.

To conclude this chapter, I would like to make two remarks, one

---

59. Sergei Esenin, "Goodbye, My Friend," in Gordon McVay, *Esenin, A Life*, 288.

60. Another famous example of such a direct line of communication between poet and reader, expressing a genuine speech act, can be found in Baudelaire's "Au lecteur," the opening poem of *Les Fleurs du mal*.

theoretical and the other historical. So far I have concluded that the *amemus* can be described according to the speech-act model, and that it is a represented speech act. But is it a representation of one (genuine) speech act of the type of (genuine) exhortation to love? This does not seem to be an adequate solution. If each of us tries to imagine (or, better, to remember) the actual methods people use in this kind of persuasion in the real world, it will become apparent that the *amemus* is not an imitation of a preexisting, genuine type of speech act. Our attempts at persuasion in reality are not only less elegant and coherent and more clumsy, but also do not usually make such a compact, focused, frontal attack on the issue. The would-be seducer in extraliterary experience is more likely to suggest that the woman come and listen to a record, or have a drink, rather than begin formulating pseudosyllogisms.

One may describe the situation as "an imitation of some speech sequence, rather than of a speech act"[61] or, even better, as a representation of a composition of speech acts. In this composition we may discern some basic, genuine speech acts such as persuading, arguing, stating. The unique combination of these in the *amemus* tradition constitutes what one could call the "literary act" of the *amemus*. This stress is important if we think that it is better to keep the number of genuine linguistic speech acts as small as possible and to describe speech sequences as combinations and compositions of a limited number of certain basic speech acts.[62]

The historical observation with which I want to conclude this chapter is that there is a move in the *amemus* tradition from the stage of establishing, crystalizing, and writing in accordance with the generic conventions, to a stage in which the generic conventions are only evoked in the form of literary allusions. Recognizing elements of the *amemus* tradition in modern literature, for instance, may remind us only of the difference or even the contrast between the established tradition and the new text. It is sometimes difficult to decide when the coherent body of rules is still in effect and when it has already disintegrated as a productive factor, and every case should be examined carefully. I think, however, that the speech-act model can provide us with a clue to such decisions. The crucial question we should ask is whether the new text complies with the *preparatory rules* of the *amemus*. These rules (as in regular speech acts) express the *cultural presuppositions* writers should share in order to participate in a successful continuation of the subgenre. As we have seen,

61. Brinker, *Representation and Meaning in the Fictional Work*, 68.
62. For some arguments against increasing the number of genuine speech acts, see Searle, "The Logical Status of Fictional Discourse," 64.

when these cultural presuppositions change, when modern attitudes toward the questions of love and life change, the genre itself ceases to be productive.

The examples of the *amemus* may also support the hypothesis that we can trace two phases in such a development. In the first, "transitional" phase, elements of the genre are incorporated into other, different poetic frameworks (Prior, Keats). Second, the generic tradition is alluded to in order to underscore a contrast between the old and the new cultivated sensibilities (Eliot). This description coincides with what Claudio Guillén calls the move from genre to "anti-genre" in literary history,[63] but I think we should not ignore the various forms of the "transitional" phase. The swing of the pendulum of literary history is more complicated than this sort of opposition suggests.

63. Guillén, *Literature as System*.

Chapter 6

Concluding Remarks

After four excursions into four different theoretical lands, it is time to adopt a bird's-eye view and make some final observations. During my discussion of the four "deep metaphors," I tried to rehabilitate old-fashioned concepts (e.g., the biological analogy) by pointing out in them aspects still viable and valid, and at other times I was obliged to express some reservations concerning too-fashionable notions (e.g., the hasty application of Wittgenstein's family resemblance). All in all, I tried to give each of the four analogies its maximum credit as a potentially fruitful theoretical perspective.

We can now ask whether any of the four deserves to be privileged. The answer is no. Each can shed some light on some of the diverse problems of literary genres, and none can supplant or displace the others.

The biological analogy can illuminate some problems of the relationships among genres and explain their evolution over long periods of time, their emergence into cultural dominance, and their eventual eclipse. The family analogy provides us with some insights into how paradigmatic works are perceived as the "founding fathers" of a genre, and how generic models and conventions are transmitted through the "family tree" of a genre: how a writer strives to shape his own version of a generic convention, growing up and achieving maturity through intricate relationships with paternal and sibling figures. The institutional metaphor brings us to dramatic genres where we may discern various conventions designed to help us accept the artifact as "natural." The idea that an institution is a system of interrelated abstract roles led me to analyze one version of comedy in such terms. Finally, the speech-act analogy is most illuminating with certain genres in which the situation of a speaker, and sometimes of an addressee, is represented. It can shed light on some short forms of poetry (as I have tried to show) and also make us more sensitive to works that evoke a speaker, or narrator, who utters his words in a speech-like situation. Each one of these analogies can do something its rivals cannot. Each succeeds in shedding light on different genres or on different aspects of how genres are structured, interrelated, and develop.

Are the four analogies the only ones that can contribute to genre theory? I would not dare to suggest such a restriction. As long as the mind strives to understand, to describe, and to explain literary genres, we may anticipate new and fruitful analogies. As long as this process of trying out new analogies is kept within bounds by the critical awareness that only a few of them can be appropriate in any given situation, the useless will not overwhelm and obscure the useful.

What makes an analogy fruitful, or at least a serious candidate for application? I cannot provide any mechanism for producing such analogies (what philosophers of science call a procedure of discovery), but there is one general observation I can suggest. Mary Hesse, in her classical discussion of the role analogies play in scientific discourse, describes the basic structure of analogies when used in a cognitive, scientific way:

> When we take a collection of billiard balls in random motion as a model for gas, we are not asserting that billiard balls are in all respects like gas particles, for billiard balls are red or white, and hard and shiny, and we are not intending to suggest that gas molecules have these properties. We are in fact saying that gas molecules are *analogous* to billiard balls, and the relation of analogy means that there are some properties of billiard balls which are not found in molecules. Let us call those properties we know belong to billiard balls and not to molecules the *negative analogy* of the model. Motion and impact, on the other hand, are just the properties of billiard balls that we do want to ascribe to molecules in our model, and these we can call the *positive analogy*. Now the important thing about this kind of model-thinking in science is that there will generally be some properties of the model about which we do not yet know whether they are positive or negative analogies; these are the interesting properties, because, as I shall

argue, they allow us to make new predictions. Let us call this third set of properties the *neutral analogy*.[1]

Thus an analogy should be embraced only if it clearly offers elements for both a *positive analogy* and a *neutral analogy* (as defined by Hesse). If the *positive analogy* justifies introducing it in the first place, it is the neutral parts that are the most intriguing. Warren, in an astute observation, points out that generic rules have a status similar to that of institutional rules: "One can work through, express oneself through, existing institutions, create new ones, or get on, so far as possible, without sharing in polities or rituals."[2] If this *positive analogy* justifies introducing the institutional analogy, it is certainly the "neutral analogy," especially the sociological concept of interrelated roles, on which I have focused my attention. One thing I have tried to do is to show that this *neutral analogy* can successfully be applied to a dramatic genre and thereby *become a positive analogy*. Or, to take another example, the fact that a "family tree" resembles how we describe the writers who participate in a certain generic tradition opens the way for exploring the relationships between these writers in the dialectical terms of parent-child relations. In other words, I have found the four analogies fruitful because there are aspects that link both phenomena beyond the ones that justified its introduction. Through this process of finding the neutral analogies that become positive ones, one develops new insights into the basic structure as well as into the diverse manifestations of literary genres. It is in these "neutral" areas of analogies that the theoretical challenge, and reward, await us.

One of the things that makes Heather Dubrow's concise introductory book on genre so suggestive is precisely her awareness of the important and fruitful aspects of analogical thinking applied to genres. At one point, when discussing *The Jew of Malta*, she introduces the analogy between how a specific text is related to generic norms and how actual physical objects may relate to the color spectrum: "no one genre, no one hue appears in isolation, and none appears in its purest state."[3] Pointing to this "positive analogy" seems to trigger other observations related to some pertinent, "neutral analogies": when a text conforms to a single generic pattern, it resembles a primary color; when it combines different literary forms, it is analogous to secondary colors (orange, violet); and when it moves between distinguishable but related genres, it reminds us

---

1. Mary B. Hesse, *Models and Analogies in Science,* 8.
2. Wellek and Warren, *Theory of Literature,* 226.
3. Dubrow, *Genre,* 28.

of intermediate colors such as yellow-green; and as colors appear in actual objects in different degrees of saturation, so a work may display, more or less vividly, the characteristics of its genre.[4]

At another point Dubrow suggests that there may be a fruitful analogy between literary genres and human personalities: "Like different person-alities, different genres are distinguished from one another by which characteristics predominate: almost all poetic forms have predilections for certain prosodic patterns, just as almost all human beings have some urge to aggression, but the extent to which such tendencies are realized and their role in the total pattern of the psyche or the form in question varies tremendously."[5]

This last analogy seems to me a bit problematic, because it presup-poses a "basic" set of characteristics of the literary text that can be expressed in different forms and degrees in different genres. In trying to define this set we may face some unresolved problems as to what exactly are those true, fundamental traits: why, for instance, should we assume that prosodic patterns are the fundamental "drives" that are differently expressed and transformed in different genres and not, say, plot struc-tures or characters, or certain attitudes toward the world? It is difficult to agree on what those "ultimates" are, and one may wonder why a narrative pattern is an expression of a "predilection for certain prosodic patterns" and not a basic textual "predilection" in its own right. Thus the personality analogy seems to rely on certain problematic assumptions about our ability to formulate the fundamental, underlying "predilec-tions" of the literary text. However, I do not wish to further analyze or evaluate Dubrow's proposed analogies, but rather to emphasize the basic *fruitfulness* of the process of analogical thinking with regard to genres as evident in her book. Note, that even when we reject a specific analogy we may, during the process of evaluating its potential explanatory force, still gain some fresh insights into how literary genres are organized and interrelated.

Is it possible to characterize any especially desirable areas from which our analogues ought to be drawn? And more specifically, need the imaginative distance between the two things compared by the analogy be as narrow as possible in order to guarantee a fruitful perspective? While I cannot answer the first question (and I suspect that such a generalization is impossible in principle), answering the second one is simpler, and it is a negative one. In the four previous chapters, I began with an analogue quite remote from literature (biological species) and

---

4. Ibid., 28–29.
5. Ibid., 7. See also a brief elaboration of this analogy on 117–18.

ended with an analogue very close to it (speech acts). Still, I do not think that this movement from more distant analogues to less distant ones can be correlated with a progression from less fruitful to more fruitful (or vice versa). In short, the conceptual distance between the subject of the analogue and the phenomenon of genre neither determines nor predicts the fruitfulness of a given analogy.

Much more useful than proximity is complexity. The analogies used here designate very complex and multilayered phenomena. If we were to list all the traits that we associate with each of the four concepts, we would end up with very long (and hierarchical) inventories. From these long series of characteristics, clearly some meaningful positive analogy eventually emerges.

In addition to being a complex and multifaceted phenomenon, I think a fruitful analogue must also combine static with dynamic elements, as do all four of the analogies used in this study. The biological analogy designates a relatively stable division of the kingdom of animals, but also evokes evolution, transformation, and mutation. Families draw boundaries between people, but also promote their interrelationships. Institutions mold human activities into distinct channels, but also act as frameworks enabling people to express their uniqueness and their new ideas. We depend on a stock of existing speech acts in order to communicate efficiently, but we can also manipulate the existing sets, refining and rearranging them to respond to everchanging situations.

Thus, although perhaps one cannot postulate any specific areas from which fruitful analogies ought to be drawn, one may reasonably stipulate that any analogy chosen should offer elements of both *stability* and *change*.

A final word about pluralism: as I stated in the introductory chapter, exploring the four analogies rather than restricting myself to only one of them is a crucial part of what I consider to be my basic pluralistic approach. "Pluralism," however, may be understood in a variety of ways, as Wayne Booth reminds us in *Critical Understanding: The Powers and Limits of Pluralism*. According to Booth, the term "pluralism" may refer to four distinguishable conceptual attitudes: disguised *monism*, which in fact would establish a single perspective and integrate the different analogies into one comprehensive theory; *skepticism*, which avoids a commitment to any specific analogy since, from the very beginning, it doubts the viability of all analogies; *eclecticism*, which gathers what seem to be the best parts of any theory and glues them together; and *methodological pluralism*, which encourages the pursuit of different theoretical frameworks even though they may clash.

Using Booth's terms, I think the best place to locate my approach would be somewhere between eclecticism and methodological pluralism. Booth himself admits that there is no clear-cut distinction between the two: "The borderline between the two attitudes is thus extremely difficult to determine, and one might do better to think simply of a continuum, ranging from full eclectics, who deliberately hack other critics' works into fragments, salvaging whatever proves useful, to the full pluralists we are coming to: those who claim to embrace at least two enterprises in their full integrity, without reducing the two to one."[6]

The slightly evaluative language Booth is using tempts one, of course, to identify oneself with the more dignified methodological pluralism. Still, I cannot deny that there is an eclectic aspect in my approach. Certainly there is one thing that explains why a radical type of pluralism is not needed here; namely, my claim that the different theoretical-analogical perspectives can, at least in principle, achieve some "division of labor" among themselves. Rather than being taxed to serve as a comprehensive explanation of all aspects of literary genres, each perspective should be left to throw light on its own particular corner of this large and heterogeneous field.

Whereas Booth tries to see how a theorist will react in the face of irreconcilable statements such as "literature is X" and "literature is Y," the statements with which I prefer to grapple have the form of "genres are *like* X" and "genres are *like* Y." Thus, instead of trying to decide between these statements, I try to see *to what extent* genres are *both* like X *and* like Y. This methodological approach perhaps does not earn me the title of a true and committed pluralist in Booth's terms, but as long as my approach can promote our understanding of literary genres, I am willing to be called an eclectic.

---

6. Wayne C. Booth, *Critical Understanding: The Powers and Limits of Pluralism*, 21.

Bibliography

The bibliography consists of two parts: (1) artistic texts and (2) theoretical and critical works. The first list includes all literary texts that have been quoted and discussed, however briefly. Of the theoretical list, most items are relevant to genre theory; the rest are primarily critical analyses of a specific genre, writer, or text.

Artistic Texts

Adams, M. H., et al., eds. *The Norton Anthology of English Literature,* fourth edition. New York and London, 1979.

Austen, Jane. *The Novels of Jane Austen,* ed. R. W. Chapman. London, New York, and Toronto, 1954.

Baudelaire, Charles. *Les Fleurs du mal.* Paris, 1972.

Beaumarchais. *The Barber of Seville and The Marriage of Figaro,* trans. John Wood. Harmondsworth, 1964.

Blackmore, Richard. *Prince Arthur.* London, 1695. (Facsimile edition, Scolar Press. Menston, Yorkshire, 1971.)

Brereton, Geoffrey, ed. and trans. *The Penguin Book of French Verse, Sixteenth to Eighteenth Centuries.* Harmondsworth, 1958.

Catullus. *The Poems of Gaius Valerius Catullus,* trans. F. W. Corish. Cambridge, Mass., The Loeb Classical Library, 1962.

Cervantes Saavedra, Miguel de. *The Adventures of Don Quixote,* trans. J. M. Cohen. Harmondsworth, 1952.

Eliot, T. S. *Collected Poems, 1909–1962.* London, 1963.

Esenin, Sergei. "Goodbye, My Friend." In Gordon McVay, *Esenin, A Life.* Ann Arbor, 1976.

Homer. *The Odyssey,* trans. Robert Fitzgerald. Garden City, N.Y., 1963.

Horace. *The Odes and Epodes,* trans. C. E. Bennet. Cambridge, Mass., The Loeb Classical Library, 1927.

Jay, Peter, ed. *The Greek Anthology, A Selection in Modern Verse Translations.* Harmondsworth, 1981.

Keats, John. *Complete Poems,* ed. Jack Stillinger. Cambridge, Mass., 1982.

Kermode, Frank, and John Hollander, et al., eds. *The Oxford Anthology of English Literature.* New York, 1973.

Marivaux. *Up from the Country/Infidelities/The Game of Love and Chance,* trans. Leonard Tancock and David Cohen. Harmondsworth, 1980.

Marvell, Andrew. *The Complete Poems,* ed. Elizabeth Story Donno. London, 1972.

Mickiewicz, Adam. *Pan Tadeusz, or The Last Foray in Lithuania,* trans. George Rapall Noyes. London, 1917.

————. *Pan Tadeusz, or The Last Foray in Lithuania*, trans. Watson Kirkconnell. New York, 1962.

Milton, John. *Paradise Lost*, ed. Merritt Y. Hughes. Indianapolis, 1962.

Molière. *Tartuffe and Other Plays*, trans. Donald M. Frame. New York and Scarborough, Ontario, 1967.

Plautus. *The Pot of Gold and Other Plays*, trans. E. F. Watling. Harmondsworth, 1965.

Shakespeare, William. *The Tragedy of Othello, The Moor of Venice*, ed. Alvin Kernan. New York, 1963.

Stallworthy, Jon, ed. *The Penguin Book of Love Poetry*. Harmondsworth, 1973.

Swift, Jonathan. *Gulliver's Travels and Other Writings*, ed. Louis A. Landa. Boston, 1960.

Tillotson, Geoffrey, et. al., eds. *Eighteenth-Century English Literature*. New York, 1969.

Virgil. *The Aeneid of Virgil*, trans. Allen Mandelbaum. Toronto and New York, 1961.

Voltaire. *The Portable Voltaire*, ed. Ray Redman. Harmondsworth, 1977.

Theoretical and Critical Works

Abelson, Raziel. "Definition." In the *Encyclopedia of Philosophy*, ed. Paul Edwards. New York, 1967.

Abrams, M. H. *The Mirror and the Lamp: Romantic Theory and the Critical Tradition*. London, 1953.

————. *A Glossary of Literary Terms*. New York, 1981.

————. "How to Do Things with Texts." In his *Doing Things with Texts*, 269–96. New York, 1989.

Ackerman, Nathan W. *The Psychodynamics of Family Life*. New York, 1958.

Alpers, Paul. "What Is Pastoral?" *Critical Inquiry* 8 (Spring 1982): 437–60.

————. *What Is Pastoral? An Essay in Literary Definition*. Forthcoming.

Alter, Robert. *Partial Magic: The Novel as a Self-Conscious Genre*. Berkeley and Los Angeles, 1975.

————. *The Pleasures of Reading in an Ideological Age*. New York, 1989.

Altieri, Charles. "The Poem as Act." *Iowa Review* 6, nos. 3–4 (1975): 103–24.

Austin, J. L. *How to Do Things with Words*. New York, 1968.

Bakhtin, M. M. "Epic and Novel." In *The Dialogic Imagination, Four Essays*, ed. Michael Holquist, trans. Caryl Emerson and Michael Holquist, 3–40. Austin, 1981.

Bakhtin, M. M., and P. M. Medvedev. *The Formal Method in Literary Scholarship*, trans. Albert J. Wehrle. Cambridge, Mass., and London, 1985.

Barthes, Roland. "L'effet de réel." *Communications* 11 (1968): 85–89.

Beardsley, Monroe C. "The Definition of the Arts." *Journal of Aesthetics and Art Criticism* 20, no. 2 (1961): 175–87.

————. *The Possibility of Criticism*. Detroit, 1970.

Ben-Amos, Dan. "Analytical Categories and Ethnic Genres." In *Folklore Genres*, ed. Dan Ben-Amos, 215–42. Austin and London, 1976.

Ben-Porat, Ziva. "Intertextuality, Rhetorical Intertextuality, Allusion, and Parody" (in Hebrew). *Hasifrut/Literature* 34 (Summer 1985): 170–78.

Black, Max. *Margins of Precision*. Ithaca, 1970.

Bloom, Harold. *The Anxiety of Influence: A Theory of Poetry*. London, 1973.

Booth, Wayne C. *The Rhetoric of Fiction*. Chicago, 1961.
————. *A Rhetoric of Irony*. Chicago, 1974.
————. *Critical Understanding: The Powers and Limits of Pluralism*. Chicago, 1979.
Bovet, Ernest. *Lyrisme, épopée, drame: Une Loi de l'histoire littéraire expliquée par l'évolution général*. Paris, 1911.
Bowra, C. M. *From Virgil to Milton*. London, 1948.
Boyd, Richard. "Metaphor and Theory Change." In *Metaphor and Thought*, ed. Andrew Ortony, 357–408. Cambridge, Mass., 1979.
Brinker, Menachem. *Representation and Meaning in the Fictional Work* (in Hebrew). Tel Aviv, 1980.
Brooke-Rose, Christine. "Historical Genres/Theoretical Genres: A Discussion of Todorov on the Fantastic." *New Literary History* 8, no. 1 (1976): 145–58.
Brooks, Cleanth. *The Well Wrought Urn*. London, 1968.
Brooks, Cleanth, and Robert Penn Warren. *Understanding Poetry*. New York, 1976.
Brunetière, Ferdinand. *L'Evolution des genres dans l'histoire de la literature*. Paris, 1890.
————. *L'Evolution de la poésie lyrique en France au dix-neuvième siècle*, second edition. Paris, 1913 (1895).
Bruser, Fredelle. "Comus and the Rose Song." *Studies in Philology* 44, no. 4 (1947): 625–44.
Bruss, Elizabeth W. *Autobiographical Acts: The Changing Situation of Literary Genre*. Baltimore, 1976.
Bush, Douglas. *English Literature in the Earlier Seventeenth Century, 1600–1660*. New York, 1962.
Butcher, S. H. *Aristotle's Theory of Poetry and Fine Art*. London, 1895.
Chatman, Seymour. *Story and Discourse*. Ithaca, 1978.
Cohen, Ralph. "History and Genre." *New Literary History* 17, no. 2 (1986): 203–18.
Cohn, Dorrit. *Transparent Minds*. Princeton, 1978.
Colie, Rosalie L. *The Resources of Kind: Genre Theory in the Renaissance*. Berkeley and Los Angeles, 1973.
Copi, Irving M. *Introduction to Logic,* fifth edition. New York, 1978.
Crane, R. S., ed. *Critics and Criticism*. Chicago, 1952.
————. *The Language of Criticism and the Structure of Poetry*. Toronto, 1953.
Croce, Benedetto. *Aesthetic as Science of Expression and General Linguistic,* trans. Douglas Aimslie. London, 1967.
Culler, Jonathan. *Structuralist Poetics*. London, 1975.
————. *The Pursuit of Signs*. Ithaca, 1981.
Darwin, Charles. *The Origin of Species*. Harmondsworth, 1982 (1859).
Dawkins, Richard. *The Selfish Gene*. Oxford, 1976.
Derrida, Jacques. "The Law of Genre." *Glyph* 7 (1980): 202–29.
Dixon, William M. *English Epic and Heroic Poetry*. New York, 1964.
Donohue, James John. *The Theory of Literary Kinds*. Vol. 1, *Ancient Classifications of Literature*. Vol. 2, *The Ancient Classes of Poetry*. Dubuque, Iowa, 1943–49.
Dubrow, Heather. *Genre*. London, 1982.
Duckworth, George E. *The Nature of Roman Comedy*. Princeton, 1952.
Ehrenpreis, Irwin. *The "Type" Approach to Literature*. New York, 1945.
Eisenstadt, Shmuel N. "Social Institutions." In *International Encyclopedia of Social Science*. New York, 1968.

Elliot, Robert C. "The Definition of Satire." *Yearbook of Comparative and General Literature* 11 (1962): 19–23.

Erlich, Victor. *Russian Formalism: History—Doctrine*. The Hague, 1955.

———. *Twentieth-Century Russian Literary Criticism*. New Haven, 1975.

Escarpit, Robert. *Sociology of Literature*, trans. Ernest Pick. London, 1971.

Even-Zohar, Itamar. *Polysystem Studies*. A special issue of *Poetics Today* 11, no. 1 (1990).

Farmer, Norman K. "A Theory of Genre for Seventeenth-Century Poetry." *Genre* 3, no. 4 (1970): 291–317.

Felman, Shoshana. *The Literary Speech Act*. Ithaca, 1983.

Fish, Stanley. "How to Do Things with Austin and Searle: Speech-Act Theory and Literary Criticism." In his *Is There a Text in This Class?* 197–245. Cambridge, Mass., 1980.

Fishelov, David. "Types of Characters, Characteristics of Types." *Style* 24, no. 3 (1990): 422–39.

———. "Genre Theory and Family Resemblance—Revisited." *Poetics* 20, no. 2 (1991): 123–38.

———. "Aristotle's Approach to Literary Genres: Classification, Description, Evaluation" (in Hebrew). *Dapim: Research in Literature* 8 (1991/92): 45–62.

Fowler, Alastair. "The Life and Death of Literary Forms." *New Literary History* 2, no. 2 (1971): 199–216.

———. *Kinds of Literature: An Introduction to the Theory of Genres and Modes*. Cambridge, Mass., 1982.

———. "The Future of Genre Theory: Functions and Constructional Types." In *The Future of Literary Theory*, ed. Ralph Cohen, 291–303. New York, 1989.

Frye, Northrop. *Anatomy of Criticism*. Princeton, 1957.

Genette, Gérard. *Introduction à l'architexte*. Paris, 1979.

Genot, Gérard. "L'écriture libératrice." *Communication* 11 (1968): 34–58.

Gerhart, Mary. "The Dilemma of the Text: How to 'Belong' to a Genre." *Poetics* 18, nos. 4–5 (1989): 355–73.

Gilbert, Margaret. "Notes on the Concept of a Social Convention." *New Literary History* 14, no. 2 (1983): 225–51.

Globinsky, Michael. "Gatunek literacki i problemy poetyki historycznej" (The Literary Genre and the Problems of Historical Poetics). In *Proces historyczny w literaturze i sztuce*, 31–60. Warsaw, 1967. A Hebrew translation appeared in *Ha-sifrut/Literature* 2, no. 1 (1969): 14–25.

Goffman, Erving. *The Presentation of Self in Everyday Life*. Garden City, N.Y., 1959.

Gould, Stephen Jay. *Ever Since Darwin: Reflections in Natural History*. New York, 1977.

Grice, Paul H. "Logic and Conversation." In *Syntax and Semantics, Vol. 3: Speech Acts*, ed. Peter Cole and Jerry Morgan, 41–58. New York, 1975.

Guillén, Claudio. *Literature as System*. Princeton, 1971.

Harshav (Hrushovski), Benjamin. "Theory of the Literary Text and the Structure of Non-Narrative Fiction: In the First Episode of *War and Peace*." *Poetics Today* 9, no. 3 (1988): 635–66.

———. "Why Can We Have Romantic Realism and Not Doggy Cats?" A lecture, University of California, Berkeley, 1978.

Harvey, Paul, ed. *The Oxford Companion to Classical Literature*. London, 1940.

Hauptmeier, Helmut. "Sketches of Theories of Genre." *Poetics* 16, no. 5 (1987): 397–430.

Hawkes, Terence. *Structuralism and Semiotics*. London, 1977.

Hernadi, Paul. *Beyond Genre: New Directions in Literary Classification*. Ithaca, 1972.

Hesse, Mary B. *Models and Analogies in Science*. Notre Dame, Ind., 1966.

Highet, Gilbert. *The Anatomy of Satire*. Princeton, 1962.

Hirsch, E. D. *Validity in Interpretation*. New Haven, 1967.

Hochman, Baruch. *Character in Literature*. Ithaca, 1985.

Hocking, Elton. *Ferdinand Brunetière: The Evolution of a Critic*. In *University of Wisconsin Studies in Language and Literature* 36. Madison, 1936.

Honzl, Jindrich. "Dynamics of the Sign in the Theater." In *Semiotics of Art*, ed. Ladislav Matejka and Irwin R. Titunik, 74–93. Cambridge, Mass., 1976.

Hough, Graham. *An Essay on Criticism*. London, 1966.

Hunter, R. L. *The New Comedy of Greece and Rome*. Cambridge, 1985.

Jagendorf, Zvi. *The Happy End of Comedy*. London, 1984.

Jakobson, Roman. "Closing Statement: Linguistics and Poetics." in *Style in Language*, ed. Thomas Sebeok, 350–77. Cambridge, Mass., 1960.

———. "The Dominant." In *Readings in Russian Poetics: Formalist and Structuralist Views*, ed. Ladislav Matejka and Krystyna Pomorska, 82–87. Ann Arbor, 1978.

Jameson, Fredric. "Magical Narratives: On the Dialectical Use of Genre Criticism." In his *Political Unconscious*, 103–50. Ithaca, 1981.

Janik, Allan, and Stephen Toulmin. *Wittgenstein's Vienna*. New York, 1973.

Jauss, Hans Robert. *Toward an Aesthetic of Reception*. Minneapolis, 1982.

Jolles, André. *Forms simples*. Paris, 1972. Originally published in German in 1930.

Kasher, Asa. "What Is a Theory of Use?" *Journal of Pragmatics* 1, no. 2 (1977): 105–20.

Kirkpatrick, Clifford. "Family: Disorganization and Dissolution." In *International Encyclopedia of the Social Sciences*. New York, 1968.

Krook, Dorothea. *Elements of Tragedy*. New Haven, 1969.

Kuhn, Thomas S. *The Structure of Scientific Revolutions*. Chicago, 1962.

———. "Metaphor in Science." In *Metaphor and Thought*, ed. Andrew Ortony, 409–17. Cambridge, Mass., 1979.

Labov, William. *Language in the Inner City*. University Park, Pa., 1972.

Lacoue-Labarthe, Philippe, and Jean-Luc Nancy. "Genre." *Glyph* 7 (1980): 1–14.

La Driere, James Craig. "Classification." In *Dictionary of World Literature*, ed. Joseph T. Shipley. Totowa, N.J., 1972.

Langbaum, Robert. *The Poetry of Experience*. New York, 1957.

Laumonier, Paul. *Ronsard poète lyrique*. Geneva, 1972.

Leech, Geoffrey N. *A Linguistic Guide to English Poetry*. London, 1969.

Lefevre, André. "Systems in Evolution: Historical Relativism and the Study of Genre." *Poetics Today* 6, no. 4 (1985): 665–79.

Lejeune, Philippe. *Le pacte autobiographique*. Paris, 1975.

Levin, Harry. "Literature as an Institution." In *Criticism: The Foundations of Modern Literary Judgment*, ed. Mark Schorer et al., 546–53. New York, 1948.

———. "Notes on Convention." In his *Perspectives of Criticism*, 55–83. Cambridge, Mass., 1950.

Lord, Albert B. "Narrative Poetry." In *Princeton Encyclopedia of Poetry and Poetics*, ed. Alex Preminger. London, 1974.

Lyons, John. *Semantics*. Cambridge, Mass., 1977.

Malone, Kemp. "Epic Poetry." In *Dictionary of World Literature*, ed. Joseph T. Shipley. Totowa, N.J., 1972.

Mandelbaum, Maurice. "Family Resemblances and Generalization Concerning the Arts." *American Philosophical Quarterly* 2, no. 3 (1965): 219–28.

Manly, John Matthews. "Literary Forms and the Origin of Species." *Modern Philology* 4, no. 4 (1907): 1–19.

Margolin, Uri. "The Concept of Genre as Historical Category." Ph.D. diss., Cornell University, 1973.

———. "Historical Literary Genre: The Concept and Its Uses." *Comparative Literature Studies* 10, no. 1 (1973): 51–59.

———. "On Three Types of Deductive Models in Genre Theory." *Zagadienia Rodzajow Literackich* 17, no. 1 (1974): 5–19.

Margolis, Joseph. "Literature and Speech Acts." *Philosophy and Literature* 3, no. 1 (1979): 39–52.

Masterman, Margaret. "The Nature of a Paradigm." In *Criticism and the Growth of Knowledge*, ed. Imre Lakatos and Alan Musgrave, 59–89. Cambridge, 1970.

Matejka, Ladislav, and Krystyna Pomorska, eds. *Readings in Russian Poetics*. Ann Arbor, 1978.

Mayr, Ernst. *The Growth of Biological Thought*. Cambridge, Mass., 1982.

Merchant, Paul. *The Epic*. London, 1971.

Milo, Daniel. "Aspects de la survie culturelle." Thèse de Ph.D. à l'Ecole des hautes etudes en sciences sociales, Paris, 1985.

———. "La Bourse mondiale de la traduction: Un Baromètre culturel?" *Annales* 39, no. 1 (1984): 92–115.

Milosz, Czeslaw. *A History of Polish Literature*. Berkeley and Los Angeles, 1969.

Moler, Kenneth L. *Jane Austen's Art of Allusion*. London, 1968.

Monod, Jacques. *Chance and Necessity*. London, 1972.

Morson, Gary Saul. *The Boundaries of Genre*. Austin, 1981.

Mudrick, Marvin. *Jane Austen: Irony as Defense and Discovery*. Princeton, 1952.

Norris, Christopher. *Deconstruction: Theory and Practice*. London, 1982.

Ohmann, Richard. "Speech, Action, and Style." In *Literary Style: A Symposium*, ed. Seymour Chatman, 241–54. London, 1971.

———. "Speech Acts and the Definition of Literature." *Philosophy and Rhetoric* 4, no. 1 (1971): 1–19.

Olson, Elder, ed. *Aristotle's Poetics and English Literature*. Chicago, 1965.

———. *The Theory of Comedy*. Bloomington, 1968.

———. *On Value Judgments in the Arts and Other Essays*. Chicago, 1976.

Ortega y Gasset, José. "Notes on the Novel." In his *Dehumanization of Art*, 57–103. Princeton, 1968.

Parsons, Talcott. *On Institutions and Social Evolution*. Chicago, 1982.

Pearson, Norman Holmes. "Literary Forms and Types: or, A Defense of Polonius." In *English Institute Annual 1940*, 61–72. New York, 1941.

Perry, Menakhem. "Literary Dynamics: How the Order of a Text Creates Its Meanings." *Poetics Today* 1, nos. 1–2 (1979): 35–64, 311–61.

Petrey, Sandy. *Speech Acts and Literary Theory*. New York, 1990.

Pratt, Marie Louise. *Toward a Speech Act Theory of Literary Discourse*. Bloomington, 1977.

———. "The Short Story: The Long and the Short of It." *Poetics* 10, nos. 2–3 (1981): 175–94.

Praz, Mario. *The Romantic Agony,* trans. Agnus Davidson. London, 1933.

Preminger, Alex, ed. *Princeton Encyclopedia of Poetry and Poetics.* London, 1974.

Propp, Vladimir. *The Morphology of the Folktale,* trans. Laurence Scott. Bloomington, 1958.

Reichert, John F. " 'Organizing Principles' and Genre Theory." *Genre* 1, no. 1 (1968): 1–12.

———. *Making Sense of Literature.* Chicago, 1977.

———. "More Than Kin and Less Than Kind: The Limits of Genre Theory." In *Theories of Literary Genre,* ed. Joseph Strelka, 57–79. University Park, Pa., 1978.

Reid, Ian. "Genre and Framing: The Case of Epitaphs." *Poetics* 17, nos. 1–2 (1988): 25–35.

Rex, Walter. E. *"Figaro's* Games." *PMLA* 89, no. 3 (1974): 524–29.

Ricks, Christopher. "Allusion: The Poet as Heir." In *Studies in the Eighteenth Century* 3, ed. R. F. Brissenden and J. C. Eade, 209–40. Toronto, 1976.

Rimmon-Kenan, Shlomith. *Narrative Fiction: Contemporary Poetics.* London, 1983.

Rosch, Eleanor. "Principles of Categorization." In *Cognition and Categorization,* ed. Eleanor Rosch and Barbara B. Lloyd, 27–48. Hillsdale, 1978.

Rosch, Eleanor, and Carolyn B. Mervis. "Family Resemblance: Studies in the Internal Structure of Categories." *Cognitive Psychology* 7, no. 4 (1975): 573–605.

Rosenmeyer, Thomas G. *The Green Cabinet.* Berkeley and Los Angeles, 1969.

———. "Ancient Literary Genres: A Mirage?" *Yearbook of Comparative and General Literature* 36 (1987): 74–84.

Rosmarin, Adena. *The Power of Genre.* Minneapolis, 1985.

Ryan, Marie-Laure. "Introduction: On the Why, What, and How of Generic Taxonomy." *Poetics* 10, nos. 2–3 (1981): 109–26.

Sabrin, Theodore R. "Role: Psychological Aspects." In *International Encyclopedia of Social Science.* New York, 1968.

Sacks, Sheldon. *Fiction and the Shape of Belief.* Chicago, 1964.

Schaeffer, Jean-Marie. *Qu'est-ce qu'un genre littéraire?* Paris, 1989.

———. "Literary Genres and Textual Genericity." In *The Future of Literary Theory,* ed. Ralph Cohen, 167–87. New York, 1989.

Schauber, Ellen, and Ellen Spolsky. *The Bounds of Interpretation.* Stanford, 1986.

Schmidt, S. J. "Towards a Constructivist Theory of Media Genre." *Poetics* 16, no. 5 (1987): 371–95.

Scholes, Robert. *Structuralism in Literature.* New Haven, 1974.

Schuur, Margje, and Gerard Seegers. "The Perception of Book Categories by Adult Users of Dutch Public Libraries," *Poetics* 18, no. 6 (1989): 471–78.

Searle, John R. *Speech Acts: An Essay in the Philosophy of Language.* London, 1969.

———. "The Logical Status of Fictional Discourse." In his *Expression and Meaning,* 58–75. Cambridge, 1979.

Segal, Ora. "The Theory of Speech Acts and Its Applicability to Literature" (in Hebrew). *Ha-sifrut/Literature* 18–19 (December 1974): 113–19.

Shipley, Joseph T., ed. *Dictionary of World Literature.* Totowa, N.J., 1972.

Shklovsky, Victor. "Art as Technique." In *Russian Formalist Criticism,* ed. Lee T. Lemon and Marion J. Reis, 3–23. Lincoln, Nebr., 1965.

Sinfield, Alan. *Dramatic Monologue.* London, 1977.

Smith, Barbara Herrnstein. *On the Margins of Discourse.* Chicago, 1978.

Solomon, Harry M. *Sir Richard Blackmore.* Boston, 1980.

Staiger, Emil. *Les Concepts fondamentaux de la poetique,* traduit et annoté par Raphaël Célis et Michèle Gennart. Brussels, 1990.

Steiner, Peter. "The Three Metaphors." In his *Russian Formalism: A Metapoetics,* 44–137. Ithaca, 1984.

Sternberg, Meir. "*Elements of Tragedy* and the Concept of Plot in Tragedy: On the Methodology of Constituting a Generic Whole" (in Hebrew). *Hasifrut/Literature* 4, no. 1 (1973): 23–69.

Stierle, Karlheinz. "L'Historie comme example, l'example comme histoire." *Poetique* 10 (1972): 176–98.

Strelka, Joseph P., ed. *Theories of Literary Genre.* University Park, Pa., 1978.

Stutterheim, Cornelis F. P. "Prolegomena to a Theory of the Literary Genre." *Zagadnienia Rodzajow Literackich* 6, no. 2 (Lodz, 1964): 5–24.

Sutherland, James. *English Literature of the Late Seventeenth Century.* Oxford, 1969.

Symonds, John A. "On the Application of Evolutionary Principles to Art and Literature." In his *Essays Speculative and Suggestive,* vol. 1, 42–83. New York, 1970 (1890).

———. "The Pathos of the Rose in Poetry." In his *Essays Speculative and Suggestive,* vol. 2, 197–224. New York, 1970 (1890).

Tillyard, E.M.W. *The English Epic and Its Background.* New York, 1966.

Todorov, Tzvetan. *The Fantastic: A Structural Approach to a Literary Genre.* Ithaca, 1975.

———. "The Origin of Genres." *New Literary History* 8, no. 1 (1976): 159–70.

Tomashevsky, Boris. "Literary Genres." In *Russian Poetics in Translation* 5, ed. L. M. O'Toole and Ann Shukman, 52–93. Oxford, 1978.

Traugott, Elizabeth C. "Generative Semantics and the Concept of Literary Discourse." *Journal of Literary Semantics* 2 (1973): 5–22.

Trilling, Lionel. *Sincerity and Authenticity.* Cambridge, Mass., 1972.

Trzynadlowski, Jan. "Information Theory and Literary Genres." *Zagadnienia Rodzajow Literackich* 4, no. 1 (1961): 31–48.

Turner, Ralph H. "Role: Sociological Aspects." In *International Encyclopedia of Social Science.* New York, 1968.

Tynjanov, Jurij. "Dostoevsky and Gogol: Theory of Parody." In *Twentieth-Century Russian Literary Criticism,* ed. Victor Erlich, 102–16. New Haven, 1975.

———. "On Literary Evolution." In *Readings in Russian Poetics,* ed. Ladislav Matejka and Krystyna Pomorska, 66–78. Ann Arbor, 1978.

Van Dijk, Teun A. *Some Aspects of Text Grammar.* The Hague, 1972.

Van Rees, C. J. "The Institutional Foundation of a Critic's Connoisseurship." *Poetics* 18, nos. 1–2 (1989): 179–98.

Vivas, Eliseo. "Literary Classes: Some Problems." *Genre* 1, no. 2 (1968): 97–105.

Watt, Ian. *The Rise of the Novel.* Harmondsworth, 1972 (1959).

Weisstein, Ulrich. *Comparative Literature and Literary Theory.* Bloomington, 1968.

Weintraub, Wiktor. *The Poetry of Adam Mickiewicz.* The Hague, 1954.

Weitz, Morris. "The Role of Theory in Aesthetics." *Journal of Aesthetics and Art Criticism* 15, no. 1 (1956): 27–35.

———. *Hamlet and the Philosophy of Literary Criticism.* Chicago, 1964.

———. *The Opening Mind.* Chicago, 1977.

Wellek, René. "Genre Theory, the Lyric, and *Erlebnis.*" In his *Discriminations,* 225–52. New Haven, 1970.

———. "The Concept of Evolution in Literary History." In his *Concepts of Criticism*, 37–53. New Haven, 1973.

Wellek, René, and Austin Warren. *Theory of Literature,* third edition. Harmondsworth, 1963.

Wittgenstein, Ludwig. *Philosophical Investigation,* trans. G.E.M. Anscombe. Oxford, 1978.

Index

Abrams, M. H., 5–6, 70–71
Ackerman, Nathan, 82
allopatric theory, 48–52
Alpers, Paul, 65–67
Alter, Robert, 54, 74n.53
amemus. See *carpe diem*
analogies, 1–7, 155–60
  conceptual use of, 5–7
  negative, 156
  neutral, 157
  ornamental use of, 4–5
  positive, 156–57
  See also scientific paradigm
Andric, Ivo, *Bosnian Story*, 34
Aristophanes, 15, 66
Aristotle, 9n.14, 68, 91, 128, 129, 131
Asklepiades, 133, 135, 138, 146, 150
Austen, Jane
  Northanger Abbey, 74–81
  Pride and Prejudice, 75
Austin, J. L., x, 126, 130, 131
autobiography, 121–22, 123

Bakhtin, Mikhail, 45–46
Baudelaire, Charles, "Au lecteur," 151n.60
Beardsley, Monroe C., 126–27, 130
Beaumarchais, Pierre Augustin, 114, 117
Beckett, Samuel, *Watt*, 96
Ben-Porat, Ziva, 38n.47
biological species, and literary genres, x,
  1–2, 3, 19–52, 155, 158, 159
  differences between, 20–23
  struggle for survival, 24–25, 45–56, 52
  See also allopatric theory, Darwinism,
    evolutionary concepts
Black, Max, 62
Blackmore, Richard, 40
  Prince Arthur, 41–45
blocking figure (*alazon*), 99, 101–2, 103–17
Bloom, Harold, 69–71
Boileau, Nicolas, 64

Booth, Wayne C., 159–60
Boyd, Richard, 7
Brinker, Menachem, 130n.30, 152n.61
Brooke-Rose, Christine, 9
Brooks, Cleanth, 139n.43
Brunetière, Ferdinand, 22–24
Bruss, Elizabeth, X, 121–23
burlesque, 28, 29, 31
Byron, Lord (George Gordon), *Don Juan*,
  34

Carnap, Rudolf, 4, 55
carpe diem, 3, 132–53
  argument and syllogism in, 133, 134,
    135, 138, 139, 141–42, 146, 147
  constitutive elements of, 133, 134, 146,
    147–48
  dynamic speech situation in, 137–39,
    141, 147
  as imitation of speech acts, 150
  as motive and as organizing principle,
    132, 144
  See also lyrical poetry
Catullus, 142, 146, 150
  "Carmina 5," 134–36
Cervantes Saavedra, Miguel de., 47, 96
  Don Quixote, 73–74, 92–94
Chalmers, Alexander, 45
Chekhov, Anton, *Cherry Orchard*, 63
Chomsky, Noam, 119
Cohen, Ralph, 10n.16, 11
comedy, 3, 14, 16, 18, 66, 86, 90, 91, 99–
  117, 130
  Attic, 15–16
  constitutive roles of, 99, 101–3, 109
  happy ending in, 90, 100, 101, 102, 103,
    105, 112
  parental figure in, 106, 110–11
  plot of, 101–3, 105, 108, 110, 114, 115,
    117
  See also roles

conventions, 2, 19, 25–27, 82, 83, 85–87,
    89–91, 96, 97, 120, 123, 155
  semiotic, 91–96
Cowley, Abraham, *Davideis,* 44, 51
Croce, Benedetto, 54, 82
Culler, Jonathan, 87, 90

Darwin, Charles, x, 2, 20, 23, 23n.11, 24,
    35, 36, 45, 46, 47
Darwinism, 35–36, 45
  and determinism, 36
  and variability, 46–47
Dawkins, Richard, 37n.45
deconstruction, 13
defamiliarization, 95
Defoe, Daniel, 45, 47
  Moll Flanders, 50
  Robinson Crusoe, 44n.61
Derrida, Jacques, 13n.21
Dixon, William M., 40n.50
dominance and periphery, 47–52, 155. *See
    also* allopatric theory, Darwinism, ev-
    olutionary concepts
Dos Passos, John, *U.S.A.,* 59
Dostoevsky, Feodor Mikhailovich, 73
dramatic genres, 85–86, 91–96, 99, 101,
    131–32, 149
dramatic monologue, 150
Dryden, John, 43
  Absalom and Achitophel, 44
Dubrow, Heather, 1n.1, 157–58

Eisenstadt, Shmuel, 88
Eliot, T. S., 145–46, 147, 153
  "The Love Song of J. Alfred Prufrock,"
    145
Elliot, Robert, 59–60
Elytis, Odysseus, *Worthy It Is,* 34
empirical approach, 64
environment, cultural and literary, 36, 39–
    40, 42, 44
epic poetry, 3, 12, 15, 18, 26, 27, 29–35,
    39–47, 66, 68, 129
  Christian epic, 27, 51–52
  See also mock epic
Erlich, Victor, 50, 52
Escarpit, Robert, 44
Esenin, Sergei, "Goodbye, My Friend,"
    150–51
Even-Zohar, Itamar, 17n.28, 38n.47

evolutionary concepts, 36–37, 45–47, 155,
    159. *See also* allopatric theory, Dar-
    winism, dominance and periphery

families, and literary genres, x, 1n.1, 53–
    83, 155, 159
  ambivalent attitude in, 72, 80–81
  autonomy within, 81–83
  logical aspect of, 53–65
  common ancestry in, 65–66
  family tree in, 67, 72, 73, 155
  parent-child relationship in, 68–81, 155,
    157
family resemblance, 54–65, 155. *See also*
    prototypical members
farce, 91, 103
Faulkner, William, *The Sound and the Fury,*
    124
Fenelon, François, *Télémaque,* 46
Fielding, Henri, 45, 47, 68, 79
  Joseph Andrews, 46
  Tom Jones, 46, 80
Flaubert, Gustave, *Madame Bovary,* 73
Forster, E. M., 60
Fowler, Alastair, x, 1n.1, 10, 25–29, 31,
    34–35, 37, 39, 54n.4
Freud, Sigmund, 69–71
Frye, Northrop, 9, 102n.39

generic productivity, 37–39, 40, 42, 43
  primary, 38, 42–43
  secondary, 38, 42
generic sterility, 39
generic survival, 37–39, 43, 46–47
Genette, Gérard, 9nn.11, 14
Genot, Gérard, 90
Geoffrey of Monmouth, *Historia Britonum,*
    41
Gilbert, Margaret, 89
Globinsky, Michael, 1n.1, 88
Gogol, Nikolai Vasilievich, 73
Gould, Stephen J., 23n.11, 35, 48
Grice, Paul H., 120, 123, 132n.33
Guillén, Claudio, 153
Gurevitch, George, 88

Harmon, Thomas, *Caveat for Common
    Cursitor,* 50
Harshav (Hrushovski), Benjamin, 20,
    76n.58
Hegel, George Wilhelm Friedrich, 45

hermeneutical circle, 26, 148–49
Hernadi, Paul, 1n.1
Herrick, Robert, 139
  "Corinna's Going A-Maying," 139
  "To the Virgins, to Make Much of
    Time," 139
Hesse, Mary, 156–57
Hirsch, E. D., 27n.21, 125
historical genres, 8–10, 125. *See also* theo-
  retical genres
Hocking, Elton, 24n.15
Homer, 15, 29, 31, 41, 42, 66
  Odyssey, 12, 30, 47
  Iliad, 47
Honzl, Jindrich, 91
Horace, 47, 60, 64, 66, 139

illocutionary act, 126–27. *See also* speech
  acts
interpretation, and literary genres, 3, 19,
  25–28. *See also* hermeneutical circle

Jagendorf, Zvi, 102n.39
Jakobson, Roman, 34, 49
Jameson, Fredric, 87
Jauss, Hans Robert, 51
Johnson, Samuel, 26, 42
Jolles, André, 124n.13
Jones, David, *Anathemata*, 34
Juvenal, 42, 47, 60, 64, 66

Kazantzakis, Nikos, *Odyssey*, 34
Kasher, Asa, 98
Keats, John, 147, 153
  "This Living Hand," 144–45
Krook, Dorothea, 63n.28
Kuhn, Thomas, 6–7

Labov, William, 123
Lacoue-Labarthe, Philippe, 13n.22
Lamarck, Jean-Baptiste, 23
Laumonier, Paul, 139n.41
Leech, Geoffrey N., 137n.39, 138n.40
Lefebre, Henri, 88
Levin, Harry, 87
life-cycle, model of, 22–23, 28–35
literary character, 73, 74, 75, 76, 86, 90,
  93, 99–102, 103n.41, 109, 110, 117,
  127, 128, 158. *See also* comedy, novel,
  roles

literary genres, and neighboring concepts,
  8, 15–16
  as colors, 1n.1, 157–58
  death of, 25–28
  definition of, 8, 13–17, 54, 56–65, 68,
    120–21
  as human personalities, 1n.1, 158
  as mines, 53
  transformation of, 24–25, 46, 124, 159
  See also biological species, families, his-
    torical genres, modes, social institu-
    tions, speech acts, subgenre, theoreti-
    cal genres
logical positivism, 4–7, 55
lyrical poetry, 18, 127, 129, 149, 156

Mandelbaum, Maurice, 65
Manly, John, 48n.71
Margolin, Uri, 9n.14, 16n.27, 19n.1, 20,
  22, 59n.18, 81n.68
Marivaux, Pierre Carlet, 117
  Le Jeu de l'amour et du hazard, 110–14
Marvell, Andrew, 146, 150
  "To His Coy Mistress," 129, 139–43,
    145
Masterman, Margaret, 6
Mayr, Ernst, 48
melodrama, 91
Merchant, Paul, 34, 41
metaphor. *See* analogies
Mickiewicz, Adam, *Pan Tadeusz*, 29–34
Milo, Daniel, 37
Milton, John
  Comus, 132n.34
  Lycidas, 26
  Paradise Lost, 12, 26–27, 29–31, 40–45,
    51
mock epic, 29, 31, 33, 43, 45, 46. *See also*
  epic poetry
modes, 8–9
Moler, Kenneth, 75–76, 80
Molière, Jean-Baptiste, 111, 114
  L'Ecole des femmes, 106–10
Monod, Jacques, 35n.42
Morson, Gary Saul, 10n.16, 11
Mudrick, Marvin, 80
Murdoch, Iris, 130

Nancy, Jean-Luc, 13n.22
natural discourse, 128–29

Neo-Aristotelian approach, 96, 129
neopragmatic approach, 10–13
Norris, Christopher, 69
novel, 3, 16, 18, 34n.40, 45–47, 50, 51, 53,
    58–62, 68, 72–81, 97, 123–24, 130,
    149
  Gothic, 74–80
  marked vs. unmarked cases of, 60n.20,
    123–24, 128, 149

ode, 90, 127
Ohmann, Richard, 129–30, 132
Olson, Elder, 90n.15, 129, 130
Ortega y Gasset, José, 53

Palamas, Koetis, *Twelve days of the Gipsy*, 34
paradigmatic cases (of genre). *See* proto-
    typical members
parody, 72, 81, 110
Parsons, Talcott, 100
pastoral, 15, 28, 65–67
Pearson, Norman, 86, 87
Perry, Menakhem, 76n.58
Perse, Saint-John, *Anabasis*, 34
Petrarch, 15, 47, 66
Petrey, Sandy, 126n.15, 131
Phèdre, 63
Plautus, 66
  Miles Gloriossus, 99, 103–6, 109
pluralistic approach, 2–3, 159–160
Pope, Alexander, 15, 40–44, 64
  Dunciad, 43–44
  The Rape of the Lock, 29
  Peri Bathos, 43
Pound, Ezra, *Cantos*, 34
pragmatics, in linguistics and literature,
    119–21, 126
Prague school, 91
Pratt, Marie Louise, 120, 123, 124, 149
Prior, Matthew, 147, 153
  "While Blooming Youth," 143–44
Propp, Vladimir, 102
prototypical members, of genres, x, 8, 12,
    17, 54, 60n.20, 62–65, 68, 133, 147,
    148, 155. *See also* family resemblance
Pushkin, Alexander, 60n.20

Reichert, John, 27n.20
represented discourse, 128–29, 156

representative cases, of genres. *See* proto-
    typical members
Rex, Walter E., 116n.66
Richardson, Samuel, 47
Ricks, Christopher, 70n.47
roles, 2, 85–86, 98–117
  complementarity of, 100, 101
  generic, 99–100, 109, 110
  institutional, 98–100, 114, 117, 156
  and literary character, 101–2, 109, 110,
    112, 115
  See also blocking figure, comedy
Ronsard, Pierre de, 146, 147, 150
  "Mignonne, allons voir si la rose," 136–
    39, 141
Rosch, Eleanor, 62
Rosenmeyer, Thomas, 9n.14, 71
Rosmarin, Adena, 10n.16, 11, 12
rules (of genres), 8, 13–15, 16, 25, 27, 39,
    43, 82, 87, 88, 90–91, 120–22, 123,
    124, 126, 129, 147–48, 152
  constitutive, 8, 14, 66n.37
Russian Formalism, 5n.5, 49–52, 73
Ryan, Marie-Laure, 14, 63, 64

Sacks, Sheldon, x
satire, x, 13, 15, 47, 59–60, 64, 66, 72, 76,
    81, 97, 103
Schaeffer, Jean-Marie, 9n.14, 10n.16,
    13n.23, 23n.11, 67n.39
Schauber, Ellen, 13n.23, 64n.29, 123n.11
Schlick, Moritz, 4, 55
Schmidt, S. J., 64
Scholes, Robert, 9n.12, 14
scientific paradigm, 6–7, 8
Searle, John, x, 14, 66n.37, 120, 121, 126,
    130–31
Seth, Vikram, 60n.20
Shakespeare, William, 15, 47, 66, 128
  Hamlet, 57, 128
  King Lear, 63
  Othello, 132n.33
  Sonnets, 47, 66
Shklovsky, Victor, 50–52, 95
simile, 137
Sinfield, Alan, 150n.58
Sinopoulus, Takis, *Deathfeast*, 34
Smith, Barbara Herrnstein, 127–29, 130,
    132, 150, 151
social institutions, and literary genres, x,

1n.1, 3, 85–117, 155–56, 159. *See also*
    conventions, roles
Solomon, Harry M., 40n.51, 42, 43
sonnet, 13, 14, 15, 16, 17, 47, 66
speech acts, and literary genres, x, 3, 85,
    119–53, 156, 159
  literary genres as complex speech acts,
    121–26, 131
  literary genres as imitation of speech
    acts, 121, 126–32, 150–51
  See also natural discourse, represented
    discourse
Spencer, Herbert, 20
Spenser, Edmund, 28
  The Faerie Queen, 29
Spolsky, Ellen, 13n.23, 64n.29, 123n.11
Staiger, Emil, 9n.10
Steiner, Peter, 5n.5
Stierle, Karlheinz, 124n.13
Strawson, P. F., x
subgenre, 16, 17, 133, 139, 147, 149, 152
Swift, Jonathan, 64
  Gulliver's Travels, 44n.61
  "A Modest Proposal," 97
Symonds, J. A., 22–23, 147n.55

Tennyson, Lord (Alfred), *Morte d'Arthur,*
    40n.52
Terence, 99
Theocritus, 28, 66
theoretical genres, 9. *See also* historical
    genres
Tillyard, E. M. W., 43

Todorov, Tzvetan, 9, 20, 124–25
Tolstoy, Leo, *War and Peace,* 94–95, 96
tragedy, 15, 16, 17, 26, 57–58, 60–63, 90,
    91, 129, 130, 149
tragicomedy, 20
Turner, Ralph, 100
Tynjanov, Jurij, 73

Van Dijk, Teun, 119
Van Rees, C. J., 66n.37
Virgil, 28, 30, 41, 42, 47, 66
  Aeneid, 12, 29, 31, 32, 33
Vivas, Eliseo, 54
Voltaire
  Henriade, 44n.60
  Micromegas, 4
  Roman et Contes, 44n.60

Warren, Austin, x, 9n.11, 86, 87, 157
Watt, Ian, 45–46, 50
Weitz, Morris, 57–62
Wellek, René, x, 9n.11, 20, 21–22, 24–25,
    86
Whitman, Walt, *Leaves of Grass,* 34
Williams, William Carlos, *Paterson,* 34
Wittgenstein, Ludwig, 2, 54–61, 65, 155
Woolf, Virginia, *To the Lighthouse,* 59
Wordsworth, William, 34, 151
  "Composed Upon Westminster Bridge,"
    151
  Prelude, 34
  The Recluse, 34

Printed in Great Britain
by Amazon

37350867R00108